T0339881

THE UPSIDE-DOWN TREE

THE UPSIDE-DOWN TREE
India's Changing Culture

Richard Connerney

Algora Publishing
New York

Library of Congress Cataloging-in-Publication Data —

Connerney, Richard D.
  The upside down tree: India's changing culture / Richard Connerney.
    p. cm.
  Includes bibliographical references and index.
    ISBN 978-0-87586-648-2 (soft cover: alk. paper) — ISBN 978-0-87586-649-9 (hard
cover: alk. paper) — ISBN 978-0-87586-650-5 (ebook) 1. India—Description and travel. 2.
Connerney, Richard D.—Travel—India. 3. India—Social life and customs. I. Title.
  DS414.2.C657 2009
  954.05'32—dc22
                          2009007798

Front Cover: Banyan tree.

Printed in the United States

For Pat Oleszko, who made this book possible.

ACKNOWLEDGEMENT

The Upside-Down Tree took many years to mature. The basis of the book was a series of newsletters I wrote for the Institute of Current World Affairs (ICWA) between January 2005 and January 2007. Upon my return to the United States, I slowly expanded, reorganized and reshaped this material, making great leaps forward during a fellowship at the MacDowell Colony in late 2007 and early 2008.

Any value found in this book is due to the cooperation and influence of a long list of muses and teachers. All shortcomings and mistakes are my own doing. An incomplete list of those to whom I owe a debt of thanks follows

Dr. Mukta Gupta's summer visits were always eventful. Our long friendship is an ongoing disaster I am lucky to have experienced.

My mother and father not only helped me out at various times during the fellowship, but, never having been to Asia before, visited me there and even enjoyed themselves.

I owe Sibte Hassan both thanks and an apology. He brought me to a new level in my understanding of Indian classical music and showed warm hospitality at every opportunity. Unfortunately, I did not know how to treat guru-ji with the respect he deserved. That he bore all my missteps on this account without complaint proves his character and his good spirit.

Biloo and his family were a godsend in Lucknow. His wife's chicken kabobs were fantastic and his children were a joy. I will always remember the good times, and good food, at his house.

Dr. Manuela Ciotti of the University of Edinburgh was an inspiration. She taught me a great deal about low-caste people in India, particularly the Chamars of Manupura. We had a few good laughs too.

My free-spirited friends in Goa — particularly Amalia, Lila, Allan, Tatiana and Natasha — taught me that learning about India was only half the problem; the more difficult challenge was learning about myself.

Elena Edwardovna of Moscow broke my heart, and in doing so reminded me that I still had one. For that, I owe her my gratitude.

The Institute of Current World Affairs provided me with an opportunity to travel and work over an extended period in South Asia. Their generosity deserves mention.

Peter Martin, former director of ICWA, edited some of my original reports from India.

Brian Hackert and the staff of the Peterborough Public Library aided me in locating the necessary research materials — some of them obscure titles rarely seen in "Our Town."

The other fellows at the MacDowell Colony between November 2007 and February 2008 made the final push not only bearable but also enjoyable. I have never before or since experienced the conjunction of artistic talent and personal warmth in such measure.

I have saved my biggest thanks to Sona, my *kaam karnewalli* and my friend. Were I to show this book to her, she could not read it, but she taught me more about dignity, determination and survival than any book ever could.

TABLE OF CONTENTS

INTRODUCTION

Uttar Pradesh (UP), in northern India, may be the place economist Kenneth Galbraith was thinking about when he called India a "functioning anarchy." Mentioning Uttar Pradesh may elicit a laugh; it is what one Indian friend once called a "loser state." Known as a home of deep poverty, incurable corruption and sticky social problems, UP is not the India that now appears regularly in *The New York Times* and *Newsweek*. This is the *other* India; the one that modernity has largely left behind. This book is the result of my repeated residencies over the last 18 years in that state.

Lucknow, the capital of Uttar Pradesh where I spent 2005–2007, does not have many international call-centers like Bangalore, or movie stars like Bombay, or even much of a tourist industry like Varanasi or Khajaraho. One thing it does have, however, is history. In the late 18th and early 19th centuries, while imperial Delhi fell into chaos and the British overran the province of Bengal, Lucknow became, briefly, the locus of the final flowering of pre-British cultural life. Here, the dancers, singers and poets of the Mughal court flocked to find their last patrons, and here in 1857, soon after the final dissolution of the Awadhi monarchy, Indians made a valiant stand against the inevitable tide of British military might.

For this reason, Lucknow gives the visitor an interesting vantage point from which to watch this century's changes. Like their ancestors of the 1800s, many of the residents of contemporary Lucknow also resist the currents of history and cling to a traditional way of life. This struggle is often interesting, sometimes comical and occasionally frightening. The battle between tradition and modernity in Lucknow today is far from over.

From Lucknow, I traveled extensively in north and central India. Chapters of this book will take the reader to Darjeeling in the state of West Bengal, to the wildly erotic sculpture of Khajaraho, the temples of Varanasi and the coast of Goa. India is a massive patchwork of different languages and cultures and no one person could possibly learn to speak all of the former or to understand all of the latter. While I speak Hindi and Urdu with some proficiency, and can stumble through a conversation in Nepali, the languages of South India remain impenetrable to me. Moreover, what I understand of Indian religion and culture becomes less relevant the further south one travels. The reader will thus find that most of the material in this book centers on Uttar Pradesh and the states of north India with the occasional foray into the Deccan peninsula. I do not mean to suggest that the people of South India do not wrestle with many of the same problems as their compatriots in North India, nor do I intend to downplay the differences between northern and southern India.

Similarly, I go on occasional junkets into Nepal. I could not ignore the troubles in Nepal over the last few years and was present in Kathmandu to witness the *jana aandolan* (people's movement) of Spring 2006 and other turning points in the nation's recent political paroxysms. At the time, I wrote extensively on politics and press freedom in the nation. Most of this material falls outside the scope of this book and does not appear here. Some anecdotes from Nepal do appear when they are relevant to the subject of Indian culture, or, in one case, to the behavior of Western travelers in South Asia.

I have tried to avoid approaching India in old, familiar ways. Contemporary press coverage of India repeats two hackneyed story lines *ad nauseam*. One is the "call-centers of Bangalore" theme (or perhaps the call-centers of Hyderabad or Gargaon) in which hard-working young Indians take technical support calls from average Americans. Hilarity ensues. The second is the "rag picker" story. In these Dickensian dispatches, a bedraggled woman picks through garbage dumps looking for tin cans to sell for scrap metal to support her suffering family. Stories like these elicit a feeling of pathos. Clean your plate, they say to us; people are collecting rags in Delhi.[1] I do not mean that the poor do not deserve our attention — they do. Turning their problems into a lugubrious tragedy, however, is something which does them no good and which most of them would not want.

Like the iconic theatrical masks of comedy and tragedy, these motifs reduce the drama of life in India to one of two pre-packaged aesthetic mode with a built-in trajectory and moral. Some Indian are happy, modern people who work with computers, these stories tell us, and some are miserable, destitute people who live in garbage heaps. This dichotomy echoes through most books about South Asia. Works like Mira Kamdar's *Planet India* depict a country that is full of CEOs and software developers, Bombay film stars and entrepreneurs.[2] At the other ex-

---

1 For but one example of the tearjerker genre, see Gentleman, Amelia. "Picking up Trash by Hand, And Yearning for Dignity," *New York Times*, 9/27/07.
2 Kamdar, Mira. *Planet India* (McMillan Library 2007), p. 96.

treme, books like Gregory David Robert's *Shantaram* show a world of slums and shantytowns, gangsters and thugs.[1]

Indians are not actors in a tragedy or a comedy, however; they are living real lives in a real world. Most Indians exist between economic extremes — neither in a Bangalore high-rise nor in a Calcutta slum. Even for those who do lead the high or the low life, the usual assumptions about them do not hold up under examination. I left India with the impression that those who work with computers are not as happy as we have been led to believe, and those who work in garbage dumps are often not as miserable as we might imagine.

I am a self-described generalist. Each chapter in this book attempts to present complex issues in a short space. Specialists could add greater levels of detail on each subject presented here. I am not an anthropologist, a linguist, a professional musician or an economist. To build my case I have relied on the work of others. In some cases, my debt will be obvious, as when I discuss economics. When I discuss music, the performing arts, and history, while I do not speak as an expert, I am at least a passionate enough amateur to use my own experiences as points of departure. The desired effect is a portrait of India painted in admittedly broad strokes but with enough sharp details to give an impression of completeness.

At the heart of this book lies a series of epiphanies I had about Indian culture. By epiphany, I mean Copernican intellectual shifts, radical reverses in the way I made sense of my environment; the evidence seemed to support one conclusion but further experience pointed to a different answer. As a lecturer of formal and informal logic at Rutgers University, I contemplated the mistakes that my students (and I) made as we reasoned inductively. I concluded that the largest obstacle to clear thinking is haste. The human mind is never happy in a state of indecision; when confronted with new and unfamiliar problems, we adopt a working hypothesis as quickly as possible. Especially in highly stressful or chaotic situations, such as wandering alone in a foreign country, we tend to adopt pat answers to complex problems.[2] Better to know than not to know, we tell ourselves, better to be confident than confused, and better to have a bad plan than no plan at all.

Visitors to India instinctively make flash decisions, adopt ideological stances, and accept the most obvious solutions to problems in an attempt to make sense

---

1 Roberts, Gregory David. *Shantaram*. (New York: St. Martin's Press 2005).

2 This idea finds support in the work of Mark Jung-Beeman, a cognitive neuroscientist at Northwestern University. Using MRI and EEG brain scans, Jung-Beeman discovered that the experience of sudden insight culminates in a burst of gamma waves originating from the brain's right hemisphere. This neurological phenomenon occurs unconsciously when the subject is relaxed and unfocused, thus explaining why intellectual breakthroughs are more apt to occur on the bus or in the shower than in the workplace. Jung-Beeman's research also suggests that certain left-brain stimulants like caffeine and Ritalin may be counter-productive when working on problems that require non-linear solutions. See Lehrer, Jonah. "The Eureka Hunt," *The New Yorker*, 7/28/08.

of all the disorder. The longer a visitor remains, the more new evidence and new experiences challenge these initial assessments. We may change our mind and later refuse to admit that we ever saw things differently. Changing one's mind has always carried the stigma of weakness and connotes a lack of understanding, clarity or confidence. In American politics changing your mind or flip-flopping has become a highly undesirable trait. If you must change your mind, the thinking goes, do it privately.

If this book has an axe to grind, it is that the process of changing our minds is worthy of our attention. Epiphanies, moments that reshape our understanding of the world, deserve examination and elucidation. I believe that the mental journey from assumption to understanding is more important than any physical journey. This book includes descriptions of my own mental maturations because it was only after traumas of bias, experience and befuddlement that I gained the occasional insight into India. I believe — hopefully without sounding like a fortune cookie — that we often find answers only by understanding why we asked the question in the first place.

I will include one final caveat; this book sometimes displays an unapologetic sense of humor. My complaints about India and Indian culture are clear but my love for India often remains unexpressed. I feel, perhaps wrongly, that I do not need to articulate the obvious — that it is clear I would not choose to live in India for so long if I did not like Indian peoples and cultures in all their wild variety. My relationship with the subcontinent is complex and, at times, dysfunctional. If it were a marriage, there would be shouting, occasional hurled objects and at least one trial separation. Nevertheless, my respect for Indian culture is sincere and I hope that readers do not take my occasional quips in the wrong way. Perhaps some will agree with me that disturbed relationships can also be meaningful, in a way that unbroken domestic harmony cannot.

A Note on Transliteration and Place Names

Although I have transliterated Hindi, Urdu, Nepali and Sanskrit words without diacritics, their meaning will, I hope, be apparent to those who know these languages. I have tried to elongate the vowels (e.g., *maalaa* for "garland") when possible. This was not always desirable where the less phonetic spelling was in common usage (e.g., in the name of Sanskrit texts like the Ramayana) or where I found the term already transliterated. In the few cases where, say, the inability to differentiate between retroflex and dental sounds makes the meaning of the word ambiguous (e.g., *moti*, with a retroflex "t" and *moti* with a dental "t" meaning "fat" and "pearl" respectively) I have tried to clarify the meaning in parenthesis.

My spelling of place names attempts to mimic common usage in contemporary India. Most residents of Mumbai still call the city by its older moniker, Bombay. Calcutta remains Calcutta for the same reason. Benares and Varanasi appear interchangeably, as both names are part of common parlance. For the archaic name of the Lucknow region, I opt for the historical "Oudh" except when the term is used as an adjective, when I use the more modern "Awadhi."

THE UPSIDE DOWN TREE: THE BI-DIRECTIONALITY OF CULTURAL CHANGE IN INDIA

One warm day in January, I found myself standing before a large banyan tree (*Ficus benghalensis*) in the Lucknow Botanical Gardens, across the street from my apartment. Banyan trees entrance me, in part because they grow upside-down. As a sprout, they grow skywards like any other tree. When they reach maturity, however, shoots develop on the tree's branches, grow straight down, and burrow into the soil. These shoots eventually take root and thicken into a trunk, so that a full-grown banyan looks more like a small forest than a single tree.

The banyan tree's inverted lifestyle continues when it reproduces. Birds eat banyan seeds and drop them onto the branches of other trees, or some equally elevated spot where the seed receives nourishment from rain and air. These traits mark banyans as *epiphytes*, meaning that they rest on other plants, or as "air plants" because they grow for a time without taking root. When the banyan seedpod finally opens, it sends a shoot downwards into the ground, there to create a rudimentary root system before turning around and growing upwards. A banyan tree thus moves in both directions depending on its stage of life. The original sapling descends from seedpod to soil, the young banyan grows like a regular tree and, when mature, the banyan pushes both skywards and earthwards simultaneously.

The idea of a tree that grows backwards, from the sky to the soil, has captured the Indian imagination for thousands of years. In the *Katha Upanishad*, an ancient Sanskrit philosophical text, an upside-down tree appears as a symbol of the world itself: "The universe is a tree eternally existing, its root aloft, its branches spread below." In this analogy, the physical world is rooted in a celestial Godhead (*Brahman*). "The pure root of the tree is Brahman, the immortal, in which the three worlds have their being."[1] The *Bhagavad Gita*, a later devotional text, calls this cosmic upside-down tree the Ashvattha Tree (the term probably originally meant "the place where the horses stand"[2]). The Ashvattha is said to have "roots above and branches below…" (15:1), and its leaves are likened to verses of poetry.[3] The god Krishna identifies himself with the Ashvattha Tree (10:26) and claims to be the foundation of human life itself. "Permeating the soil, I support beings by my vital energy," (15:13).[4]

The Ashvattha tree, the banyan tree and other sacred epiphytes in Indian mythology (e.g., pipal trees) function as symbols for the transcendental origins of human existence. A contemporary commentator remarks:

> The root of this material existence is upward. This means that it begins from the total material substance, from the topmost planet of the universe. From there the whole universe is expanded, with so many branches, representing the various planetary systems. The fruits are the results of the living entities' activities. They include religion, economic development, sense gratification and liberation.[5]

In this traditional worldview, our human nature and all the distinctive institutions of human society — artistic, literary, cultural and economic — originate in the great beyond. They may exist in the physical universe, the soil, but they have their origin in a higher realm. Culture is, literally, a piece of heaven on earth.

On the day I contemplated the banyan tree in the Lucknow Botanical Gardens, however, India did not seem like heaven on earth. I had just returned to the subcontinent after a decade's absence and saw changes that bewildered me. When I was a student studying in Varanasi in the early 1990s, most cars on the roads were Ambassadors (a car based on a late 1940s design), similarly antiquated Fiats and the occasional boxy Maruti vans. Now, dozens of new models from every car manufacturer imaginable fought each other for space on the ancient byways of north India. As recently as the mid-1990s, when I returned to India as a graduate student, television consisted of a few channels with low production values and simplistic programming. Now the airwaves carried a full array of cable and satellite programming from every nation and culture.

The way that people dressed had changed as well. As a student living in Varanasi in the early 1990s, I enjoyed wearing the traditional, loose-fitting *kurta pa*

---

1 Manchester, Frederick, trans. *The Upanishads: Breath of the Eternal* (Mentor: New York 1975).

2 Monier-Williams, Monier. *Sanskrit-English Dictionary* (New Delhi: Munshiram Manoharlal Publishers 1988), p. 115.

3 *Urdhvamulam adhahshaakhamashvattham* 15.1. Besant, Anne, trans. *The Bhagavad Gita: Text and Translation* (Theosophical Publishing House 1998), p. 206. The meaning of verse 15:13 is debatable. Some deny that it refers to the Ashvattha tree, but rather to the sun and moon in verse 15:12.

4 *Ibid.,* p. 211.

5 Prabhupada, Swami Bhaktivedanta, trans. *Bhagavad Gita As It Is* (New York: Bhaktivedanta Book Trust 1972), p. 228.

jama as I walked to class. Many men wore traditional dress at that time and I did not feel self-conscious in these clothes, even as a *farangii* (foreigner). Now, many young men had adopted Western-style dress; only older men, musicians and politicians still wore a *kurta*. As a result, I now usually kept my traditional Indian clothes in the closet.

Beyond cars, televisions and clothing, a subtler shift had occurred as well. When I first arrived in India in the early 1990s, India was just beginning to shake off the quasi-socialist system that predominated since Independence in 1947. Western goods were still hard to find in the market and the call-centers and software companies of Bangalore and Gargaon did not yet exist. Average Indians did not look to the West, its business models, or its culture when they considered their future.

By the time I returned to Uttar Pradesh in early 2005, however, new trade policies had transformed India and the nation seemed ready to emerge as a world power. With all this economic momentum and foreign investment came new cultural forms, some modeled on the West, some hybrids of Western and Indian ideas. In film and the arts, new avenues for the exposure and dissemination of traditional Indian art forms to Western audiences had caused changes in the art forms themselves. Relations between workers and managers had changed. Changes in the environment had altered the way people practiced their religion. In people's personal lives, newfound affluence and openness was altering the way Indians raised families, married and fell in love.

For many Indians, India was moving in a new direction, upwards. In opposition to the traditional, transcendent view of human life and culture, modern Indians were adopting, implicitly, the alternate view: if India could continue to develop adequate sanitation, sewage, potable water, agriculture, transportation, hospitals, schools and functioning law courts — what is often called infrastructure — then the higher branches of Indian culture, commerce, art, and literature would flourish. The tree was growing from the ground to the sky, like other trees.

Traditional culture in India has adapted to these changes in surprising ways. As Indians lurched towards the West, religious and intellectual conservatives led a counter-reformation of sorts. The 1990s saw the rise of right-wing Hindu political parties that challenged the hegemony of the long-ruling Congress Party. The newspapers now talked of *hindutva*, Hindu-ness, and *saffronites*, Hindus who felt that their traditional culture was under siege from Western cultural imperialism (the color saffron has a special significance in the Hindu religions). Likewise, Muslims in India, along with Muslims across the world, had embraced their own traditions with a renewed passion, and it seemed as if more Muslim women now wore the veil and more Muslim men wanted to talk to me about the Koran.

The changes I noticed in Indian culture over the last 18 years were of two types. On the one hand, Indians were moving towards Western lifestyles. At the same time, however, they were embracing re-formulated Indian traditions. Like the Banyan tree in the Lucknow Botanical Gardens, India was moving in two different directions. Some Indians, like the downward hanging branches of the tree, continued to live according to a belief in a transcendent order for human life shaped by tradition. Other people, like the banyan's central trunk, saw India's future as an upward rise brought on by Western technology, education and lifestyles, toward universal material development and a secular, open society. Most Indians incorporated both into their lifestyles, so that they were an amalgam of two distinct cultural movements wrapped in a single skin.

As I began to notice when I first returned to India, and as I continued to see over the next several years, these two opposing worldviews shaped Indian culture from top to bottom. When tradition met progress, the results were unpredictable. At times they conflicted and at times they complemented each other, but mostly these two cultural movements slid past each other as if each was unaware of the other's existence.

This idea of modern Indian culture as a bi-directional banyan tree provides the inspiration and the organization of this book. The first section concerns the environment in which India grows, its oceans, rivers and land. From here, I examine the supporting institutions of Indian society, education, law courts, politics and family life. Finally, we come to the flower of Indian culture, arts, music and dance. I include a chapter on Indian culture and economics and find an oddly apt message about Asian development in the pages of the late Kurt Vonnegut's novel *Slapstick: or Lonesome no More!*

This is a book about Indian culture, and I did not originally intend to address the subject of Indian national politics. I have neither the expertise nor the access to operate as a political correspondent, nor the desire to posture as a political pundit. During the course of my research, however, I saw what I perceived as a pervasive misrepresentation of recent developments in Indian politics. More specifically, a number of recent books consistently paint the Hindu right wing in India as essentially fascist or theocratic. I will argue that these claims are untenable and misrepresent a positive development in the history of Indian democracy.

In the last chapter, the tree grows downwards again. The most profound revelation I experienced while writing this book was that progress is as much a "mythology" as any found in India's religious literature. Progressives become passionate about "development" as a vaguely defined panacea for the world's ills; they assume that India is moving forward from an ignorant and deprived past to an affluent, enlightened future. Cogent reasons exist to doubt whether this is necessarily the case for India, however, and prophecies about the rise of Asian mega-economies are just that, predictions made by true believers in a quasi-religious concept called Progress. If an economy developing in simple opposition to traditional Indian life were all that Indians had to look forward to, then the future would be bleak. I believe that progress as usually formulated for India promises much more than it could ever deliver, and includes a hidden cost.

As this book concerns cultural evolution, the concept of culture itself requires some elucidation. Culture, says scholar Leslie White, "...rests on its own principles, it is governed by its own laws."[1] Culture can only be explained in terms of itself and has a course and an internal logic all its own. People and governments, according to this view, have a limited ability to change the course of culture by their volition and even radical changes in environment or trade do not necessarily alter a culture's course.[2]

Unchecked population growth — to take but one example that will receive further attention in later chapters — continues despite widespread acknowledgement of its destructive effects. The reason is culture. The same holds true for water pollution; Indians realize that the Ganges River is highly polluted, but their culture requires its use for a variety of religious and social functions and no amount of pontification about bacterial contamination seems able to lessen popular demand for the river's holy water. In a chapter on language in India, I will argue that Uttar Pradesh has many more English-medium schools than it needs because of entrenched cultural values rather than economic necessity. Time after time, I saw Indian culture develop independently of material and economic conditions.

Some imagine that economic advancements in South Asia will alter the very fabric of Indians' lives. But this is only indirectly true, if it is true at all. Open markets and airwaves will eventually leave their mark on South Asian culture but only through the medium of cultural symbols and values whose shape we cannot predict with any surety. White postulates — and my own experiences confirm — that culture moves in patterns divorced from external stimuli. Thus, the familiar metaphors about cultural change, the usual picture of tradition smashing into modernity like two trains speeding down opposite sides of the same track, have perhaps outlived their usefulness.[3] To think clearly about the changes in today's India we require a new model, our bi-directional banyan tree, a symbol borrowed, ironically, from ancient Sanskrit verses.

---

1 White, Leslie. *The Science of Culture: A Study of Man and Civilization* (New York: Grove Press 1949), p. 340.

2 White's views on culture are sometimes baffling. His student, Marshall Sablins, skewered White's theory of "energy" and culture, which attempts to relate technology and cultural movement. "He [White] was not amused when I objected that energy 'per capita' was the same as in the Old Stone Age, since the primary source remained the human body." In Salbins, Marshall. *The New York Times Magazine*, 9/22/08, p. 82.

3 Or cars bumping into bushes. See Friedman, Thomas. *The Lexus and the Olive Tree* (New York: Anchor Books 2000).

Pindar claimed, "Custom is King of all," and this serves as a succinct expression of the central thesis of this book.[1] India's future will be determined not only by economic development, but also by a dynamic traditional culture that continues to develop along its own lines — sometimes in concert, and sometimes in conflict with material enrichment. India develops not, as one writer has suggested, "in spite of the gods."[2] Rather, the seed for the creation and the fuel for the sustenance of India's economic boom lay in its traditions, as does, I will argue, the animating spirit of its future.

1 Cit. Herodotus. *The Histories* translated by Aubrey de Selincourt (New York: Penguin 1980), p. 220.
2 See Luce, Edward. *In Spite of the Gods: The Strange Rise of Modern India* (New York: Doubleday 2007).

Tameez aur Tahazeeb: Lucknow, Home of Manners and Civilization

Lucknow reminded me of Natchez, Mississippi, where I once traveled on business. Like Natchez, Lucknow was a place where people tried to preserve the genteel customs of a former age, called *tameez aur tahazeeb*, manners and civilization. Politeness in conversation was highly valued. Restaurants served finger bowls after meals and haggling in the market place rarely became contentious. On one trip to the bazaar, a shopkeeper gave me a free meal simply because he was "happy to meet me" and on many other occasions total strangers went out of their way to make me feel welcome.

Like some city of the Old South, Lucknow even had antebellum buildings. By "antebellum," I mean before the Indian Mutiny of 1857. The city was the site of some of the bloodiest fighting of this conflict. Prior to this, it was the capital of the Kingdom of Oudh (or Awadh), and was ruled by the Grand Nawabs (a title roughly equivalent to Duke) and independent Kings of the 18th and 19th centuries. Many building survived from this era, making the city a mix of Mughal-era mausoleums, Raj-era ruins, and huge, decaying estates with carriage houses and verandahs.

By the time I had arrived in Lucknow, one of these old homes had become Mrs. Sharma's Guesthouse, a port of call for foreign scholars where I spent my first week. There I made the acquaintance of the two other guests, Manuella, an anthropologist from the London School of Economics, and Matthew, a linguist from Kansas who translates Urdu fiction into English. Both Matthew and Manuella had been working in Lucknow for years, and both were fluent in Urdu and Hindi respectively. In the coming weeks, they both helped me make contacts with the local community.

Years earlier, while living in Varanasi, I met several people who studied Hindustani classical music in Lucknow, so I expected to find a small expatriate community there. At dinner, I asked Matthew and Manuella about this.

"Expatriate community?" said Manuella incredulously.

"You're looking at it!" she and Matthew said in unison.

They were only half joking. Most of the Western music students had forsaken Lucknow in favor of New Delhi and over the next few weeks, I met few foreigners in Lucknow. The city was never a major destination for travelers, but I was surprised to see so few in January, is peak tourist season in India.

Lucknow is the capital of Uttar Pradesh, the most populous state in India. This area has largely missed out on India's recent windfall in the computer and technology industries and remains poor, especially when compared to states like Karnataka, Maharashtra and Punjab. The state suffers from serious infrastructure problems that include water and air pollution, poor sanitation, power shortages and high illiteracy rates.

The rough appearance of Lucknow's streets perturbed my wife Deborah, who was in India for the first time. She had found Delhi enjoyable enough but had difficulty seeing the charm in Lucknow. After touring several neighborhoods, including some of the city's most exclusive areas, she asked me where the "modern section" was located. I did not know how to answer this question except to say that the word "modern" is relative.

At about 5:30 AM on our first night in Mrs. Sharma's Guesthouse, the Muslim call to prayer awakened us. Deborah groaned and rolled over, pulling the covers over her head. I stayed awake listening to the rise and fall of the imam's voice in the pre-dawn twilight. I am not religious in any sense, but I liked the melancholy sound of these Arabic verses.

> By the morning hours,
>
> And the night when it is stillest,
>
> Thy Lord hath not forsaken thee nor doth He hate thee,
>
> And verily the latter portion [of life] will be better for thee than the former...[1]

In the evening, we traveled by rickshaw to the neighborhood of Gomtinagar to see a film and crossed the Gomti River by bridge. Along the riverbanks, we noticed blazing bonfires from the holy burning *ghaats* (steps), where Hindu priests cremated the dead and immersed the ashes in the river. Bright orange flowers — thrown into the river as part of the funeral rites — floated on the green, brackish water giving it the appearance of a viscous, pea soup sprinkled with paprika.

---

1 See Pickthall, Mohammed Marmaduke, trans. *The Meaning of the Glorious Koran* (Tahrike Tarsile Quran, Inc., 2001).

The air on a still, hot night in a place like Lucknow carries smells impossible to describe, burning cow dung (a cheap source of fuel), sandalwood, kerosene and pollen. They mix together into a miasma that the visitor initially finds nauseating. For me, all these scents add up to something greater than its parts, an atmosphere of total stasis, as if the air had been hovering over the same ground for eons without change and would have hung there forever but for your arrival. On this night, it seemed as if it had all been waiting there for me, this air, this river, the bridge with rhesus monkeys chattering on its railings, the water buffalos staring at me with their pitch black eyes. I felt, as I do every time I arrive in India, as if I had finally arrived home — paradoxically to a place that I did not understand.

Gomtinagar was one of the more exclusive neighborhoods in Lucknow and the Gomti Picture Hall was as modern as any movie theater in America. There was one significant difference, however; the volume was deafening. The movie, *Mughal i Azzam* (The Great Mughal), is a classic Hindi film from the 1950s that tells the story of a Mughal Emperor, his son and the latter's impolitic love affair with a beautiful courtesan.[1] The first half of the movie was enjoyable enough to watch and included excellent Hindustani singing and dancing. The interaction between Akbar, his son the Prince, and the courtesan entranced me, even if I could not always follow the Urdu-laced dialogue.

Sadly, the idea that you should "leave them yelling for more" never caught on in India. The second half of *Mughal i Azzam* slowed to a crawl and, with the volume blaring, the experience soon became torturous. The emperor gave several long speeches on the meaning of leadership; the imperial army broke out into an endless song and dance number and the courtesan shamelessly overacted. More singing followed. The beautiful courtesan was condemned to death and entombed alive in the castle walls. A woman shrieked a song in a glass-shattering falsetto.

Just when I felt I could stand it no longer, the courtesan fled through a secret passageway, the credits started to roll, and the lights went on. Like the film heroine, we had escaped from *The Great Mughal* at last.

The next night, the staff of Mrs. Sharma's Guesthouse informed us that Mrs. Sharma had given permission for a wedding to take place in her house. As the guests arrived, the mother of the bride made sure to invite us to all of the festivities.

"No member of my family smokes, drinks or chews betel nut," she boasted. "We are quality people!"

---

1 The courtesan is played by the legendary Madhubala (d. 1969), the Indian equivalent (roughly) of Marilyn Monroe. Madhubala had a meteoric career. She was stunningly beautiful, driven, wildly promiscuous and dead by age 36. A painful degenerative disease ended first her film career, and then, nine years later, her life. See Akbar, Khatija. *Madhubala* (UBS Publishers and Distributors 1997).

The bride's family was not only "quality" but prolific as well — about four hundred guests arrived over the next few days. From the first light of dawn until after midnight, Mrs. Sharma's Guesthouse pulsed with the sound of Bollywood's loudest hits.

Looking for some peace and quiet one morning, Matthew, Deborah and I took a walk in the Lucknow Botanical Gardens. While sitting in the warm sunshine, Matthew pointed to a building that overlooked the park and remarked that the residents of this building must have nice views. Deborah and I later approached the gatekeeper of the building and asked whether any flats were available. We were in luck, and within two days, we had signed a lease for a third floor apart- ment in an area full of interesting historical memorials. Across the street lay the Sikandarbagh, or Garden of Alexander, the site of some of the bitterest fight- ing of the Mutiny of 1857 (see the chapter entitled *Uda Devii Zindabaad*, below). Just a short distance down the street in the other direction stood the Imambara Shahnajaf, the sprawling tomb of Ghazi-ud-din Haidar, King of Oudh 1814–1827. An early 20ᵗʰ century Indian history summed up his reign with the statement, "Ghazi-ud-din Haidar was most polite in his manner, and during his reign no event of importance took place."[1]

The haggling necessary to furnish the apartment was dizzying. Retailers in Hazratganj, Lucknow's main bazaar, posted grossly inflated prices that grew even larger when we walked through the door. Worse, the workmanship was often poor. One alternative was to seek out the carpenter's colony on the far bank of the Gomti River and order our furniture from the carpenters themselves. This was a time-consuming prospect, however, and we were eager to move out of Mrs. Sharma's (now very loud) Guesthouse as soon as possible.

Lucky for us, there was Gandhi Ashram, a state-operated worker's collective that manufactured and sold clothing and furniture. The prices were non-nego- tiable but fair and the workmanship simple but solid. Gandhi Ashram did not advertise, and all of the signs were in Hindi without English translation. The store in Lucknow included a statue of Gandhi himself in every corner, and the staff acted as if infused with the Mahatma's kindly spirit.

The shopping went smoothly until Wednesday night when we climbed into a cycle rickshaw at about 5 pm, intending to meet some deliverymen at our new apartment. With all the city buses, motorcycles, cows and water buffalos, riding a rickshaw through a large Indian city at rush hour can be frightening. During my time in India, however, I had managed to avoid any major collisions or accidents. The ability Indian drivers had to miss each other always amazed me.

My luck changed suddenly on this account when our rickshaw smashed into a motorcycle and tipped over. The rickshaw driver and I were both unharmed but Deborah was not so fortunate. She caught her hand between the rickshaw

---

1 Beg, M.A. *The Guide to Lucknow* (Lucknow: Royal Printing Press 1911), p. 25.

and the motorcycle and injured her fingers. By the time we arrived at the city hospital, one of her fingers had turned purple. But before we could rush into the emergency room, I needed to settle with the rickshaw driver, who insisted on extra money "because it is an emergency."

The doctor seemed competent enough, but his bedside manner was more appropriate for a veterinary clinic than a hospital. Without warning, he approached Deborah with a large hypodermic needle and tried to push me aside when I asked him what he was doing. As I had heard that Indian hospitals did not always use disposable needles and there was an outside chance of contracting serious infections (including HIV/AIDS) from dirty needles, I insisted that the doctor tell me the purpose of the injection. As it turned out, he was trying to give Deborah a shot for tetanus, against which she was already inoculated. After hearing this, he put the needle away but I got the feeling that he did not appreciate my meddling. Upon examination, the injury was not serious. With a few stitches and some dressing, the prognosis was that Deborah's hand would be as good as new in a week or so.

I took Deborah, with her bandaged hand, back to Mrs. Sharma's Guesthouse just in time to see the arrival of the groom and his accompanying marching band. As he paraded around the neighborhood on a horse, the bride's friends and family ushered us into the courtyard for dinner.

I asked the bride-to-be whether her parents had arranged her marriage or whether it was a "love marriage." She answered that it was both, explaining that although she met her fiancé in college, she still considered it an "arranged marriage" because she had sought the full agreement of both families before announcing the engagement.

Although the bride's family was solidly middle-class — consisting of hotel managers, bank tellers and cell-phone peddlers — the wedding was an opulent affair. The vegetarian, alcohol-free reception took place in a massive tent on the front lawn of Mrs. Sharma's Guesthouse. The men wore three-piece suits and colorful turbans while the women sparkled in silk saris and expensive jewelry. I realized too late that I had not brought a tie to India and had to get through the evening wearing nothing flashier than a smile.

Eventually the groom's procession returned. After a simple ceremony involving the exchange of flower wreaths (*maalaa*), the music and dancing started again and continued throughout the night.

We moved into our apartment the next day bringing a single table and bed as furniture. The rest would have to wait for the workmen at Gandhi Ashram. Some additional items proved to be surprisingly difficult to find. Mosquito nets, for example, were available only at a single store, *Kapoor's Macchardaanii Bhavan* (Kapoor's Mosquito Net Palace).

Even more difficult to find than a mosquito net was an Internet connection. Despite several misleading ads, broadband service was hard to come by. Installing a dial-up service was not very attractive because having a landline installed in a private residence is a prolonged process, especially for foreigners. One Delhi-based company promised to give me a price quote in 24 hours, but after two weeks of persistent badgering, I still had not heard from them.

To make matters worse, the Lucknow Police had started raiding Internet cafes looking for people who were downloading obscene materials. Each edition of the Lucknow papers carried endless stories about the arrests of 16-20 year olds caught offending public morality by accessing unwholesome websites. The crime of viewing obscene material in public carried a five to ten year imprisonment and a fine of 10,000–20,000 Rs.[1] *The Times of India* quoted the Lucknow police chief as saying, "We will . . . ensure that internet cafes do not turn into cozy nests of love bugs."[2]

The raids not only prevented Internet cafes from becoming "cozy nests," they had created a siege mentality. The staffs of most Internet cafes were evasive and jumpy, and not inclined to help a strange *farangii* (foreigner) with his computer problems.

Perhaps the most challenging problem we encountered while settling into our apartment was hiring a servant.[3] Although employing servants sounds luxurious, for us it was the lesser of two evils. As a foreigner with limited language skills, I was an easy mark for the vendors in the marketplace. A native-speaking servant could find a fairer price at the bazaar than I could, so hiring one made good economic sense. I also needed answers to a myriad of questions that arose about mundane day-to-day life in our adopted city — Where could I buy a bicycle? Is the insect in the bathroom dangerous? How do you know if a mango is ripe?

On the other hand, servants often required more time and attention than I would have needed to do the work myself. The first woman I hired spoke very quickly in an idiomatic version of Hindi and I had some difficulty communicating with her effectively. Either by mistake or by design, she ended up with the impression that we required three servants, not one. The doorbell started to ring every few hours with another servant who wanted to buy our groceries or dust our furniture.

Rectifying the situation was not easy. They took umbrage at our insistence that we only needed one servant to come *once* a day. It was hard to convince them that we were not in any way dissatisfied with their work, but that we simply did not generate enough disorder (or have enough furniture) to require so much

---

1 Roughly $225-$550 by the rate of exchange in early 2005.

2 "City cyberians land in police custody," *Times of India: Lucknow Edition*, 2/1/05, p. 3.

3 I realize the term 'servant' (*naukar*) sounds archaic and insensitive to the Western ear. It is in common usage in India, however, and does not carry the same negative connotations as it does in the West.

domestic help. I was afraid that some of them ended up with hurt feelings. Out of the lot of them, we selected Sona, a woman with a mischievous smile, as our *kaam karniwaalii* (worker). I would later regret the decision (see the chapter "Sona's Blue Refrigerator" below).

While wrestling with these issues Manuela, our anthropologist friend from Mrs. Sharma's guesthouse, stopped by and invited us to a Republic Day celebration at a nearby school scheduled for the next day. Unfortunately, she neglected to tell us that we were the guests of honor. When we arrived at 9:30 the next morning, the entire student body was waiting for us, standing in ranks. They refused to begin the celebration until we had taken our seats in front of them.

Once we had taken our seats, they marched around the school's courtyard and sang the Indian national anthem. It was all good fun until, during the martial arts display, some students began breaking fluorescent light bulbs with their bare hands, scattering shards of glass uncomfortably close to us.

Broken light bulbs aside, the students extended a warm welcome to us and we were touched that the entire school had spent their own national holiday entertaining a group of complete strangers from a distant land. This, I thought to myself, must be the meaning of *tameez aur tahazeeb*. I turned and looked at Deborah, who was sitting next to me. She seemed to be enjoying herself; perhaps she was thinking that there were more important things than being modern.

The International Museum of the Latrine: Sewage and Scavengers

My first stop in New Delhi was a nondescript building near Indira Gandhi International Airport, the Sulabh International Museum of the Latrine. This may seem like an odd choice; Delhi has a wide range of mosques, temples and shrines that would make a more picturesque starting point from which to initiate a survey of contemporary India. I was still thinking about the upside-down tree, however. If cultural change in India was bi-directional and today's India was moving in a radical new direction, then, I decided, the way I looked at India should be similarly inverted.

The problem of sewage may sound mundane, but it is one of the most vital issues confronting India today. Functioning sewage systems make large urban areas into hospitable environments for businesses and residents while their absence leads to grave ecological and public health problems. Ultimately, the flowering of human culture — literature, music, commerce, fine art and education — rises from this humblest of roots.

If you are tempted to laugh at the idea of a museum dedicated to commodes, then consider this: More than 1.5 billion liters of untreated sewage enter the Ganges River every day, increasing the already catastrophic number of deaths from water-borne diseases in the Ganges River plain.[1] According to the U.S. Agency for International Development (USAID), over 40% of India's urban population is "without any significant access" to a functioning sewage system and basic sanitation.[2] When you consider the environmental and public health problems that

---

1 Sharma, Sudhirendar. "Delhi: Demanding More from the Ganga," *Disputes Over the Ganga* (Kathmandu: Panos Institute 2004), p. 145.
2 http://www.usaid.gov/pubs/cp2000/ane/india.html.

arise from inadequate sewage systems in India, nothing is funny about the Sulabh Museum at all; latrines are serious business.

This is not to say that I did not have a few laughs while looking at the collection of loos on display or listening to the curator of the museum, Mr. Bhageshwar Jha. Mr. Jha took me on a tour of 2,500 years of sanitation history with an infectious passion and an irreverent humor. He showed me displays of water-closet memorabilia from the ancient city of Harappa to the modern age. The collection included archeological evidence for indoor sanitation systems in ancient India, placards explaining personal hygiene as described in the sacred texts of Hinduism, and examples of seemingly every indoor plumbing device ever invented.

According to Mr. Jha, the museum was the idea of Dr. Bindeshwar Pathak, the founder of the Sulabh International Social Service Organization. Dr. Pathak invented the *Sulabh Sauchaalaya* (literally, "easily-obtained latrine") system, a simple two-pit design for a public latrine that can be used without access to a functioning sewage main — an important feature in India, where most villages and cities are not connected to a public pipe system. The *Sulabh Sauchaalaya* system conserves water and allows for easy maintenance and using a *Sulabh Sauchaalaya* has a gentler impact on the environment than other forms of septic latrines. Over the last 30 years or so, Dr. Pathak and his organization claim to have built more than a million such facilities in India for both public and private use. Today Sulabh International is one of the largest NGOs in India.

The effort to improve sewage in modern India stretches back to Mahatma Gandhi himself. Gandhi-ji was reportedly so concerned with sanitation problems in India that he once requested that attendees to the All-India Congress Convention clean their own latrines.[1] Dr. Pathak sees himself as Gandhi's successor in the fight for a sanitary India. On the day I visited the Sulabh Museum, employee were singing religious hymns in the reception area in front of a statue of Gandhi.

Perhaps the comparison between Dr. Pathak and Mahatma Gandhi goes a little too far. The biography of Dr. Pathak provided in the press packet begins:

> Dr. Bindeshwar Pathak is a great humanist and social reformer of contemporary India. To the weaker sections of society especially, his is the compassionate face of a paternal redeemer. He has the vision of a philosopher and the undying zeal of a missionary. He is the icon of a new culture which embraces the poor and extols the dignity of labor. His boundless love for the downtrodden of India finds examples in myriad and tangible ways. No wonder those who know him intimately swear that Dr. Pathak is born to help the helpless.[2]

I wanted to see what this "paternal redeemer" and his organization had provided for Lucknow so I later visited the Sulabh facility in Hazratganj, the city's

---

1 Pathak, Bindeshwar. *Road to Freedom*, p. 39-40
2 "A Profile of Dr. Bindeshwar Pathak", p. 1.

main bazaar. It was qualitatively different from any public rest room I had ever entered. Sunshine descended through skylights, illuminating the immaculately clean interior, spotless tiles, and gleaming fixtures. The caretaker laughed when I asked him for permission to take photographs of this temple of plumbing.

The Sulabh facility in Hazratganj was opulent, but it paled next to the public rest room that Sulabh International built for the controversial guru Sri Sai Baba and his devotees.

> [A]n aesthetically exquisite and visually appealing, colourful toilet-cum-bath complex, spread over an area of over two acres at a total cost of Rs. 1.53 crores [approximately $350,000]....The toilet complex provides a variety of facilities to its users including 120 Water Closets, 108 bathing cubicles, 28 special toilets, sex dressing rooms [sic] and rows of urinals, immaculately laid out to avoid congestion.[1]

As I left the Sulabh latrine in Hazratganj, the caretaker asked for a rupee, which surprised me. I thought that Sulabh's facilities were for the use of the lower economic strata of India and I wondered how many people are discouraged from using the Sulabh Comfort Center because of this fee. A spokesperson from the local Sulabh office later claimed that the fee is voluntary. Still, I often saw men urinating in public within walking distance of the facility, and the Center itself was usually deserted.

THE SCAVENGERS

In addition to the public health and environmental problems they create, poor sewage systems engender social problems as well. The task of removing human waste (also called night soil) falls to members of the Scavengers caste, for whom sanitation has become a hereditary occupation. Believing it will make them ritually unclean, some upper caste Indians have an aversion to physical contact with Scavengers. Traditionally even the shadow of a Scavenger can temporarily make a Brahmin impure. Scavengers and similar castes are thus sometimes called "untouchables" and occupy the lowest level of the caste hierarchy.[2]

Uttar Pradesh currently has more Scavengers (between 1.5 and 2 million) than any other state in India.[3] Soon after my arrival in Lucknow, one of them appeared at my door offering to clean the bathroom.[4] I agreed to pay Rajkumar the Scavenger about 300 Rs. a month (about $8) to scour the commode three times a week. When I asked him about Scavengers in Lucknow, he told me that there were several Scavenger colonies in Lucknow, including one, Bhapunagar, which was less than a mile from my apartment.

---

1 *Sulabh Sanitation Movement* Sulabh International Social Service Organization, p. 69.
2 M.K. Gandhi called untouchables the Harijan, or "children of God." The current euphemism is *dalit*, a word meaning "oppressed."
3 *"Safai Karmachaariyon se Kede-makodon Jaisaa Bartaav," Dainik Jaagaran,* 2/17/05, p. 4.
4 A strict division of labor exists in India between cleaning the lavratories and other domestic work. The former was outside the domain of Sona, our servant.

I rode my bicycle to Bhapunagar the next day. After all that I had read about the oppression of the Scavenger caste, I expected to see a shantytown of some sort. What I found instead surprised me; the streets were lined with small, clean shops and the houses, while modest, were sturdy and well maintained. Bhapunagar was not the Hamptons, but neither was it the Howrah slums of Calcutta.

Rajkumar later explained that the City of Lucknow employs Scavengers to repair and maintain the city's aging sewage system. In this capacity, they earn about 5,000 Rs a month, or about $1,500 per year. While this is not exactly affluence, neither does it add up to complete destitution. Lucknow's Scavengers may inhabit the lowest level on the caste hierarchy, but they are not necessarily impoverished. Scavengers are in some ways similar to undertakers in our own society; the nature of their profession may disgust some people, but this disgust creates a level of job security. Moreover, in the night-soil trade — as in the funeral trade — business is always good.

> It means that employment is not a serious problem because of the nature of the job that scavengers do. There is no competing claim on the job....
> Hence, these families do not face difficulty in getting jobs in municipalities and corporations for scavenging work.[1]

At another Scavenger colony, Balmikinagar, I saw much the same thing I had seen at Bhapunagar — sturdy, working-class dwellings that displayed neither destitution nor opulence. Balmikinagar had the added attraction of a park dedicated to Maharish Valmiki, a low-caste Hindu sage who wrote and important Hindu epic, the *Ramayana*.

The Scavengers I met in Balmikinagar felt a strong sense of pride in their community's association to Maharish Valmiki and posed for pictures in front of his statue. Articulate and friendly, with some sporting costly Western-style clothing, the Scavengers hardly seemed like the destitute group I had learned about from Sulabh International. They all confirmed what Rajkumar had told me; the average salary for a Scavenger on the city payroll is 5,000 Rs a month, or about $1,500 a year.

In fact, the only real eyesore in Balmikinagar was the Sulabh Comfort Station. Unlike Sulabh's palace of personal hygiene in Hazratganj, Lucknow's main shopping district, the facility in Balmikinagar was in a state of complete disrepair. On the day I visited, it was filthy and swarming with flies.

After my trips to Bhapunagar and Balmikinagar, I started to wonder about some of the conclusions reached about the Scavenger community by Sulabh International. Dr. Pathak's book, *Road to Freedom*, for example, paints a monochromatic picture of Scavengers as oppressed and impoverished. This picture does not necessarily represent the Scavenger community that I found in Lucknow, however. Moreover, some of Dr. Pathak's claims about the destitution of the Scavenger

---

1 Pathak, p. 103.

community seem much less dramatic when placed in context. For example, he decries the high illiteracy rates among Scavengers, but neglects to mention that the illiteracy rate in Uttar Pradesh as a whole is not significantly higher.[1] Other statistics compiled by Dr. Pathak also require a grain of salt. It is not surprising, for example, that most Scavengers say they do not like their job and do not want their children to follow them into their profession.[2] I wonder how many plumbers and sanitation workers in America would express a similar sentiment. What these statistics do *not* show is the Scavengers' appreciation for job security and for respectable wages given to them in exchange for unskilled labor.

A New Sewage System for Lucknow?

Change may be in the — somewhat fetid — air for the Scavenger community. The Lucknow Municipal Corporation (LMC) and the government of Uttar Pradesh, in association with the Japan International Cooperation Agency (JICA), are planning a full-scale upgrade of the sewage systems of some of the largest cities in Uttar Pradesh. The government's $96-million plan includes Varanasi, Kanpur and Allahabad in addition to Lucknow.

Lucknow sorely needs an upgrade to its current system. The antiquated sewer system, originally built in 1917, covers only one-third of the city's neighborhoods and reaches only 60% of its population. [3] In many of the older neighborhoods, a constant stench arises from open sewers that run along the side of the roads.

Neither the residents of Balmikinagar nor Rajkumar express any worry about the government's plan to build a new, automated sewage system. When I suggested that this system might mean fewer government jobs for members of their community, they smiled politely and changed the subject. These unfortunate Scavengers, I said to myself, must be blind to their own self-interest.

Over the next few weeks, the coverage in the newspapers about the anticipated sewage system changed from unbridled optimism, to guarded optimism, to thinly veiled despair. The Japan International Cooperation Agency had difficulty understanding the Indian bureaucratic system and complained of "gaps" in the coordination of relevant ministries. At a stakeholders meeting, members of Uttar Pradesh's ruling Samaajwaadi (Socialist) Party ridiculed Japan International's plan and made scatological jokes at their expense.[4]

Then — silence. The story disappeared from the media. As it turned out, this was not the first time that grandiose plans for the rehabilitation of Uttar Pradesh's sewage problems had appeared in the papers. Many optimistic development organizations have sailed this rancid sea, only to founder on the reefs of Indian bureaucracy and political apathy.

---

1 *India Today, Special Issue*, May 19, 2003.
2 Pathak, Bindeshwar. *Road to Freedom*, p. 115.
3 "US, Japan plan to unclog city sewers," *Times of India* (Lucknow edition), 1/25/05, p. 3.
4 "Will sewer project be the 'link'?," *Times of India: Lucknow Edition*, 2/3/05, p. 3.

Suddenly, the Scavengers of Balmikinagar did not seem so blind.

Uttar Pradesh's sewage problem will remain serious for some time to come. While the zeal of Sulabh International is admirable, it offers only a stopgap solution. Sulabh's public facilities may lessen the toxification of the water table in some areas, but cannot serve as an adequate sewage system for Uttar Pradesh's roughly 170 million residents.

The only real solution to the sewage problem in Uttar Pradesh — and the water problems and health problems that it creates — is the creation of a modern, statewide sewage and treatment system. Unfortunately, the state has a long history of development projects that have not come to fruition and there is little promise that the latest efforts by JICA will be any different.

Why sewage development projects fail so often in India is difficult to grasp. The government of Uttar Pradesh could organize public works; Lucknow was full of massive monuments and parks to a wide range of historical figures. Ambedkar Park, for example, included a massive, elaborate ziggurat dedicated to Dr. Ambedkar, a low caste political leader. When it came to mundane (and politically neutral) projects like irrigation and sewage, however, the UP government seemed to lose interest.

Novelist Kiran Nagarkar's examines this blind spot in the civic life of Indians in his novel *Cuckold*. In one telltale scene, the practical crown prince of Mewar tries to interest a minister in repairing the kingdom's sewage system, only to find that the project fails to capture his imagination.

> The town planner, Sahasmal himself looked a little abashed and was making genteel squeamish noises and wondering why we didn't discuss architectural plans for a new complex of marble temples of the order found in Ranakpur or a new Victory Tower what would be twice as tall as the one that the great Rana Kumbha had built. After all, Father's victories are no less than my great grandfather's. I told him that they were excellent ideas and I was sure that he could find the finances for these projects...but that as far as the exchequer was concerned, it would stick to more mundane matters like discharge and outlet systems.[1]

With so much disdain for the inglorious cause of sewage modernization, the government's planned "eradication" of traditional scavenging by 2007 did not seem realistic, and has since failed to materialize.[2] As neither government-sponsored programs nor NGOs offer much hope for a long-term solution to the sewage problem, the day-to-day job of the removal of night soil will continue to be performed by the Scavenger caste, acting in their traditional role for some time to come.

This might not be so bad. Sulabh International claims to have "liberated" 60,000 Scavengers from their "sub-human profession" through the use of their

---

1 Nagarkar, Kiran. *Cuckold* (New Delhi: Harper Collins 1997), p. 20.
2 "Scavengers rotting in UP," *Times of India: Lucknow Edition*, 2/17/05, p. 3.

Sulabh system.[1] But no group stands to lose as much from the eradication of scavenging as do the Scavengers themselves. Traditional Indian society has provided a societal niche for them. Since Independence, the Scavenger community has enjoyed a growing sense of communal pride and a weakening of the social stigmas attached to their inherited profession. As long as the sewage systems in large cities like Lucknow remain dysfunctional, the government of Uttar Pradesh will continue to offer many Scavengers steady work unclogging and repairing the existing sewers. In the end, while few people would choose to be a Scavenger by choice, it's a living. Moreover, it is not clear what organizations like Sulabh International or the government of Uttar Pradesh can offer the Scavengers in place of their traditional lifestyle. Scavengers certainly desire freedom from discrimination and ostracism. Until a viable development scheme creates an attractive alternative, however, it is not in the Scavengers' best interest to be "liberated" from their jobs.

---

1 Pathak, Bindeshwar. *Road to Freedom: A Sociological Study on the Abolition of Scavenging in India* (Delhi: Motilal Banarsidas 1991), p. 6.

In Search of Flesh-Eating Turtles: Death Rituals and Water Pollution

If we could follow human excrement down the latrines of Lucknow and into the cracked pipes beneath the streets as it oozes through the aged sewage system, perhaps through an aged treatment facility — if it is functioning on that day — we would soon find ourselves in the Gomti River. Once there, fecal matter mixes with industrial waste, fertilizers and pesticides from nearby farms and the rotting carcasses of water buffalos, goats, cows and swine.

Mixed in with this pungent stew floats the fully or partially cremated remains of Lucknow's inhabitants. Traditionally, Hindus cremate their dead and scatter the ashes over the waters of a nearby river. Normally, this would not be a serious problem because small amounts of ash are relatively harmless to the health of a large river such as the Gomti. Unfortunately, the cremation ritual requires the erection of a wooden funeral pyre and, wood being expensive, poor families often cannot afford enough to incinerate their departed relative's remains fully. In other instances, funeral workers extinguish the funeral pyre prematurely so that they can salvage and re-sell the logs. In either case, many bodies end up floating in the river half-cremated.

To make matters worse, some bodies drop into the river without any cremation at all. The corpses of lepers, monks of certain ascetic orders, young children and those who have suffered a "bad death" (e.g., victims of accident or violence) are traditionally weighted and immersed in the river rather then burned. Although this is now illegal in many areas, it continues to happen with regularity.

However they end up there, human carcasses are disastrous for any waterway. They increase the levels of biological agents like bacteria, which are already far above normal in many Indian rivers. Near the city of Varanasi, a Hindu-pilgrimage center with extensive cremation grounds, the Ganges River is notoriously filthy. One prominent environmentalist, considering water pollution near Varanasi, remarked:

> When the 15th century poet Kabir wrote of the Ganga [Ganges], "Hell flows along that river, with rotten men and beasts," few would have believed his impious lament would one day prove so prophetic.[1]

Although Lucknow's cremation grounds are much smaller than Varanasi's, half-burned cadavers add significantly to the Gomti's contamination as well. Water contamination from half-burned bodies and body parts contribute to a catastrophic public-health crisis in Uttar Pradesh, where roughly one person dies of dysentery every minute.[2] Effective, alternative methods for the disposal of the dead will not solve all the Gomti's problems, but they would be a step in the right direction.

THE ELECTRIC CREMATORIUM

A traditional Hindu funeral requires a small army of ritual specialists. The Dom (pronounced "dome") caste is responsible for erecting the funeral pyre itself. Members of the lowest, or untouchable, castes, the Dom nevertheless have a lucrative monopoly on the sale of wood at the cremation grounds, and they extract as much money as possible from the mourners. If the deceased's family balks at the price, the result could be a small pyre that does not fully burn the corpse. Reportedly, the Doms are not very polite when they demand their due, either. One anthropologist overheard a Dom say the following to the bereaved family of an elderly man:

> "Your respected father won't die again and again. You won't perform his last rites time after time. Your father raised you, educated you. Now you must give with an open heart.... Do the work happily. You will die also. You too will arrive here.... So how did he die? Did you poison him?"[3]

Other than the Dom, the family of the deceased must employ a Mahabrahmin, a member of a sub-group of the Brahmin (or priest) caste, who performs elaborate rites for the repose of the soul of the dead over a period of several weeks. The Mahabrahmins also drive a hard bargain. Their leverage in these negotiations is supernatural; if the ceremonies are botched, the ghost of the departed (called a *pret*) could return to haunt the living.

The list of required funerary specialists does not end there. The family also must hire an additional Brahmin priest for subsequent observances, as well as a barber, who cuts the hair of the mourners and acts as a type of "gofer" during

---

1 Sharma, Sudhirendra. "Delhi: Demanding More from the Ganges," *Disputes Over the Ganga: A Look at Potential Water-related Conflicts in South Asia* Subba, Bhim ed. (Kathmandu: Panos Institute 2004), p. 146.

2 *Ibid.*, p. 135.

3 Parry, Jonathan. *Death in Benares* (New Delhi: Cambridge University Press 1994), p. 92.

the funeral rites. Each of these specialists takes his cut, and by the time the ordeal is over, a family could spend many thousands rupees. This cost is simply too high for many poor Indians. Often the families of the deceased must canvass their neighbors and relatives for funds to cremate the body. In many cases, this leads to cutting corners, such as not using enough wood.

In an attempt to solve this problem, the Government of India has built several electric crematoriums that allow people to cremate the dead at a bargain price. In Lucknow, the use of the electric crematorium costs only a few hundred Rupees. Despite this low price, however, the impact of these facilities on water pollution remains unclear. Although most Indians realize that the traditional Hindu funeral is expensive, prolonged, and ecologically destructive, they have not embraced the use of electric crematoriums in large numbers.

Some of the reluctance to use the electric crematorium arises from religious tradition. Brahmin priests objected that they could not perform the proper solemnities if the cremation occurred in an electric crematorium. *Kapaal Kriya*, or "skull breaking," for example, is essential to an orthodox Hindu funeral. This ritual requires the "chief mourner" (usually the departed's son or other male relative) to break open the head of the corpse as it smolders on the pyre. Accomplished by means of a bamboo stave, *Kapaal Kriya* marks the emancipation of the soul from the body. An electric cremation makes proper skull breaking impossible and could result in the spirit of the dead hanging around as an angry ghost (or *bhuut pret*) — a serious peril for the family of the deceased.

Despite these problems, the first electric crematorium in Varanasi enjoyed a brief period of popularity. "Brief" because, by accident or design, the facility suffered from surprisingly frequent electrical outages and repair problems that left it inoperable much of the time. Some people believed that the Doms and the Brahmins conspired to sabotage the operation of these facilities. Whether this allegation is true or not, both the Brahmins and the Doms stood to lose a great deal from the widespread use of electric crematoriums. The Doms would no longer be able to exact a high price for wood, and the Brahmins would have a need to curtail their elaborate rituals.[1]

I visited Lucknow's cremation grounds on the banks of the Gomti one morning to see for myself why people prefer expensive wooden funeral pyres to the reasonably priced electric crematorium. When I arrived, the traditional funeral grounds were full of mourners, Doms, Brahmins and the bodies of the dead wrapped in saffron cloths. Following the directions of the Brahmin priest, mourners circled the blazing pyres to the accompaniment of rhythmic Sanskrit chants. A large statue of the god Shiva looked on. Shiva has a special connection to the funeral grounds; a medieval hymn says of him "You play in the cremation

---

1 *Ibid*, pgs. 67, 97.

grounds, your friends are flesh-eating demons, you cover your body with the ashes of the dead, and you wear a garland of human skulls."[1]

The "City Department's Electric Body Burning House," just a short distance away, appeared to be empty. A metal gate barred the door of the imposing, factory-like building. I found my way in through a side door, where I met Muhammad Rashid, the facility's Electrician, and Ram Grish, the Operator. They told me that they were just finishing the morning's third cremation. Behind them, I could see smoke billowing out from one of the cremation chambers. No mourners were present, however. Muhammad and Ram told me that the most people who end up in the electric crematorium have no family. Even when they do, the cremation often occurs without them. The bodies usually arrive in the morning and they return the ashes to the next of kin in the afternoon.

Muhammad estimated that 90–95% of cremations occur on traditional wooden funeral pyres. Those who end up in the electric crematorium are often wards of the state, the homeless, vagabonds and those who have suffered a "bad death." When asked why the electric crematorium is so unpopular, both Muhammad and Ram told me that wooden funeral pyres are an "ancient tradition" and that people do not want to change it, regardless of environmental concerns. Both men denied that the electric crematorium closed frequently due to electrical shortages or repairs.

Muhammad doubted the validity of the Brahmins' objection to the electric crematorium on the grounds it precluded skull breaking. "Actually," he said, "the extreme heat of the electric crematorium will break open the skull anyway, naturally. You do not have to break it open yourself. If people just realized this, they would use our facility."[2]

I left with the impression that funerals at the electric crematorium were drab events. The facility was set back from the river and the architecture was boxy and inelegant. Moreover, while the regular cremation grounds contained religious icons of the various Hindu deities, the inside of the electric crematorium had all the charm of the Brooklyn Department of Motor Vehicles. I wondered whether the city would have more success in promoting its use if they invested in some cosmetic changes to the building and put some thought towards interior design.

The Electric Body Burning House was not only ugly, but inconvenient as well. While regular cremations continued late into the night, a sign outside the electric

1 Translation mine, Sanskrit text found in Pavitrananda, Swami trans. *Siva-Mahimnah Stotram: The Hymn on the Greatness of Siva* (Calcutta: Elm Press 1976), p. 49.

2 As a Muslim, Muhammad may not have understood the subtleties of the Hindu cremation rituals. In actuality, the *Kapaal Kriya* or "skull breaking" bestows spiritual benefits on both the deceased and the chief mourner. Thus, even if the skull does break under the intense heat of the electric crematorium, the chief mourner would not reap any spiritual benefit. Parry, Jonathan. *Death in Benares* (New Delhi: Cambridge University Press 1994), p. 184.

crematorium insisted, "The last body must be received by 4pm." In Lucknow, perhaps the Dom did not need to sabotage the electric supply; the facility operated under so many constraints that it could not compete with traditional funerals anyway.

After wandering down to the traditional cremation grounds, I spent some time talking to mourners participating in traditional death ceremonies. They all complained about the cost of the funeral rituals and all of them seem aware of rising pollution levels in the Gomti River. They all agreed, however, that only criminals and lepers use the electric crematorium; they would never use it themselves.

I met a young man named Ranu Shuklu, who held a PhD in Botany. Dr. Shuklu was mourning the death of his friend's father. He ridiculed the superstitions and chicanery that surround the funeral rites and expressed concern over the pollution of the Gomti and its effect on local animal and plant life. I asked him if, upon his own death, he would prefer a cremation in the city's Electric Body Burning House. "Well," he said slowly, "in that case, the funeral is really for the benefit of my family, not me, so I would let my family decide."

Dr. Shuklu thought for a moment and then added that people in Lucknow preferred traditional funerals because of the relatively cheap cost of wood. "In Calcutta, it would be too expensive for many people to have a ceremony like this. Here, though, it is possible..." he said with a shrug.

Funerals and cremations are a time of great emotional stress and mourners are often happy to let tradition dictate their actions. While survivors grieve, it is easy for savvy professionals like the Dom and Brahmins to prey on their psychological insecurities and to pressure them into paying more for a cremation than they intended. While most people care about the environment to some extent, the bereaved's chief concern is giving their family member or friend a dignified send-off. As long as Lucknow's electric crematorium looks like some sort of "dark satanic mill," it will never be a viable alternative to traditional cremation.[1]

In Search of Flesh-Eating Turtles

In the late 1980s, the state government of Uttar Pradesh and the *Ganga Pariyojanaa Nideshaalaya* (Ganges Project Department, or GPD) came up with an innovative idea to control water pollution. If people spurned the use of electric crematoriums, then perhaps they could eliminate "floaters" *after* the bodies were already in the river. Their plan was to re-introduce a species of animal into the

---

1 Herodotus preserves an anecdote about the Persian emperor Darius, who once offered Greek prisoners any price if they would eat the bodies of their ancestors. He made the same offer to a cannibalistic tribe (supposedly from India!), except he insisted that they burn their dead rather than eat them. Each group refused Darius's money, choosing adherence to cultural norms over material advantage. See, Herodotus. *The Histories* translated by Aubrey de Selincour (New York: Penguin 1980), p. 220.

Ganges and its tributaries that would eat floating corpses and body parts, cleaning the water in the process.

Several species of turtles fit the bill.[1] In tests, they had a ravenous appetite for rotting flesh. Moreover, they were easy to breed in large numbers by using incubators. Scientists discovered that they could habituate the turtles to human flesh before their release to ensure that *homo sapiens* was their dinner of choice. Lastly, because turtles had a religious meaning in Hinduism — Hindus believe that the god Vishnu once incarnated as a divine turtle — the Indian public could, in turn, easily digest the idea of turtles swallowing their final remains.

By the mid 1990s, the GDP had released over 24,000 flesh-eating turtles into the rivers and streams of Uttar Pradesh with the hope that the turtles would prosper and reproduce. A rumor that the turtles had developed a taste for human flesh and had begun to nip living bathers proved to be wholly untrue. Between the inception of the project and the present day, however, that optimism has faded. The Ganges and its tributaries, including the Gomti, are just as polluted as ever, and no apparent change in the number of half-burned bodies floating in the waterways of North India has occurred.

So what happened to the turtles? To find out I contacted Dr. Suhendhir Sharma, an ecological expert and the author of an important article on flesh-eating turtles in *India Today*.[2] Over lunch, I asked him where to find the animals that he wrote about in his article. Surprisingly, he told me that the flesh-eating turtles had disappeared.

"What happened to them?" I asked.

Nobody knows, he told me, because the government never conducted a follow-up study. Dr. Sharma offered several theories, however. One conjecture holds that local villagers discovered that the flesh-eating turtles were themselves quite tasty. Over time, these villagers decimated the turtle populations through poaching. Another plausible explanation from the missing turtles is that they found their way to Chinese food markets as part of an illegal trade in endangered animals. Sadly, experts realized this danger even before the project's completion. In Dr. Sharma's article, the director of the GPD, K. Mohan remarked, "Until some areas of the Ganges are given the status of a sanctuary, it could be fatal to the turtles to be released."[3]

After my lunch with Dr. Sharma, I despaired of ever seeing the flesh-eating turtles. Then one day, I stumbled upon a reference in the newspaper to a "Crocodile- and Turtle-Release Program" at a place called the Kukeral Crocodile Reserve, located on a tributary of the Gomti about 10 km from Lucknow. I wondered whether the turtles in this program were the ones I was looking for.

---

1 *Kachuga kachuga, Kachuga tecta,* and *Geoclemys hamiltonii.*
2 Sharma, Sudhirendra. *"Jalacharon ka Jauhara," An Advanced Hindi Magazine Reader,* Mishra, Awadhesh ed. (Varanasi: Abhaas Prakashan 1994). Reprinted from *India Today.*
3 *ibid.* Translated from the Hindi.

I hired a car and headed out to the crocodile reserve. As it turned out, three species of turtles lived in the facility's animal pens. A brief chat with the game-keeper, Mr. Shaam Laal, confirmed that these were the same species used in the GPD program. I asked Mr. Laal what had happened to the turtles after their release. He threw up his hands and said simply, "The government did not invest money in the project, so they died."

Not only did Mr. Laal let me see one of the remaining turtles, he also opened up one of the cages and let my wife Deborah photograph it up close. This particular turtle, a female *Kachuga kachuga*, was camera shy. Mr. Laal roused her from a pool of muddy water with his hand, but she swam away and hid in a corner. So he reached into the pool with both arms and lifted the flesh-eating creature out of the water, placing it not more than two feet in front of us.

To tell the truth, the *idea* of flesh-eating turtles is much more frightening that the actual animal itself. This *Kachuga kachuga* stuck its head out from its shell and considered us with a slightly peeved look. Her expression was not ferocious, just irritated. I am not going to eat you, she seemed to say to us, but don't expect a Christmas card.

I asked Mr. Laal if this particular turtle had a name.

"Like I told you," he said. "It is *Kachuga kachuga*."

I explained that it was not the species I was asking about but rather the personal name of this particular animal. I told him that in America, many zoos name the animals that they keep — like Mai Xiang, the Panda at the National Zoo in Washington DC.

He found the idea ridiculous. "You can just call it *Kachuga kachuga*," he answered curtly.

As I looked into *Kachuga kachuga*'s eyes, I saw more than a bored reptile; I saw Uttar Pradesh's cremation problems in all their grotesque totality. In lieu of effective policies that would prevent the dumping of half-burned bodies into rivers and streams, India had turned to this innocent turtle to solve its problems. Sadly, the result of this experiment was that thousands of *Kachuga kachugas* disappeared without a trace. It occurred to me that she had much more to fear from us than we did from her.

In the end, neither electric crematoriums nor flesh-eating turtles had much effect on the pollution levels in the Gomti River. What bothered me most was that both schemes *seem* like good ideas. I wondered whether a public relations campaign and redesigned facilities, which allowed for the full range of traditional rites, people would use the electric crematoriums in larger numbers. Perhaps a properly funded turtle release program really could perhaps also make a difference, were the government of Uttar Pradesh willing to try again.

When I was living in New York City, I often found myself stuck in traffic on the Brooklyn-Queens Expressway near the Calvary cemetery. When I was not looking at the license plate of the truck in front of me, I would gaze out over the vast field of headstones towards the East River. How foolish, I thought, to give so much good real estate to people who can no longer enjoy it.

Maybe I was the fool. After all, why should I expect people to think rationally about their most irrational fear, death? At the fault line between being and nothingness, when that special somebody becomes "some body," all of our otherwise sensible thoughts give way to mortal terror. The realization that a beloved family member has now become an inanimate public-health hazard does not come easily to us. Like Prince Hamlet, we are too busy contemplating (or maybe breaking) the skull of "poor Yorick," to give much thought to the ecological impact of death. On a planet of six billion people, however, we need to find a better place to put all those bones once our soliloquy has ended.

EATING BABY SHARKS: THE FAILING FISHERIES OF GOA

Hindu mythology tells the story of Manu, a type of oriental Noah, who one day finds a little fish swimming in his bath water. The fish begs Manu to spare him. "Preserve me," says the fish, "and I will preserve you." Manu accepts the deal, raising the fish until he becomes so large that Manu must set him free in the ocean. To repay his kindness, the fish warns Manu about the imminent deluge and instructs him to build an ark to ride out the storm, much as Noah does in the Book of Genesis. The fish then tows Manu's ship in the direction of dry land, saving him and — as Manu and his wife end up repopulating the decimated earth — indirectly saving the whole human race as well.[1]

Preserve me and I will preserve you. The fish's offer came to mind as I sat at Felice and Zeon's Italian Restaurant in the village of Chapora on the coast of Goa and stared down a baby shark. Felice, the head chef, had offered to make me

---

[1] See Cotterell, Arthur *A Dictionary of World Mythology* (New York: Perigee Books, 1979), p. 75. In some versions of the story the fish reveals himself to be Matsya, an avatar of Vishnu. The *Srimaad Bhaagavatam* adds that the fish was golden in color and had a single horn. Swami Bhaktivedanta Prabhupada further glosses the relevant verse (8.44) by saying that the fish was "8 million miles long." He reads *niyutayojanah* as a measurement of Matsya's massive dimensions. Alternately *yojana*, originally a measurement of the distance covered by one yoking of draught animals (about 8 miles), may mean "harnessing." *Niyutayojana* thus becomes loosely "a million harnessings-strong," a compound describing Matsya's ability to pull Manu's ark to safety, or even "he of a million harnessings" referring to the circular nature of Hindu cosmology. This interpretation foreshadows the action of the succeeding verses, which describe Manu tethering his craft to Matsya's horn, and suggests yogic discipline — both *yog* and *yojana* derive from the root, *yuj* — while avoidsing Bhaktivedanta's fantastic claim of piscine enormity. See Prabhupada, Bhaktivedanta, ed. *Srimad Bhagavatam: Eighth Canto* (Los Angeles: Bhaktivedanta Book Trust 1977), p. 255 and Monier-Williams, Monier. *Sanskrit-English Dictionary* (New Delhi: Munshiram Manoharlal Publishers 1988), p. 858.

something special for dinner. A native of Naples, Felice makes the best Italian food in Goa, possibly in all of India, and I was sure that whatever he made would be excellent. When the waiter later appeared with an eleven-inch-long grilled baby shark, however, I did not know what to say. I knew that catching and serving a baby shark violated fishing laws, depleted the adult shark population and removed an important link in the food chain. I mulled on the environmental irresponsibility of serving illegal catch like baby shark. I had half a mind to confront Felice for including it on the menu. I even considered telling him the story of Manu and emphasizing how a little fish, like the one on the plate before me, had once saved the human race.

I couldn't pontificate on an empty stomach, however, and I thought I would try a bite first. It was delicious. A well-prepared baby shark is a culinary rapture with few bones to get in the way. Adult sharks sometimes acquire an ammonia taste from years of swimming in polluted water, but a young shark lacks these impurities. Prepared correctly, baby shark is the veal of the sea, with a heavy, white flesh that needs little seasoning. One bite turned into two or three and, as the shark was minnow-sized, I soon cleared my plate. Having now fallen down the slippery slope of environmental sin, I could not think of a good reason to stop and ordered a second baby shark to follow the first. One fewer shark is not the end of the world, I reasoned.

Shark is not the only seafood delicacy available in Goa. The area is famous for fish. Goan fish curry is the local culinary favorite and, until the tourist industry came along, fishing was the bread-and-butter occupation of coastal Goans. Even today, villagers often spend Sunday afternoon walking without shoes into the muddy shallows to collect mussels and clams and people still greet each other when entering their neighbor's homes by asking, "What you bring, fish?"

In Chapora harbor, a fleet of about 50 fishing boats left daily from the pier beneath the Chapora Fort, an old Portuguese fortress guarding the mouth of the Chapora River. One December day shortly before sunrise, I boarded the *Sahil*, a 32-foot trawler with a crew of three. The captain, Ramesh, had been fishing the waters off Goa for 16 years, following a family tradition that went back generations. He knew the waters intimately: where the reefs fell and how to follow the currents out of the harbor according to the tides.

Soon after reaching open water, Ramesh pointed to a dark spot on the water's surface about a kilometer from the boat. "Sardines," he said. "You can tell by the way the water shimmers." His sharp eyes were professional assets; the law prohibits sonar devices on fishing boats. To find fish, he followed the schools of dolphins as they fed; for prawns, he trawled near submerged rocks and reefs. Tuna, he told me, are difficult to catch because they stay in deep water and are active only at night.

After a few hours of trawling, the crew hauled in the nets and emptied a menagerie of flailing sea life onto the *Sahil's* deck. Prawns, pomfret, kingfish, squid, rockfish and kite fish all squirmed and flopped on the slippery wooden surface. Large crabs in a variety of shapes and colors snapped their claws in the air and, sometimes, at the crew's feet. Some species got a second chance. The crew returned poison puffer fish, kite fish, sea snakes and cuttlefish to the sea. I asked about shark, and Ramesh told me that they usually only pulled in a few small ones close to shore. Later in the day, the crew found a dead baby shark tangled in their nets. The captain threw it back in the ocean.

As we trawled the waters, Ramesh told me that the fishing industry in Goa had changed drastically over the last 15 years. The fleet of approximately 50 boats was only a remnant of a 100-strong fleet that sailed from Chapora 20 years ago. The four other active ports in Goa had seen a similar reduction in fishing boats, while the Tirakol River fleet in the extreme north of the state was wholly defunct. The future of the fishing industry did not look bright and Ramesh did not want his son to follow in his footsteps.

"Computers," he said. "Computers aren't going away. I want him to be a programmer, not to spend his life looking for fish that aren't there."

Ironically, this reduction in fishermen coincided with an increase in market demand for fish. High-end catch like full-grown tuna and large tiger prawns often ended up in a sushi bar in Japan where they sold for high prices. An influx of tourists into the area also pushed up the prices of most species. A report from the Washington-based International Food Policy Research Institute showed that demand for fish, while stable in developed countries, had skyrocketed in developing nations.[1] Overall, the world's appetite for fish had doubled in the last 20 years.

In South Asia, fierce competition for fish sparked an undeclared "fish war" between India and Pakistan. Every year the Indian and Pakistani navies incarcerated foreign fishermen who invaded their coastal waters in search of fish. In early 2007, Pakistan freed 115 Indian fishermen accused of violating Pakistan's marine territory. The Pakistani government impounded their boats in the hopes that this would reduce the number of incursions in the future.[2]

The Goan fishing industry suffered not from a fall in demand but from declining yields in the catch. The Goan catch skyrocketed from 17,000 tons in 1963 to a high of 101,922 tons in 1993. Technological advances, such as mechanized winches, increased productivity, allowing crews to cast their nets more frequently each day. By the mid-90s, however, catches had dropped to about 60,000 to 70,000 tons annually despite these mechanical improvements, indicating a fishery under extreme stress.[3]

---

1 See http://news.bbc.co.uk/2/hi/science/nature/3156340.stm.

2 "Pak releases 115 Indian Fishermen," *Kashmir Images*, 1/10/07, p. 2.

3 See Z A Ansari, C T Achuthankutty, and S G Dalai. "Overexploitation of fishery resources, with a particular reference to Goa," (*National Institute of Oceanography*, 2006), p. 287.

GOAN FISH CATCH IN TONS

Year	Total fish catch	Growth
1963	17,000	
1970	36,616	+115.3
1980	25,715	-29.77
1990	56,225	+118.6
1991	75,622	+34.5
1992	96,333	+27.3
1993	101,922	+4.76
1994	95,840	-5.0
1995	81,856	-15.58
1996	92,737	+13.29
1997	91,277	-1.57
1998	67,236	-26.33
1999	60,075	-10.65
2000	64,563	+7.47
2001	69,386	+7.47
2002	68,462	-1.3

From Z.A. Ansari, C.T. Achuthankutty, and S.G. Dalai, "Overexploitation of fishery resources, with a particular reference to Goa" (*National Institute of Oceanography*, 2006).

On the day I spent aboard the *Sahil*, the crew pulled in 10 large tiger prawns, about four kilos of crab, another seven kilos of high-value fish and a few kilos of low-priced "junk" fish for sale to poor locals. The sale of this meager catch provided for captain Ramesh and his crew of three. I conducted an informal survey of the daily catches over the next few weeks which showed that this problem is common. Ships often came in without enough fish even to pay for the cost of fuel.

With such meager catches, just keeping the *Sahil* in the water was a feat. The rising price of diesel alone could ground a boat, as can repairs on an aging ship. The *Sahil* was about 30 years old and it showed some wear and tear. Deck planks were splintered and rotting; the engine looked more rust than metal. Ramesh signed a deal with the devil just to keep the *Sahil* in business; intermediaries from the nearby cities of Panjim and Mapusa provided money for the *Sahil's* fuel and repairs. In return, Ramesh agreed to sell his catch to them for a fixed price, far below market price. Many ships' captains are, metaphorically speaking, in the same boat:

> The result is a vicious circle: as catches per vessel fall, profits plummet, and fishers overfish to maintain supplies, causing serious depletion of

stock and thus endangering long-term availability. With falling returns, the asset stock value of vessels goes down, compelling owners to continue fishing at uneconomic rate [*sic*] of return, incurring losses and damaging the resource base.[1]

The decline in Goa's fishing fleet reflected a global crisis in fish stocks. A 1997 report by the UN Food and Agriculture Organization (FAO) estimated that 69% of the world's fish stocks were over-exploited. Recently, a panel of maritime experts predicted that all of the world's commercially viable fish stocks could fail in the next 50 years, thus eliminating roughly 40% of the world's available food.[2] Biologist and environmentalist Jared Diamond, in his recent book *Collapse: How Civilizations Choose to Fail or Succeed*, lists failing fish stocks as one of the 12 potential environmental catastrophes that could lead to a sudden, drastic, planet-wide reduction in living standards.[3] The fish crisis is thus not a "green" cause, or an environmental nicety; it is a problem of almost eschatological import.

Mr. Vishnajit Parab, the chairman of the Chapora Boat Owners Fisheries Co-op Society Ltd., initially blamed the feebleness of the Western Ghat fish stocks on the GATT agreement of 1994. Before this agreement most boat owners were local fishermen, using small boats with hand-pulled nets. Following the passage of GATT, however, large trawlers from Taiwan, Japan and other Asian nations began to fish the waters off India. Although regulated to the ocean beyond 100 kilometers from shore, Mr. Parab told me that they often approached close to land as well. Equipped with Fishfinder radar systems, these foreign ships decimated the local cuttlefish, ribbonfish, salmon and shark populations. From what I understand about the GATT agreement, I failed to see how its passage affected local fish stocks as Mr. Pranab claimed. When I asked him to explain the connection between the two, he changed the subject, alleging that the real cause of the depletion of Goa's fish stocks was the tsunami of December 2004. "After the tsunami, everything changed," Mr. Parab said ruefully. "Before [the tsunami] about 50% of the local population were involved in fishing; now it is only 10%. The price of diesel has skyrocketed while the profits from fish sales have remained stagnant."

According the Mr. Parab, few fishermen made any profit at all from their work in Chapora. He explained that many local boat owners continued to fish simply to defray the cost of maintenance, which could amount to 50,000 rupees annually for a boat in dry dock. Mr. Parab predicted that in 10 years the Chapora port would close for the same reason as the Tirakol River port. In Tirakol, a sandbar

---

1   ZA Ansari, CT Achuthankutty, and S G Dalai. "Overexploitation of fishery resources, with a particular reference to Goa," (*National Institute of Oceanography*, 2006).

2   See http://www.newscientist.com/channel/life/endangered-species/dn10433-no-more-seafood-by-2050.html.

3   Diamond, Jared. *Collapse: How Civilizations Choose to Fail or Succeed* (London: Penguin 2005), p. 488.

closed off the harbor except at high tide. The costs of dredging the port were prohibitively expensive for the local community, so the port closed permanently. The Chapora harbor faced a similar fate, but Mr. Parab hoped that the government would help defray the cost of dredging, thus allowing the fishing industry in Chapora to flounder on for a few years.

The government intervention Mr. Parab hoped for, however, may only make the situation worse by creating a "perverse subsidy."

> The main reasons behind all these failures [of fish stocks] are the tragedy of the commons...which makes it difficult for consumers exploiting a shared renewable resource to reach agreement despite their shared interest in doing so; the widespread lack of effective management and regulation; and so-called perverse subsidies i.e., the economically senseless subsidies that many governments pay for political reasons to support fishing fleets that are too large in relation to their fish stocks, that lead almost inevitably to overfishing, and that yield too low profits to survive without subsidies.[1]

I asked him about baby shark, telling him that I often saw it on the piers in Chapora and in the local restaurants, despite it being illegal catch. He explained that the sharks are often dead when pulled aboard the ship, "Why not get some benefit from the shark?" He asked, "We cannot bring it back to life."

Adding to the woes of the Goan fisheries, pollution has sullied the waters and made life for the fish that remain even more difficult. A 2006 report from the *European Journal of Parasitology* noted that pollutants in the water had been especially bad for sole, mackerel, sardines and ribbonfish.[2] At the Panjim Jetty, a large port in the city of Panjim, fishermen complained of the small catches and the long distances they traveled just to find any fish at all.

The tsunami, GATT, pollution, Fishfinder radar, everybody offered a different reason why the Goan fisheries were failing. In the end, however, the reason for the impending demise of the world's fish stocks rests "not in the stars but in ourselves." Humanity, in principle, possesses the foresight to understand the crisis, the compassion to worry about the future condition of the planet and the intelligence to draw up clever plans for fish conservation. If food were the direct result of calculated self-interest, everyone in India — myself included — would forego seafood like baby shark for more sustainable fare.

Choices about food are often more an issue of culture than reason, however. Environment sometimes dictates what appears on our plates; but more often tradition and habit shape our diet. Consider the medieval Norse who colonized the west coast of Greenland. For four hundred odd years they clung precariously to the icy shore, but by the 15th century the Greenland Norse were extinct. The causes contributing to the colony's failure are complex, but some suggest a cul-

---

1 Diamond, p. 280.
2 "Pollution Killing Goa's Fishing Industry," *Herald* [Goan edition], 12/26/06, p. 1.

tural disdain for seafood was an important factor in their demise. The Greenland Norse, like most Scandinavians of the time, preferred beef and a believed that seafood was useful only animal feed. This cultural attitude did them no favors in Greenland, where their cattle herds froze to death. Surrounded by seas teeming with edible species of fish that they stubbornly refused to exploit, the Norse suffered from a protein poor-diet, grew weak and eventually succumbed to Inuit raiders.[1]

Goa and much of the world has just the opposite problem; fish remains a food of choice despite rising prices and limited availability. One day, from a café on the shore of Chapora harbor, I watched the weekly, Sunday procession of Goan women into the shallow waters at low tide to collect shellfish. The women chatted as their arms dipped into the water and plucked clams and cockles from the harbor floor. The event was as much a social event as a fishing trip. Later, catch in hand, these women would visit relatives who would great them with a jolly "What you got, fish?"

I wondered how many generations of Goans had done the same, Sunday after Sunday, generation after generation back through the centuries to a time when the oceans seemed inexhaustible. As the tide rose I imagined the legendary, ancient deluge; how Manu, the progenitor of mankind, rode the endless seas, his ark pulled by a grateful, giant fish. In my imagination, Manu's ark grew ever heavier and larger, and the fish ever smaller until it slipped from the noose and disappeared, now only a squiggly tadpole, into the blue. "Preserve me and I will preserve you," the fish had said. If only we had listened.

---

1 See Diamond. Modern Mongolians have much the same problem. Outer Mongolia has many lakes and streams with edible local fish. Traditionally, however, water was the residence of evil spirits and Mongolians avoid even washing in them. As of 1999, the remote Mongolian steppes were still home to full-grown adults who claimed to have never taken a bath.

KIPLING'S VERMONT: SURVIVING THE MONSOONS

So far, this book has followed the flow of water from latrine to river to ocean. Only one part of the cycle is missing, the return of water to land that comes with the summer monsoons. Monsoons in India are, literally, feast or famine. Parts of the nation sink beneath torrential rains; others remain as dry as bones. In the summer of 2005, an unprecedented amount of rain fell on Bombay, submerging the city. The rising water stranded commuters for days on buses and trains and hundreds of people died from water-borne illnesses. Likewise, in parts of Himalchal Pradesh, surging rivers and mudslides destroyed roads and isolated remote villages. Much of Rajasthan and Uttar Pradesh, on the other hand, remained arid. Rains fell erratically in these areas, and farmers lived in a constant state of anxiety about their crops.

Summer in Lucknow was an ordeal, a time when every sensible traveler was somewhere else. With its scorching heat, sauna-like humidity and dust-filled air, the season tried my patience, burnt my skin and stretched my intestines. Tempers flared with the blazing sun, traveling was a misery and eating a hazard. The atmosphere changed from one extreme condition to the next — extreme heat, extreme humidity, extreme rain, and extreme aridity. Most of all, it was extremely uncomfortable.

In Lucknow, hot weather divided Indian society into two *ad hoc* castes, those with AC and those without. People who could afford air conditioners hid in their houses until September, invisible to the rest of the city. Those without AC did just the opposite; they took their beds into the streets and alleyways, or even perched them on rooftops, hoping to catch a breeze in the hours before dawn. For half the city summer was akin to hibernation; for the other half, it was like an extended camping trip.

MARILYN MONROE, ERROL FLYNN AND ME

Although I had an air conditioner installed in the bedroom, it was not enough to keep Deborah around. When the weather became unbearable, she departed for America, leaving me on my own for the next two months. In seven years of living together, this was to be our longest separation. Before she left, we rented *The Seven Year Itch* and watched it on our laptop computer. The parallels were impossible to ignore — a seven-year relationship, oppressive summer heat, an absent wife, and a coveted AC unit. "All that's missing is Marilyn Monroe," I quipped. Deborah did not laugh.

After she left, the temperature rose even further. It was not a static or constant annoyance, however. The summer heat in India goes through a number of stages. May was hot (often hitting 110° Fahrenheit) but as they say, it was a dry heat; you baked, but you did not boil. When the monsoon rains arrived in mid-June, the temperature dropped a bit (100° on average) but the humidity shot up to a horrific level. For much of the day, I found it impossible to go outside. Downtown Lucknow only came alive at night as people gathered in the bazaar and lined up for air-conditioned movie theaters and roadside ice cream stands.

To relieve the tedium, I went to Ram Advani's Bookstore in downtown Lucknow to buy some summer reading. As soon as I stepped inside, the owner, Mr. Advani, rushed over and introduced himself — again. Ram was in his late 80s and had been selling books in Lucknow for the last 60 years. While he could easily recall the author and title of books published over three decades ago, he could not remember who I was, despite having met me more than a dozen times. So I told him my name once more. As always, Ram was happy to meet me and insisted I stay for tea. I sat with him and let him talk. Ram was a walking library of local history, and I knew that if I listened long enough, he would tell me something that I had never heard before.

I was not disappointed. He began to talk about the La Martiniere School, a dilapidated building on the banks of the Gomti River. The structure was the creation of a French military officer, General Claude Martin (d. 1800), an advisor to the Nawab of Oudh. Nobody is quite sure what the General was thinking when he built La Martiniere, but it is an architectural monstrosity. Leering, misshapen lions and Roman deities gaze at the visitor from the rooftop. A staircase to nowhere rises above the main spire. Completing the structure's ornate creepiness is an elaborate sarcophagus under the central hall, which once preserved the General's mortal remains.

General Martin's will dictated that his haunted castle be converted into a boarding school for boys. The school opened in 1840, survived the Mutiny of 1857 and remains a popular English-medium academy today. In the 19th century, the famed writer Rudyard Kipling, perhaps sensing some literary value in the building's gothic horror, made the La Martiniere School the setting of his novel *Kim*. The young protagonist of the book, a half-breed named Kim, suffers through the year as a student at the stultifying school (which Kipling renames St. Xaviers), awaiting vacations, when he engages in espionage on behalf of the British government.

This much I knew. What I did not realize was the Errol Flynn connection.

"Do you like Errol Flynn?" Mr. Advani asked me.

"I'm not sure I've seen any picture with him in it," I admitted.

"He was in the film adaptation of *Kim*, you know. They filmed part of it right here in Lucknow."

"Really? Did Errol Flynn come to Lucknow?" I asked. Mr. Advani was doubtful that the Hollywood star actually traveled to India for the movie, but the thought of Captain Blood wandering through Lucknow's bazaar was enough to make us both laugh.

He told me that a group of American students had arrived in Lucknow for a crash course in Urdu. With the help of several local scholars, Ram had organized a lecture series for them at a nearby hotel. He suggested that I attend. Starved for good conversation in idiomatic American English, I said that I would. When I arrive at the hotel three days later, Mr. Advani greeted me at the door. "And what is your name?" he asked me. "Have we met before?"

Sadly, the visiting students did not share Mr. Advani's interest in Lucknow's history. While professors from Lucknow University delivered talks on local festivals and temples, the students became noticeably restless. Most of them seemed unable to follow the lecture and some fell asleep in their chairs. They awoke only when the speakers stopped for lunch. Over a meal of rice and lentils, I introduced myself to my fellow Americans. They asked me who I was. A tourist? A relief worker? When I explained that I lived in Lucknow, they became nonplussed. "You *live* here? What do you *do*?" they asked.

I gave several students my telephone number and told them to stop by my apartment for coffee, lunch, a beer, anything. They did not call. A few weeks later, I saw one of them in an Internet café. He was wearing a Red Sox T-shirt. A native of Boston, I wanted ask him if he was a baseball fan, if he was from Boston, if the Red Sox were still in the playoffs. He did not want to talk, however. He ignored my greeting and walked away without a word.

LITTLE SISTERS, MOTHER GANGA, BHANG-EUPHORIC FATHER

Feeling a bit restless myself, I took a trip to Benares to re-visit the neighborhood where I lived as a student. I reserved a train ticket for the Inter-city Express, which leaves Lucknow at 7 AM and arrives in Benares by noon. I reached the station at a quarter to seven, confident that I had time to spare. I could not find the correct platform, however, and by the time I finally located it, the Inter-city Express was pulling away from Lucknow at a slow chug. I chased it down the platform, threw my suitcase through the open door of the caboose and took a flying leap into the moving train. I was unhurt, but I had landed on my laptop computer, which began to make ominous clanking noises.

In Bengali Tola, my old neighborhood in Benares, everything had changed. The alleys, which once contained only temples and tea stalls, now included Internet cafés, restaurants and gift shops. The press of beggars and fakirs that I remembered was also largely gone, replaced by tour guides, souvenir sellers, travel agents and touts hawking yoga retreats. I inquired about several people I once knew in the area only to learn that they had moved elsewhere. I recognized nobody and nobody recognized me.

I went to visit the Little Sisters. When I was a student, I lived around the corner from a group of Catholic nuns from the Order of the Little Sisters of Jesus. When they discovered that I had been born into a Catholic family (a rarity in Bengali Tola), they began knocking on my door early in the morning, insisting that I accompany them to mass. They would not take no for an answer, even when I told them that I had not attended church in years. To appease them, I would sometimes stop by their headquarters, Yesu Ashram, and help with their gardening. Over time, I grew fond of the Little Sisters. Before I returned to America, I donated some of my equipment, most of my clothing, and my entire student stipend to their community-outreach program.

Yesu Ashram was still there, hidden in the alleyways overlooking the Ganges. When I knocked on the door, the mother superior, Sister Lordia, recognized me immediately. "How long has it been?" she asked. When I told her 15 years, she was incredulous. She told me that some of the older nuns had left due to poor health and the community-outreach program was now defunct. "There are no poor people in this neighborhood anymore," Sister Lordia explained. "The program only made sense when everybody was destitute."

The good news, according to Sister Lordia, was that conversions were up. In the past, converts to Christianity were scarce in Benares because few Hindus would undertake the rite of baptism, a public rejection of their religion and their caste. To remedy this situation, some local priests came up with a new strategy — inviting local Hindus to become *Christa Bhaktas* (yogis for Christ). This sidestepped the issue of baptism and recast Christian doctrine in the familiar language of Hinduism. In some villages around Benares, the mother superior told me, the number of *Christa Bhaktas* had skyrocketed.

Before I left, Sister Lordia took a long look at me. "You have become, so...so large," she said.

"Too much dessert," I explained.

Now thinking about sweets, I headed to Godaulia, Benares' main bazaar. As a student, I frequented a local shop called Baba Thandai. Wondering if it is still there, I walked through the twisted streets until I found the correct alleyway.

The familiar, cave-like décor, the peeling orange paint, and the faded icon of Lord Shiva — here, at least, nothing had changed.

The menu was the same as well. For about fifty cents, the staff at Baba Thandai will serve you *pistaa* (sweetened milk), *sharbat* (syrupy beverage) or even a *bhaang lassi* (hashish milkshake). *Bhaang* consists of hashish mixed with spices and oils. Although illegal in most places, the laws allow for the consumption of cannabis in Benares as a religious practice. The city has an ancient association with the god Shiva, also called Bhangeri Baba or "Bhang-euphoric Father."

After leaving Baba Tandai's, I walked to the banks of Mother Ganga (the Ganges River) and watched an *aaratii* (fire ritual) dedicated to Shiva as the sun set over the sacred city. Sanskrit-chanting Brahmin priests waved incense in the air, surrounding me with pungent smoke. The spirit of the ceremony possessed me and I joined the swaying throngs of devotees, clapping my hands in time with the beating drums. When the ritual ended, a young girl pressed a candle into my hands. She told me it was an offering to the river goddess and demanded five rupees. Descending the *ghaats* (stone steps) to the Ganges, I floated the candle on a leaf and watched it rushed downstream in the fast monsoon current. My eyes followed the flame as it wavered unsteadily, flared for a moment and then went dark.

A Pound of Flesh

Back in Lucknow, I looked at myself in the mirror one morning and decided that Sister Lordia was right — I could lose ten pounds. Donning my running shoes, I crossed the street to the Lucknow Botanical Gardens for a jog. It was 5:30 AM and I assumed that this was a good place for exercise before the heat of the day began. Unfortunately, everybody else had the same idea. By 6:00 AM, hundreds of people clogged the paths of the garden and I was unable to move.

Following Robert Frost's suggestion, I took the path "less traveled" and ran into an empty field where bright yellow Brazilian trumpet trees in full bloom imitated a New England autumn. For a few moments, I was completely alone and experiencing something rare in Lucknow, solitude. Then a gardener chased me down, chided me for leaving the "proper road," and led me back to the herd. Exasperated, I realized that few people read Robert Frost in Lucknow.

If one park did not work out, Lucknow had many others from which to choose. Ambedkar Park, on the far bank of the Gomti River, had a mile-long circular track. Unfortunately, it did not open its gates until 11 AM, the heat of the day upon it. I arrived the next day at eleven and ran a few miles anyway, but with the temperature topping 105 degrees, I did not get far. By my third lap, I was feeling dizzy and stopped. I did not return a second time. Only "mad dogs and Englishmen go out in the mid-day sun."[1]

---

1 Coward, Noel. *Mad Dogs and English Men: Complete Recordings Vol.2* (Naxos Nostalgia 2001).

Frustrated by these failed attempts at exercise, I all but gave up the idea of losing weight. Then one day I made the mistake of ordering fish for lunch and contracted a severe bout of dysentery.[1] Although I was bedridden, my stomach bug had a flattering effect on my physique. Within a week, the reflection in the mirror was noticeably thinner — victory at last.

ALL'S WELL THAT ENDS WELL

Still suffering from a gastrointestinal infestation, I traveled to Delhi to pick up Deborah. She called me from London and told me that she would be several days late. Her flight collided with a bird on takeoff, cracking the cockpit window, and had to return to Heathrow. I lay for days in my hotel room waiting for her, watching the BBC while suffering from fever and stomach pain.

On TV, I learned that I was not the only one who was sick in India. The rains had brought mosquitoes, and the mosquitoes, disease. The media reported several cases of Japanese Encephalitis (an often-fatal type of brain fever) in Gorakhpur. The next day there was news of more cases and several deaths. The outbreak spread from Gorakhpur to the surrounding countryside. By late August, the disease reached Lucknow and the body count rose into the hundreds. Unfortunately, neither Deborah nor I had received an inoculation against Japanese Encephalitis. Our physician in America had told us that it was a rarity in India.

When Deborah finally touched down in New Delhi, we decided to celebrate her return with a quick trip to Rajasthan where we spent a few nights at Neemrana Fort, a 15th-century fortress-cum-luxury-hotel. Each room had a special name, The Palace of the Moon, the Palace of the Queen. We lodged in *Sheesh Mahal*, the Palace of Mirrors, while Deborah recovered from her jet lag. When she was rested, she unpacked some duty-free pinot grigio, which we drank on the fortress battlements, watching the sun set over the dusty plain.[2]

The next day, we took a walk through a nearby village. A young boy led us to the 18th-century Neemrana Stepwell, a massive, subterranean labyrinth, hundreds of feet deep. A local Maharaja had built the stepwell to alleviate his subjects' discomfort during the long, hot summer. As the water table rose, villagers could descend to the appropriate depth, eliminating the need to wait in line to use a well bucket. All of the Maharaja's efforts were ultimately in vain, however. The boy told us that nobody used the stepwell any more. "The water is bad for drinking," he said.[3]

---

1 In Lucknow, the prevailing wisdom was that you should not eat any fish in a month without an "R" in the name, i.e. May through August.

2 Oenophiles will find that fine wine is a rare luxury in India. Nevertheless, certain domestic vintners (e.g. *Grover Vineyards*) produce some drinkable wine and the number and variety of domestic vineyards is growing yearly. Alcohol remains a regulated and heavily taxed industry and imports are difficult to find in many areas.

3 Lucknow's Great Imambara also has a step well, home, last I checked, to a flock of fruit bats. Step-wells seem to be a late-Mughal craze.

As I wandered through the stepwell's maze of arches and stairways, I thought about the monsoons in India. They have always been fickle, and even the most elaborate preparations could not protect people from their unpredictable behavior. Inequitable and inadequate monsoon rains are a recurring and seemingly unsolvable problem. Fear of drought is on ongoing theme in Indian literature all the way back to the oldest Sanskrit texts. In the Rig Veda (1:32) the god Indra receives praise for slaying Ahi, the dragon of the mountains, and "releasing the waters." For the pre-scientific mind, a malevolent creature retained the sustaining waters during the dry season and the situation required the violent intercession of Indra's *vajra* (lightning bolt).[1] All through India's history, people have dreamt of controlling the inconsistency of nature by building wells, canals, reservoirs and holding tanks — all to no avail.

In Lucknow, Nassar-ud-din Haider, King of Oudh (1827–1837) tried to alleviate the seasonal suffering of his subjects by altering the courses of his kingdom's rivers. He planned a 50-mile canal that would connect the Gomti with the Ganges, thus diverting water from wet areas to drought-ridden ones. Excavation began with high hopes, but the effort soon faltered. The King had squandered the royal treasury on "a life of pleasure and debauchery" and the resulting lack of funds and a "want of engineering skill" led to the abandonment of the project long before its completion.[2] The remains of Haider's Canal lay about a mile from our apartment, a river to nowhere.

The modern-day Ministry of Water Resources gave King Haider's dream of linking rivers new life when it proposed to connect no fewer than 37 of the Ganges' tributaries by 2016.[3] Ultimately, the project will link not only rivers in the Ganges Plain, but many rivers in western and southern India as well. Theoretically, once construction is complete, water from the waterlogged state of Bihar could flow through a series of locks and canals and emerge in dusty Rajasthan.

The environmental impact of the river-linking project is potentially catastrophic, however. By mixing the water of highly contaminated rivers such as the Ganges with cleaner waterways like the Brahmaputra, the government may make the problem of water pollution, which is already severe, worse than ever. Moreover, it is an open question whether such a project is politically possible. The Ganges river basin alone draws water from four different nations. Linking rivers successfully would require the cooperation of every country in South Asia and every Indian state simultaneously, a detail that makes the success of the river-linking project doubtful.

In the end, despite centuries of schemes, modern India remains at the mercy of the weather. Like their ancestors in the 18th century, people today can still do

---

1 Sanskrit text and notes found in Lanman, p. 70.

2 Beg, M. A. *The Guide to Lucknow* (New Delhi: Asian Educational Series 2000), p. 56.

3 *Interlinking Rivers: Contradictions & Confrontations* (New Delhi: South Asian Dialogues on Ecological Democracy 2004), p. 5.

little more than watch the sky and wait. Waiting, after all, is the defining characteristic of monsoons — waiting for the rains to come, waiting for the heat to pass, waiting for a lover's return, waiting, finally, for the day when, as expressed by Ogden Nash in his poem "Kipling's Vermont,"

> The summer like a rajah dies,
> And every widowed tree,
> Kindles for Congregational eyes,
> An alien sutee.[1]

---

1 Nash, Ogden. "Kipling's Vermont," *Candy is Dandy: The Best of Ogden Nash* (London: Andre Deutsch 1983), p. 277. *Sutee* (or *sati*) is the traditional rite of widow burning, in which the living wife of the deceased joins her husband on his funeral pyre. Outlawed by the British in the 19th century, *sutee* still occurs in rural areas of India on occasion. Rudyard Kipling lived near Brattleboro Vermont between 1892 and 1896. There, he wrote *Jungle Books* and enjoyed the fall foliage. See Murray, Stuart. *Rudyard Kipling in Vermont: Birthplace of the Jungle Books* (Bennington: Images from the Past Inc. 1997).

The Tower of Babu: Hindi, Hinglish, English

Before we left for Asia, a friend, recently returned from New Delhi, told my wife Deborah, "You don't need to learn Hindi. Everybody in India speaks English." She half believed this fiction until we arrived in Lucknow and hired Sona, our kitchen maid. Sona was a great cook but did not speak a word of English. Worse, she assumed that if we did not understand her when she spoke at a normal volume, then we would surely fathom her meaning if she yelled. During those first weeks, we lived in fear of dinnertime. From the kitchen, Sona would scream "*mirch!*" (pepper), "*tail!*" (oil) or "*namak!*" (salt) at the top of her voice while we flipped through our Hindi dictionary trying to translate her request before the lentils burned.

The claim that all Indians know English is inaccurate especially in Uttar Pradesh.[1] While some cities in India, such as Madras and Bombay, have long-standing traditions of indigenous English-speakers that stretch back to the origins of British involvement on the subcontinent, Lucknow is not one of them. Never widespread, English literacy declined further at the end of the British Raj with the exodus of British administrators, soldiers and residents.

Christ Church Cemetery in Nishatganj, Lucknow bears witness to a once-thriving British and Anglo-Indian community in Lucknow. Today, rows of unvisited headstones are all that remain. A casual survey of the inscriptions indicates that fatalities from diseases like typhoid and cholera were common. Most of the

---

1 The expectation of widespread English literacy in India is common among Western travelers. Filmmaker Chris Smith was shocked to discover while filming *The Pool*, a drama about Goan street children made with non-professional actors, that many of the children who auditioned for the lead role could not speak English. See Anderson, John. "Let Them Speak Hindi," *The Village Voice*, 9/3/08.

deceased passed away before the age of 40. Overgrown and neglected, the site's correct name was unknown even to the gatekeeper, who called it simply *gora kabristhaan* or "white man's cemetery." As I walked through the ranks of marble and slate headstones, it occurred to me that the tiny number of English-speaking residents of Lucknow today probably represents a smaller percentage of the overall population than in the past. If this is true, contemporary residents of Lucknow have less opportunity to talk to a native-born English speaker than did their ancestors a century ago.

Located smack in the middle of the Hindi belt, Lucknow's residents should benefit from being members of India's largest linguistic group. Of all indigenous Indian tongues, only Hindi has enough speakers to claim the title of a national language. The 1991 census showed that Hindi had some 337 million speakers compared to its nearest rival, Bengali, with about 70 million.[1] Hindi's popularity receives a further boost from the Bombay entertainment industry, which produces slews of Hindi-language films that show in theaters all over India, even in areas where Hindi is not native. Fans from Kerala to Kashmir have learned enough Hindi to follow their favorite star's latest film.

As a language, Hindi has a lot going for it. With a syllabary that allows for a greater range of sounds than the Roman alphabet and spelling that is far more phonetic than English, Hindi is relatively easy to learn. It has neither the perplexing tonal system nor the difficult, character-based writing system of Mandarin and other East Asian languages. As part of the Indo-European linguistic family, Hindi is a distant cousin of almost all European dialects and shares phonetic characteristics with them; in Hindi, "me" is *main* and mother is *Maataa-ji*.

The most difficult part of learning Hindi was neither grammar nor pronunciation but rather the reluctance of native speakers to converse with foreigners in anything but English. In the hallway of our apartment building, I tried to speak Hindi to my neighbor's children. They responded by saying, "Why are you talking like that? Please speak English." I persisted, explaining that I needed to work on my pronunciation. Still, they refused to answer me in Hindi. I wondered whether this was an attempt at hospitality or if these children were ashamed of their own mother tongue.

Some fluency in Hindi made me privy to certain information hidden from foreigners. At a pond near the temples of Kujaraho in Madhya Pradesh — a site that attracts a large number of tourists — an untranslated sign warned about *magar*, crocodiles, that sometimes lay hidden in the pond's muddy waters. At Benares Hindu University's gleaming, marble Shiva temple, all of the Sanskrit inscriptions have accompanying English translations, except for one behind the temple's sanctum sanctorum (*garbha griha*) that lionizes the practice of *sati* (widow burn-

---

1 Brass, Paul. *The Politics of India Since Independence* (Cambridge: Cambridge University Press 1990), p. 159.

ing). At the State Museum inside Delhi's Red Fort, a display in honor of Sarat Bose, an ultra-nationalist and friend of Adolf Hitler, had Hindi-only placards, a unique feature among the museum's collections. I am convinced that the most interesting signs in India are the ones that foreigners are not intended to read.

The Remarkable Rise of Native-Language Media

Between Sikhandarbagh Crossing, where I lived, and Narahi Bazaar, where I shopped, lay the Lucknow offices *Dainik Jaagaran* standing alongside the offices of such venerable publications as *The Hindustan Times* and *The Times of India. Dainik Jaagaran* (Daily Vigil) is a fast growing Hindi-language media company, originally based in Kanpur, and its fortunes have grown with the rebirth of Indian-language media over the last thirty years. As the percentage of dailies in English fell from over 20% in 1960 to less than 18% in 1987, the number of Hindi newspapers grew from less than 20% to over 30%.[1] The next decade saw even faster change; by 1996, English-language press accounted for only 12.5 % of India's daily newspapers, while Hindi rose to roughly 40% of the total.[2] In Uttar Pradesh, Hindi's reach now far exceeds that of the English language press in terms of both readership and revenue.[3]

These changes follow a nation-wide trend in native-language media. The development of Indian-language media after Independence hinged on improving the typefaces of Indian scripts, a surprisingly difficult problem. Indian scripts are notoriously ornate; the most common, Devanagari, in which Hindi, Marathi, Nepali and other languages appear, not only has more characters than English (roughly 36 to 26), but also requires innumerable compound characters.[4] Other Indian languages suffer from similar problems.[5] This made setting type for an Indian language newspaper difficult, particularly with the antiquated equipment

---

1 See www.languageinindia.com.

2 Jeffry, Robin. *India's Newspaper Revolution: Capitalism, Politics and the Indian-Language Press 1977-99* (New York, St. Martin's Press 2000). p. 46.

3 Hindi is also replacing regional dialects, such as Urdu. Urdu was the language of business and law during the Mughal and Raj eras. Since Partition, however, the emergence of Hindi as national language has largely eclipsed its importance. In Lucknow, the former center of Urdu publishing, many Urdu-language presses and newspapers have closed, one prominent exception being *Sahara Urdu Edition*. Hindi and Urdu are mutually intelligible, the main differences being script, vocabulary and some minor points of grammar. Since Independence, Hindi and Urdu have pulled further apart as they are now part and parcel of communal identification. The term 'Hindustani' refers to the half-Hindi, half-Urdu dialect in common usage.

4 Devanagari uses a separate character for each consonant cluster. For example, the sound "pr" as in "apron," appears as a hybrid character composed of elements of the constituent phonetic elements.

5 Reportedly, South Indian scripts, such as Telegu and Tamil are even more difficult for a typesetter. Urdu script is simpler, but the morphology of the character still depends upon its position in the word, e.g. finals appear graphically different from initial and medial characters.

---

available to most Indian newspapers until the 1990s. With the advent of computer-based typesetting, Indian newspapers finally achieved parity with English newspapers in terms of possible output in sheets per hour.[1]

Once dependable native-language types appeared, Indian publishers could tap into a vast reservoir of enthusiastic readership in the Indian heartland. Much of India still lay beyond the reach of the Internet and television programming, and newspapers still fulfilled the role they once held in America as a printed public forum. Between 1976 and 1996, the production of newspapers increased four-fold. This dizzying growth in native language publications expanded civic culture into every village, causing vast social changes and increased political awareness.

> Once an event became a "story", it acquired a life of its own. Once published, "a story" — police beating villagers, for example — could spread across Andhra Pradesh, reach the capital, Hyderabad, be translated into other languages, including English, and travel to New Delhi and overseas. A host of possibilities arose. Official inquiries might be ordered, police reprimanded, villagers beaten in retaliation, even a prime minister's visit organized. Countless daily events — the actions, one might say, of what had once been the audience — now sometimes found themselves on stage, part of, and thereby able to influence, a far larger political play. [2]

India today boasts a vibrant array of Indian-language dailies available on almost any street corner. They are cheap (usually less than 15 cents a copy) with lively, distinct personalities and they give voice to every imaginable political ideology. Dailies like *Dainik Jaagaran*, and *Aaj* (Today) a long-standing daily out of Varanasi, provide national politics as well as local color. Jeffrey credits this local coverage with some of the success of Indian newspapers in the 60s and 70s. In their quest for readership and advertising dollars, Indian newspapers began reporting on local issues in a way it had never done before. Jeffrey takes it as a given that localization leads to larger readerships because "...new readers were enthralled by the coverage of local events — by reading about themselves and the things that pleased, amused and annoyed them."[3]

This would explain why reporters and photographers in Lucknow were so intent on taking my picture. *Times of India: Lucknow Edition* tailored itself to the expectations of their readership and Lucknow residents liked to consider themselves urbane and cosmopolitan. Foreigners thus often found themselves the prey of ambitious photographers from the Indian press, which wanted to sprinkle their newspapers with the faces of the very few Western foreigners who lived in the city. This would have been pleasant enough if they were not also in the habit of inventing quotes and adding sarcastic captions. A *Times of India* photographer once took a surprise snap of me at a wedding, catching me with an unfortunately

---

1 See Jeffrey, pgs. 20-41.

2 Jeffry, Robin. *India's Newspaper Revolution: Capitalism, Politics and the Indian-Language Press 1977-99* (New York, St. Martin's Press 2000).

3 Jeffrey p. 97.

sour expression that resembled aloof disdain. The caption in the paper the next day disingenuously complimented me on my "warm smile."

If I sometimes annoyed them, I also amused them, however. A *Hindustan Times* reporter stopped me in the street one Christmas to ask me about Western Christmas traditions for a human-interest piece. She enjoyed a story I told her about the loss of my childhood belief in Santa Claus, which faltered in the face of a geometric conundrum (a ping-pong table had appeared one Christmas, supposedly a gift from Santa, but I could not reconcile the dimensions of the ping-pong table with our home's narrow chimney). Both the reporter and her editor apparently liked the anecdote and the paper sent a photographer to my apartment to photograph a Christmas tree that my wife Deborah had fashioned out of wire — actual evergreens were difficult to find in Lucknow.

Author Jill Lapore writes about how newspapers in Revolutionary America created a culture of public dissent and "loyal opposition," a crucial development in the political history of our nation.[1] In India, the native-language press has cultivated just this type of public debate and dissent at the corner tea stall, where Indians gather every morning for tea, *puri subzee* (flatbread and vegetable curry) and the morning's news. In 1997, a Tamil daily estimated that an average of 18 people read each copy of its newspaper. In Lucknow, the number could be even higher. Each morning at Sikhandarbagh Crossing and at countless thousands of other tea stalls in Uttar Pradesh farmers, rickshaw drivers, traders and laborers gather to pour over tattered copies of *Dainik Jaagaran*, and inadvertently lay the foundation for widespread civic culture in India.

The Internet, often experienced in isolation, cannot compete with newspapers as an inspiration for this type of public, tea-fueled symposia.[2] The recent rise of Internet culture in India thus threatens to mitigate the social and political achievements — both deliberate and inadvertent — of the Indian-language press. Furthermore, Internet-based businesses and the social changes they engender could retard the growth of Hindi language as India's premier native tongue. In contemporary India, I saw young people using as many English words as possible, a change that some saw as a step forward because of English's immediate utility in the Indian economy. In light of India's social and linguistic history, however, this rebound romance with English is undeniably regressive. Just as India emerged from a dark age of domination by foreigners who did not speak any Indian language, the outsourcing and Internet boom has turned the tables once again.

---

1 Lapore, Jill. "The Day the Newspaper Died." *The New Yorker* 26 January 2009 pgs. 68-73.
2 See Heffernan, Virginia. *The New York Times Magazine* "Click and Jane" 2/1/2009. Heffernan questions the relative value of on-line reading and reading from printed material and expresses doubts that her three year old can benefit from exposure to the Internet in the same way as exposure to books. "I sadly suspect he needs the shelves and dust."

HUNGRY KYA? THE RISE OF HINGLISH

When we needed a break from Sona's cooking, Deborah and I ordered pizza from Dominos. American-style pizza is a growing fad in Uttar Pradesh and large Western pizza chains such as Dominos and Pizza Hut have opened up branches all over the state. In Lucknow, the cover of every Dominos Pizza box displays the company's slogan, "Hungry Kya?" A conjunction of the Hindi question-word "*kya*" and the English adjective "hungry," "Hungry Kya?" apparently means, "Are you hungry?"

Phrases like "Hungry Kya?" characterize the widespread Indian pseudo-language popularly referred to as Hinglish. Hinglish, like "Hungry Kya?," exists in a grammatical no-man's-land that has lays between Hindi and English. Currently in vogue, Hinglish appears in newspapers, magazines and Bollywood scripts. Even the daily proceedings of the Indian parliament often occur in a bewildering mixture of Hindi and English. Many urban Indians feel that sprinkling their sentences with English words makes them sound cosmopolitan.

Sometimes, English words make their way into common parlance by virtue of their brevity, as happens when speaking about modern technology. The Hindi word for "television" for example, *doordarshan* (literally, "sacred vision from afar") is much clumsier than the English abbreviation TV. Likewise, the term for "advertisement," *vigyaapan*, is less succinct than "ad." Other words such as "computer" and "IT" seem to have no widely accepted parallels in Hindi and have joined the vernacular without alteration.

Changing social realities have similarly lead to adoptions of English words. This summer I visited an old friend, Dr. Mukta Gupta, in the state of Punjab. Mukta and I met in graduate school, became friends and have kept up a lively correspondence ever since. While visiting the Gupta household in Chandagarh, I made the mistake of referring to her as my *yaar*. Yaar is a slang word that means "friend" and commonly refers to any casual acquaintance. Formerly, however, when a man used the term to refer to a woman, it had the connotation of "lover." Mukta warned me that her father understood the word in this sense and that I should not use it in front of him. "You can call me *sahelii*," she said.

Even this term was a poor choice because it is traditionally only used between women. By saying *sahelii*, I was effectively labeling myself as female. The masculine equivalent of *sahelii*, *dost*, was no better because it is usually only used between men. Remarkably, proper Hindi has no term for a platonic, mixed-gender friendship between two unrelated individuals. Given linguistic conundrums like this, it is no wonder that the gender-neutral word "friend" is gaining currency.

In other instances, English words have entered the speech of average Indians for reasons that remain obscure. In the last decade, I have noticed the words "left" and "right" taking the place of the equally handy Hindi words *baayaan* and *daahinaa*, while the perfectly serviceable Urdu term *waqt* has given way to its English equivalent, "time." English has even inserted its Anglo-Saxon nose into the sphere of family relations, where Hindi has an expansive variety of words from which to choose. In Hindi, each relative has a unique title. A paternal uncle, for example, is *chacha*, while a maternal uncle is *mama*. Lamentably, it is now common to hear "uncle" used to refer to a family relation, even though the English word is less precise than the Hindi.

As almost any English word or phrase may enter the popular vernacular, Hinglish has a potentially goliath vocabulary. When the lexicon of English (the largest vocabulary of any language on earth) combines with the considerable vocabulary of Hindi, the possible choices for expressing any idea in Hinglish are legion. To refer to a book, for example, one may use the Sanskrit-derived "*pustaka*," the Arabic "*kitaab*" or the English "book." Even this list omits numerous other choices such as *grantha, adhyaaya*, tome, volume and edition, to name but a few.

Hinglish is thus an extremely awkward means of expression. Any given speaker may know one or more English synonyms or a few Hindi equivalents. Rarely, however, is an individual erudite enough to know all the possible terms. This leads to endless snags in conversation as speakers of Hinglish wrack their brains for allusions that all their audience will understand. In Lucknow, I used a mash of Hindi, Urdu and English words to convey a single idea.

Moreover, if the intent of speaking Hinglish was to sound sophisticated, the effect was often just the opposite. Many Hinglish speakers are effectively monolingual; they speak neither proper English nor proper Hindi. One writer laments, "A ridiculous situation is developing in which people are earning B.A.s and M.A.s but cannot speak or write any language well."[1] He goes on to say that college courses in English rarely progress beyond potboilers written by popular authors like Sidney Sheldon and Jeffery Archer, while Hindi literature is omitted entirely.

Grade-school students may not find much literature on their syllabi either. Ms. Bhattra, principal of Children's Intercollege Academy in Lucknow, admitted that the curriculum at her school did not require students to read any work of either Hindi or English literature from cover to cover. Given these trends in both primary and secondary education, it is not surprising that few Lucknowites can hold a conversation on either English or Hindi letters. Sadly, the question that arises regarding many Hinglish speakers is "Educated Kya?"

English

Citizens of Uttar Pradesh share a common notion that proficiency in English is a requirement for landing a good job. As one columnist put it:

---

1 Agravaal, Daamodar. "*Padhe so Pandit Hoya*," *An Advanced Hindi Magazine Reader* Mishra, Awadesh ed. (Varanasi: Aabhaas Prakashan 1994), p. 162. Reprinted from *Dainik Jaagaran*.

> Far from being a colonial hangover, any accent today on English is a pragmatic acceptance that if you want to walk the talk [sic] of a globalised world, you've got to do it in English.[1]

For this reason, parents increasingly prefer English-medium schools for their children. Although English literacy overall may be declining in Uttar Pradesh (based on the number of English-language media outlets), English-medium secondary schools have proliferated during the last decade and now comprise up to one fifth of the available secondary schools in some areas of the state.[2]

Wondering how Indian students lived in a linguistic world that was moving in two different directions, I visited Children's Academy Intercollege, a private grade school in Lucknow, to ask about their English-medium curriculum. The principal, Ms. Swaran Bhattra, told me that the law requires a single Hindi course per year. Otherwise, all interaction between the faculty and the students takes place in English. I asked her if the students find it difficult to switch from one language to another. "Actually," she answers, "because it is such a competitive place they practice [English] on the playground as well."

While these children may have spoken English on the playground, they often used only Hindi at home. Our neighbor Meenu sent her two boys to English-medium schools but was unable to communicate with them in English herself. This was a source of embarrassment for her husband Raju. One evening, Meenu and Raju invited Deborah and me to their apartment for a cocktail. When we arrived Raju was congenial enough, but Meenu was sullen and spoke little. Later, we learned that Raju had insisted that she remain silent during our visit because her English was poor.

This unfortunate woman was not alone. Much of the English I heard spoken in Lucknow was rudimentary, and the English-language newspapers were not much better. While most journalists at the local office of *The Times of India* could earn a passing grade in the average high school English class, indefinite articles remained a mystery for them:

> The traffic system went haywire on Friday as huge gathering of Bahujan Samaj Party workers took toll on the movement of vehicles in the city.[3]

As did definite articles:

> Visit New York and Washington for their skyscrapers (and opera lovers may spend an evening or two at the Broadway of course)....You could then

---

1 *Times of India: Lucknow Edition*, 6/4/05, p. 1

2 Based on a study of schools in the Bijnor district. Jeffery, Roger and Patricia with Jeffrey, Craig. "Social Inequalities and the Privatisation of Secondary Schooling," *Educational Regimes in Contemporary India* Chopra, R. and Jeffery, P. eds. (New Delhi: Sage 2005), p. 52.

3 *Times of India: Lucknow Edition*, 6/4/05, p. 4.

isit the Miami Beach and cross over to the western coast for some real fun at San Francisco, Las Vegas, and Los Angeles.[1]

At first, the broken English I heard from my neighbors and read in the press did not bother me. Rather, it was endearing — like hearing a young child speak his first words. Moreover, this obsession with English made Deborah's and my life easier. If knowing some English created employment opportunities, I reasoned, then all this bad grammar must be a good thing.

PLEASE LEAVE A MESSAGE AT THE SOUND OF THE APPOGGIATURA

Certain aspects of people's linguistic behavior still mystified me, however. I found people's obsessive interest in good English spelling particularly flabbergasting. At the Scripps / Howard National Spelling Bee in Washington DC, Indian children regularly take first prize. In the last decade, South Asian competitors have dominated the contest, producing five of the last eight champions. The Indian juggernaut rolled on in 2005 with the victory of Anurag Kashyap, who triumphed by spelling "appoggiatura" (a word meaning "a melodic tone") correctly. Coverage of the National Spelling Bee was impossible to ignore in Uttar Pradesh and the media treated Mr. Kashap like a star athlete.

As a poor speller, I found Anurag Kashyap intimidating. Ever since I failed my third-grade spelling test, I have tried to master the peculiarities of English spelling without success. To make matters worse, since the introduction of spellchecking software, my motivation to improve my spelling has wholly evaporated. If someone like me — who writes for a living — was content to let SpellCheck do his dirty work, then what motivated Indian people to attain spelling glory year after year? More importantly, what made the idea of the National Spelling Bee so fascinating for the residents of Uttar Pradesh? Anurag Kashyap's star status was not simply an expression of the high regard in which Indian parents hold academic and financial success. This fascination with spelling was a fetishization of lexical minutiae that was of limited value in the marketplace. After all, no candidate for a programming position — the career to which, incidentally, young Anurag aspired — has needed to spell appoggiatura during a job interview.

In fact, the closer I looked, the more suspicious I became of the idea that learning English was essential to landing a good job. For several consecutive weeks, I conducted an informal and non-scientific survey of the Help Wanted section of the Lucknow edition of *The Times of India*. Counting the number of positions advertised and comparing it with the number of positions that explicitly required English, I arrived at some surprising conclusions. Out of 1,444 open positions,

---

1 "Zip Off on a Loan Trek," *Times of India: Lucknow Edition*, Times City, 6/5/05, p. 1. Fact checking is also rare. This author cared neither that Washington DC has no skyscrapers, nor that both the Metropolitan Opera and City Opera are at Lincoln Center rather than "the Broadway" (if by that term he means the theater district near Times Square), nor that Las Vegas is not on "the western coast."

only 59, or about 4%, listed English as a necessary requirement for employment.[1] Moreover, I saw no relation between the salary offered and the need to know English. In fact, most high-paying technical positions (e.g., programmers, mechanical and electrical engineers) did not explicitly require fluency in any dialect unless, perhaps, it was a computer language.

Most of the positions that did require English consisted of jobs in other Indian states or in the Middle East (e.g., Oman and Qatar). Despite producing large numbers of English-speaking graduates in recent years, Uttar Pradesh has failed to interest many large foreign businesses. As the director of a technological institute in Kanpur remarked, "...it pains me that cities like Lucknow and Kanpur, which supply English-speaking graduates to call centres operating from Noida and Gurgaon [towns near Delhi], don't have a single centre of even 100 seats."[2] The few *local* jobs that required English were teaching positions at English-medium schools.

The want ads also showed that certain fields remained the exclusive domain of Hindi-speakers. All government positions required Hindi, as did most legal professions (excluding the High and Supreme Court where most proceedings were in English). June Mishra, director of Children's Academy Intercollege, told me that her son, an employee of a large multi-national bank, discovered too late that his job required him to read complex legal documents in Hindi. After years of exclusively English-medium education, he hired a tutor to teach him the finer points of Hindi grammar.

If the results of my survey were at all indicative of the regular demand for English-speaking professionals, then it was doubtful that employment furnished a sufficient cause for the rise of English-medium instruction in Uttar Pradesh. Not enough positions required English to legitimize the number of English-medium schools. Nor was this situation likely to change any time soon. Serious obstacles (e.g., lack of infrastructure, inept government, general lawlessness and rampant corruption) precluded any large-scale influx of IT or BPO business into the state any time in the near future. Like teaching Hawaiian children to ski, instructing all the children of Uttar Pradesh in English grammar was out of step with local realities.

---

1 Like most statistics, these figures require a grain of salt. The number of available positions was necessarily an approximation because the exact number was often not printed (e.g. an ad for an unspecified number of "drivers"). When estimating, I tended towards the conservative side. If an advertisement listed a position in the plural (e.g. "managers"), I counted it as two positions, if in the singular, one position. The randomness of the sample is also suspect because I used editions printed within a short span of time. Lastly, *The Times of India* being an English newspaper, it is possible (although, in my opinion, not likely), that some employers considered the need to speak fluent English to be self-evident.

2 Srivastava, Prashant. "Is UP 'hot' enough for IIT-Kanpur alumni?," *Times of India Lucknow Edition*, 7/25/05, p. 3.

If people in Uttar Pradesh did not learn English solely to find work, then why *did* they learn it? Perhaps the answer lay in the linguistic history of the Deccan peninsula. In ancient India, a divide separated vernacular and literary languages. The upper classes used Sanskrit as a social shibboleth, and, to this end, the language deliberately retained a maddeningly complex grammatical structure.[1] You could not learn Sanskrit in a month, a year or even ten years. It required a lifetime of continual study to conquer, and its use was largely exclusive to Brahmin priests, for whom mastery of Sanskrit was a religious imperative, and to the ruling castes, which had enough leisure time to make sense of it all. Like Anurag Kashyap, upper-class Indian boys and girls through the ages have sat before their elders and recited arcane linguistic formulae as part of their education and social conditioning. Average people, engaged in trade or agriculture, could not foster pretensions of becoming a priest or a prince because they could never imitate the jargon of the upper castes. A linguistic wall encircled Brahmins and Kshatriyas (warrior caste) and ensconced them in the halls of power. In short, Sanskrit kept the rabble out.

With the dawn of the Mughal era, Sanskrit gave way to Persian (Farsi) as the language of the political and religious elite. Those seeking royal patronage, whether they were Hindu or Muslim, improved their chances by speaking Persian. The pattern, however, remained the same; linguistic barriers reinforced the social hierarchy. In the modern period, English replaced Sanskrit and Farsi as the language of prestige and entitlement. In a similar way, it inhibits social mobility by creating a linguistic passkey that, unlike appearance, resists easy replication.

You could see the social and economic multi-valance of English easily by looking at store signs in Lucknow. Signs for fancy sari shops appeared in English. Signs for businesses hoping to reach a general audience, such as banks and cell phone services, were in both Hindi and English. Stores with a proletarian clientele (e.g., smoke shops, tea stalls) used signs exclusively in Hindi.

Most English-medium education in Uttar Pradesh was privately funded and enrolling a child in a private English medium school, like Children's Academy Intercollege, was expensive and often beyond the means of the lower classes. Unfortunately these institutions, whatever their benefits, also function as social barriers between castes and economic strata. The spread of such institutions was therefore not a modernizing trend at all; rather it receives its impetus from ancient cultural tensions and serves to perpetuate a medieval set of inequalities. Many Indians considered English less a way of connecting to the modern world than a means of disassociating themselves from the Hindi-speaking masses.

> Over the years, English has confirmed, consolidated, and deepened its position as the language of the pan-Indian elite. The language of the colo-

---

1 The term *Sanskrit* means, roughly, "refined" or, "cultivated."

nizers has, in independent India, become the language of power and prestige, the language of individual as well as social advancement.[1]

Uttar Pradesh suffered from a dichotomy between the goals of the state and
the goals of the individual. The state as a whole would have benefited from a population that spoke and wrote a single language with a high degree of proficiency,
and, on a national level, the continued spread of Hindi could only have been in
Uttar Pradesh's self-interest. For many individuals, however, English was a far
more attractive choice. Ambitious students dreamt of technology jobs in Bangalore and Hyderabad, or even the rare posting in America. More significantly,
fluency in English promised respectability in a culture obsessed with the social
pecking order. The tension between collective benefit and individual advantage
shaped the linguistic edifice in Uttar Pradesh — an edifice in which English was
just one more steep staircase for the poor to climb.

Confusion over language is not limited to contemporary Uttar Pradesh. India
as a nation has struggled with the status of Hindi from the birth of the nation.
Nehru and other founders of modern India hoped that Hindi would ultimately
emerge as the official national language of India. In deference to the opposition
of the southern states, where fluency in Hindi was uncommon, and due to the
difficulty of switching suddenly from English to Hindi, the constituent assembly
that framed the Indian constitution allowed English to share the status of official
language for the first 15 years after Independence. The government planned to
use this time to promote Hindi literacy in South India and to translate official
documents from English to Hindi.[2]

The change was not so simple. By the early 50s the language issue had become a political morass, with various ethnic and religious groups seeking official
recognition for their regional dialects. When the time came for the inception of
a Hindi India in 1965, political parties in South India objected. As January 1965,
the deadline for the imposition of Hindi as India's official language, approached,
Tamil-speaking political parties in the South launched a bitter agitation against
what they considered linguistic imperialism. Prime Minister Lal Shastri caved
into the demands of southern constituencies and allowed English to continue as
an official language indefinitely.[3]

In the wake of Shastri's failure of political will, South Indian states opted
for English over Hindi in official government business and civil service exams
and promoted English-language instruction in public institutions. When the
Internet later made outsourcing possible, the southern states, which retained
larger percentages of English speakers than the northern, became the preferred
location of business outsourcing projects. The Hindi-speaking majority of north

---

1 Guha, Ramachandra. *India After Gandhi* (New York: Harper Collins 2007), p. 751.
2 *Ibid.*, pgs. 128-131.
3 *Ibid.*, pgs. 393-397.

India thus found its numerical advantage turned into a disadvantage by politics and circumstance.

Some see Western investment in the English-literate South as a validation of southern state's resistance to Hindi dominance. But Hindi's future is far from bleak; it remains the largest linguistic group in India by far. A truly indigenous language, Hindi has intimate links to India's culture and history. Hindi-language press continues to grow and Bombay films have brought Hindi to millions outside of the Hindi belt. Moreover, the impetus behind the English language craze will, in all probability, turn out to be ephemeral. Call-centers requiring English speakers will undoubtedly move on to other, cheaper regions as India's economy develops. Untied to financial gain, the social pressure to learn English may wane and India may finally fulfill the vision of its founders, a nation where everybody shares a common language.

UDA DEVI ZINDABAD? THE ASSAULT ON HISTORY AS ILLUSTRATED BY THE
HISTORY OF AN ASSAULT

In the center of the intersection outside my apartment in Lucknow stood a statue of a patina-covered, sexually ambiguous figure carrying a rifle and walking forward with a determined glare. The inscription on the base of the statue named the figure as Uda Devi Pasi, a heroine of the Mutiny of 1857. Curious about the identity of Uda Devi Pasi and the meaning of the monument, I delved into local history. The story of Uda Devi Pasi ended up being much more complicated than I imagined, however, and led to a wider consideration of the uses and misuses of history in India.

In the fall of 1857, northern India was in a state of virtual anarchy. A general revolt against the growing hegemony of the British East India Company consumed the cities of Delhi, Jhansi and Kanpur.[1] In Lucknow, a small British garrison clung tenuously to life at The Residency, a collection of buildings on the banks of the Gomti River. Surrounded by rebels and lacking adequate supplies, the dwindling detachment of British soldiers, loyal Indian auxiliaries (often called *sepoys*) and non-combatants teetered on the edge of annihilation throughout the summer of 1857. A relief column of British soldiers broke through in September but lacked

---

1 Formerly spelled 'Cawnpore,' the site of a horrific massacre during the Mutiny. After resisting the rebels, the British garrison at Cawnpore negotiated a retreat with the rebel leader Nana Sahib. In June 1857 the entire British force boarded several ships intending to navigate the Ganges to British-held Allahabad. Either deliberately or accidentally the rebels fired upon the ships, setting them aflame. There were few survivors. A short time later, rebel forces, facing a renewed British offensive, massacred the remaining prisoners, mostly women and children, and threw the bodies down a well, an event known as the Bibighar massacre.

the firepower to leave again. This so-called "first relief of Lucknow" left the encircled Residency with more mouths to feed and in even greater need of supplies.

In November, General Colin Campbell broke through the rebel lines again and eventually saved the entrapped garrison.[1] During this "second relief of Lucknow," Campbell's 93rd Highlanders Regiment advanced along the Southern bank of the Gomti until they reached the Palace of Sikandarbag, the ruins of which laid across the street from our apartment.[2] There British forces met desperate resistance from rebels who had fortified the position. In the sanguineous battle that followed, over 2,000 rebels and many soldiers lost their lives in hand-to-hand combat.

After the British overran Sikandarbag, an officer noted that many of the British casualties had bullet wounds indicating a steep, downward trajectory. Suspecting that a sniper remained hidden in a nearby pipal tree, British officers fired at the tree and dislodged a rebel who fell to the ground with a thud, dead. Further investigation revealed that the rebel was, in fact, a low-caste woman named Uda Devi Pasi, who had donned men's clothing to participate in the uprising.

Or so the story goes.

Today Uda Devi Pasi is an inspiration to low-caste women in Uttar Pradesh State. Each year on November 16, members the *Pasi* caste gather at the sight of her final plunge and celebrate her as an anti-imperialist rebel who defied convention and struck a blow for the embryonic cause of Indian Independence. For *Pasis*, traditionally a caste of pig-herders and toddy-tappers, Uda Devi Martyrdom Day is an occasion to revel in the bravery and martial spirit of their ancestors and to chant the rousing slogans, *Uda Devi amar rahe!* (Uda Devi is deathless!) and *Uda Devi Zindabaad!* (Long live Uda Devi!).[3]

On November 16, 2005 Sikandarbag Park filled up with members of the *Viranga Uda Devi Pasii Sansthaan* (Heroic Uda Devi Pasi Institute). They came from West Bengal, Madhya Pradesh and Bihar to offer oblations to the image of Uda Devi Pasi. Many were women from remote villages who had traveled long distances to attend. As I looked at their faces, it occurred to me how much the day must mean to them, low-caste women, the least-esteemed position in all of Indian society.

---

1 The siege of Lucknow still elicits strong feelings among Indians. On 25 September 2007, BJP activists protested the arrival of a contingent from the British Association for Cemeteries in South Asia (BACSA), which intended to visit the remains of the Residency on the anniversary of Campbell's 2nd Relief. The violent BJP protest confined BACSA members to their hotel rooms. They left Lucknow without paying tribute to British casualties. See www.thehindu.com/2007/09/26.

2 Sikandarbag means "Garden of Alexander," a reference to Alexander the Great. Of Persian origin, the word *Sikandar* (Alexander) denotes a rising young talent or a Young Turk as in the phrase *takdiir ka Sikandar*, "Alexander of fate."

3 A toddy-tapper was a person who tapped palm trees for sap, from which an alcoholic punch was made.

They sang songs in honor of their heroine, and recited poetry expressing their outrage at the injustices of the caste system.

> Do not give us a monument or a stage,
>
> Give us a new society,
>
> We want freedom today from the unfair traditions of the world,
>
> We want a new society![1]

Unfortunately, a monument and a stage was all they would get on Uda Devi Pasi Martyrdom Day this year. Politicians, well aware of how much Uda Devi Pasi means to the Pasi caste (a large voting bloc), attended the gathering in a herd. The stage filled with ministers and officials from competing political parties — all of them men and few of them members of the Pasi caste. At one point in the program, an old Pasi woman stepped up on the stage to ask for a *maalaa* (flower necklace) to offer before the picture of Uda Devi. A well-dressed man refused to give up any of the officials' *maalaas* and told her to sit down.

As inspiring as the story of Uda Devi may be for Pasis and the politicians who want their votes, the tale suffers from a serious problem — no reliable historical evidence for Uda Devi Pasi exists. Although an eyewitness did mention a woman sniper killed at Sikandarbag on November 16, 1857 in his memoir, he recorded neither her name nor her caste.[2] In fact, the name Uda Devi and her association with the *Pasi* caste do not seem to pre-date the 1980s, when Pasi organizations began "re-discovering" the history of their people. This was part of a widespread trend fostered by Hindu reform groups like the *Arya Samaj*, who wanted to include traditionally marginalized groups in the history of Independence.[3]

The name Uda Devi does not even appear on the original monument in Sikandarbag Park erected in 1973. The inscription on the monument's base originally read "The Unknown Hero." Sometime between the erection of the monument and the present, the letters "Un" received a coat of white paint, leaving the visible phrase "known hero." If Uda Devi is deathless, it is because she was never born in the first place.

The "rediscovered" history of the Pasi caste does not end with Uda Devi Pasi. Pasi leaders claim that a dilapidated ruin outside Lucknow is the remains of the castle of Maharaja Bijalii Pasi (King Lightning). Maharaja Bijalii — so-named because he was, according to his statue's inscription, "as fast and enthusiastic as lightning" — was the leader of an extensive 12th-century kingdom ruled by Pasis.

---

1 Varma, Preety. "*Ham nayaa samaaj chaahie,*" (Viiranganaa Uudaadevii Smaarak Samsthaan 2005).

2 See Forbes-Mitchell, William. *Reminiscences of the Great Mutiny 1857-59* (New Delhi: Asian Educational Service 2002), p. 57.

3 Narayan, Badri. "Inventing caste history: Dalit mobilization and nationalist past," *Caste in Question*, Gupta, Dipauter, ed. (New Delhi: Sage Publications 2005).

As with Uda Devi, King Lightning has a murky history, however. His name does not appear in histories of medieval India, nor, as far as I am aware, have the ruins that stand at Maharaja Bijilee Memorial Park ever been identified or dated.

In light of these historical realities, Uda Devi Pasi Martyrdom Day seemed a bit ridiculous. Many of the Pasi women who came in such large numbers for the occasion were illiterate, and most of them were probably only dimly aware of the history of Lucknow or the Mutiny of 1857. The politicians of Uttar Pradesh were taking advantage of their credulity by trading manufactured history, in the form of memorial parks and statues, for votes. I doubted that many of the Pasis in attendance understood the flimsiness of the story of Uda Devi or the manipulative behavior of the politicians.

I expressed these thoughts to Dr. Manuela Ciotti, an anthropologist and expert on low-caste women from the University of Edinburgh, as we drove away from the Martyrdom Day festivities. She did not share my outrage. The actual history of the Pasi caste is wholly lost to the world, she explained. Whatever contributions they made passed without record. The Pasis, like numerous other low castes of India, have existed for millennia under the boot of the Brahmins, the Muslims and the British. As unscrupulous as it seems to barter votes for history, this manufactured history is dear to many Pasis.

"Look," she said, "nobody was worried about the historical basis of Uda Devi today except you. Over a thousand Pasis gathered because of this story. What is wrong with that?"

Perhaps she was right. After all, Westerners also utilize shadowy historical figures to promote a wide range of ideas. What connection, for example, does the historical St. Valentine have with a Hallmark Valentine's Day card? Although a Pasi named Uda Devi may never have fallen out of the pipal tree in Sikanderbag Park, it is equally untrue that George Washington chopped down his father's cherry tree.[1] So, if early Christian bishops and America's first president can be enlisted to promote squishy romantic sentiments and the value of honesty, why can't Pasis edit Lucknow's historical record to accommodate the aspirations of a long-suffering group of poor village women? All cultures create their own historical myths. As Manuela asked, "What is wrong with that?"

MANGAL PANDEY

With this idea in mind, I went to see the Bombay film *The Rising-Ballad of Mangal Pandey*. Critics had heaped negative press on the movie because of its loose adherence to the historical facts of the Mutiny of 1857. The British government objected to a fictional scene that depicted the massacre of villagers by British-led *sepoys*. Others griped about the free hand that producers had taken with the facts

[1] The story first version of the cherry tree story appeared long after Washington's death in *The Life of Washington* by Parson Mason Locke Weems.

of Mangal Pandey's life. Still others felt that certain scenes could be offensive to white people, many of which die bloody deaths at the film's conclusion.

The historical basis of the film rests on the story of an ordinary *sepoy* (soldier) named Mangal Pandey, stationed near Calcutta in the spring of 1857.[1] A rumor, later proved false, that the British East India Company's new Enfield rifles required cartridges greased with cow fat, angered the Brahmin Mr. Pandey, for whom eating beef was a mortal sin. One day, stoned beyond sense on *bhaang* (hashish), Mangal confronted his commanding officers, killed one of them and injured another before turning his gun on himself and attempting to commit suicide. Unsteady from excessive cannabis consumption, he missed his own head and inflicted a non-mortal wound upon his shoulder. The British finished the job for him a short time later, hanging him on April 8, 1857.[2]

The film re-makes the story of Mangal Pandey into a nationalistic morality play. In *The Rising*, the British East India Company does indeed slaughter sacred cows to grease its rifles and then, in turn, uses the rifles to inflict a promiscuous slaughter on inoffensive villagers. Mangal Pandey, on the other hand, receives gentler treatment. He comes across as a sensitive, if mercurial, young man with a passing resemblance to 1970s rock star, Frank Zappa. Before the shooting starts, Mangal makes friends with his European officers, has a love affair with a beautiful dancing girl (played by the stunning Rani Mukherjee) and does some hoofing himself in some of the film's many energetic dance numbers.

To the film's credit, British soldiers did not always appear as inhuman monsters. One officer, Captain Gordon, befriends Mandal and becomes the film's voice of conscience. Indian leaders are not always innocent in *The Rising* either. In one scene, a group of men attempts to enact the ritual of *sati*, in which a widow self-immolates on her husband's funeral pyre. Gordon, the good *gora* (white man), interrupts the barbaric custom and rescues the widow. Neither did the film shy away from the fact that Mangal Pandey's actions were inspired as much by *bhaang lassi* (hashish milkshakes) as by nationalistic fervor.

With all of the bad press, I did not expect to like *The Rising* half as much as I did. Although the film did take some liberties with history, it was neither more nor less honest than other historical dramas in India — or in America, for that matter. The liberties taken in *The Ballad of Mangal Pandey* were no more glaring than the countless anachronisms and inaccuracies found in Western historical films (e.g., *Gone With the Wind*). History, after all, is written by the winners and only tells part of the story. What is wrong with writing the other half ourselves?

---

1 A sepoy was an Indian employed as a soldier by British authorities.
2 Mangal Pandey's rampage immediately preceded the outbreak of a general uprising against the British East India Company, which began in earnest about a month after his death. Certain historians reason *post hoc ergo propter hoc* that the Mutiny of 1857 occurred *because* of Mangal Pandey's execution.

AYODHYA

The answer to my question lay beneath the rocky soil of Ayodhya, about six hours by Jeep northeast of Lucknow. The word *Ayodhya* literally means "without war." Never, since Eric the Red named a glacier-covered island in the North Atlantic "Greenland," has a place had such an inappropriate moniker. The city of Ayodhya has been a flash point for Hindu / Muslim tensions for at least a century and a half, and the very name of Ayodhya has become battle cry for extremists of both religions.

The origins of the conflict over Ayodhya are lost in the distant past. Many Hindus claim that Ayodhya is the birthplace of Ram, an incarnation of the god Vishnu and subject of the Hindu epic *Ramayana*. A popular story endures that Ayodhya was the site of a huge temple that stood on the very spot of Ram's earthly incarnation, called the Ramjanambhoomi (Place of the birth of Ram). Muslim invaders in the 16th century, according to this version of events, razed the temple and built a large mosque, the Babri Masjid, from its stones.

A persistent belief that the Babri Masjid mosque sat atop a Hindu holy site stoked the fires of communal hatred in the 1980s and 90s. The Bharatiya Janata Party used the issue of the Ramjanambhoomi to construct a populist platform with a wide appeal to working-class Hindus. In one infamous BJP-lead agitation called the *Rath Yatra* (chariot journey), right-wing politician L K. Advani traversed India in an economy van decorated to look like a primeval war chariot, all the while urging Hindu mobs to march on Ayodhya to fight for the glory of Ram. A short time later, on December 6, 1992, a massive mob of Hindu nationalists converged on the city, overran security barriers and leveled the four-and-a-half-century old Babri Mosque with pickaxes and shovels. Even years after the destruction of the mosque, the issue of Ayodhya can indirectly spark new outbreaks of communal violence, as it did in the 2002 Gujarat riot.[1]

The archeological record does not offer much support for the existence of a medieval Hindu temple at the site of the now-atomized Barbri Mosque. Most early surveys of the Ramjanambhoomi by the Archeological Survey of India (ASI) failed to find the remains of any large, pre-existing structure. Later, under political pressure from the Hindu right wing, the ASI re-examined the site, this time claiming to have found the sought-after evidence for a massive, 11th century temple of Ram. Meanwhile, independent archeologists have objected that geological evidence suggests the site remained abandoned from the 4th to the 13th centuries due to flooding.[2]

---

1 For more on the *Rath Yatra* and the rise of the Hindu Right wing in general, see the chapter "Caste and Communal Politics" below.
2 Romey, Kristen M. "Flashpoint Ayodhya: Did Hindu hard-liners recruit archeologists to rewrite history?," *Archeology Magazine*, July 2004, p. 53.

Some scholars even claim that a belief in the birthplace of Ram beneath the Babri Mosque dates only to the mid-19th century. Historian K. N. Panikar suggests that the origins of the conflicting over the Babri Mosque stem from an 1855 dispute over the nearby Hanumangiri Temple. In this conflict, a group of Sunni Muslim zealots, claiming that the Hanumangiri Temple rested on the remains of a pre-existing *mosque*, engaged in pitched battles with local Hindus. The head priest of the Hanumangiri Temple then pressed the accusations about the Ramjanambhoomi and the Babri Mosque as a "defensive ploy."[1]

This is an interesting idea, but the issue is far from decided. European travelers in the late 18th century recorded popular accounts about the Ram temple. Panikkar dismisses the account of Joseph Tieffenthaler as "garbled."[2] Quoted at length by historian Harsh Narain in his book *The Ayodhya Temple-Mosque Dispute*, however, Tieffenthaler's 1771 memoir provides a readable telling of the destruction of the Ram temple and the construction of the Babri Masjid complete with descriptions of local festivals.[3] If Tieffenthaler did intend to describe the Babri Masjid / Ramjanambhoomi, it would place belief in a pre-existing temple under the Babri Masjid into the mid-18th century, long before the Hanumangiri episode described by Panikkar.

To complicate matters further, some of the columns of the Babri Mosque apparently contained Hindu (or perhaps Jaina) motifs. While inconclusive — Babar could have salvaged the columns from an abandoned nearby temple — these pieces of evidence undermine any attempt to date the belief in the Ramjanambhoomi in the recent past. Narain includes a long list of sources supporting the view that Babar replaced a pre-existing temple with a mosque. A number of the sources he lists, including an 1838 work by Montgomery Martin, and an 1854 work by Edward Thornton pre-date the Hanumangiri event of 1855.[4] Thus, although no hard evidence proves the existence of a pre-existing temple, popular belief in the story, at least, is centuries old.[5]

---

1 Panikkar, K.N. "A Historical Overview," *Anatomy of a Confrontation*, Sarvepalli Gopal ed. (New Jersey: Zed Books 1991), pgs. 30-33.

2 *Ibid.*, p. 11.

3 Narain, Harsh. *The Ayodhya Temple-Mosque Dispute* (Delhi: Penman Publishers 1993), p. 10-11. Tieffenthaler's wrote his account in Latin. Jean Bernoulli translated the work into French in 1786. The various renderings of Bernoulli's French are not without differences.

4 Narain, Harsh. *The Ayodhya Temple-Mosque Dispute* (Delhi: Penman Publishers 1993), p. ix. Narain also invokes the elusive *Sahifah-i-Chihal Nasa'ih-i-Bahadurshahi*, a lost work attributed to Aurangzeb's grand-daughter by mid-20th century author Mizra Jan. Jan claims that the text contains an explicit account of the destruction of the Ram temple and the construction of the Babri Masjid. The authenticity and even the existence of the *Sahifah-i-Chihal* are in doubt, however.

5 Gopal, Sarvepalli. "Introduction," *Anatomy of a Confrontation* (New Jersey: Zed Books 1991), p. 11.

By the time Deborah, Dr. Manuela Cotti and I visited Ayodhya in January 2005, the site looked less like a Hindu temple or a mosque and more like a high-security prison. Rings of barbed wire and steel barriers surrounded the site and visitors were restricted to a rat's maze of chain link fences that wound past guard towers and bunkers. Overzealous security personnel subjected all visitors to repeated body searches and confiscated cameras and bags at the gate. The site itself amounted to little more than a few holes in the ground and a makeshift shrine to Ram. Little is left of the Babri Mosque. By the time I left, I thought that the Ramjanambhoomi must be the least pleasant tourist site in the world. More disturbingly, the line between fiction and reality had blurred. While the producers of *The Rising* had created a movie based on real life, the City of Ayodhya had made a real place look like the film set for *The Great Escape*.

If I found the level of security at the Ramjanambhoomi overbearing, however, I was unaware of the looming threat to the site. On July 5, 2005, a group of Islamic terrorists attempted to breech the walls and destroy the site with rocket-propelled grenades. In the 90-minute gun battle that followed, five extremists, one policeman and two bystanders died. Ayodhya, the place "without war," had become a battleground once again. When I read about this attack in the newspaper, I realized that tampering with history in India is not at all analogous to re-conceiving the biography of George Washington to include a vivisected cherry tree.

India: Mother to Us All?

The re-evaluation of history in India occurs among many different groups and on different levels of the social hierarchy. Individual castes such as the Pasi see themselves as heir to a lost kingdom and martial tradition; the Bombay film industry created a narrative of national unity in *Mangal Pandey* and Hindus a feeling of communal redemption at Ayodhya. It does not stop there. In recent years, historians in India have engaged in a contentious war of words over world history and the respective roles of Indians and Europeans at the dawn of recorded history.

Many books on the history of South Asia begin with an event called the Aryan Invasion. Somewhere around the year 1500 BCE, the story goes, nomadic tribes from central Asia poured through the mountain passes on the northwest border of present-day Pakistan and conquered the Indian subcontinent. They brought with them their language, Sanskrit (or perhaps proto-Sanskrit), horses, chariots and a host of deities that included Agni, god of fire and Indra, the thunder god.

No archeological evidence directly proves the occurrence of this Aryan Invasion, and no texts clearly record the event. Belief in the Aryan Invasion rests primarily on linguistic evidence, philological reconstructions, and horse bones (or the lack thereof). Early European visitors to India discovered, much to their bewilderment, that Sanskrit, the ancient language of India, bore an uncanny resemblance to ancient European languages such as Greek and Latin (see figure 1).

English	Latin	German	Sanskrit
Father	Pater	Vater	Pitr
Mother	Mater	Mutter	Matr
Brother	Frater	Bruder	Bhraatr
Sun	Solis	Sonne	Suurya
Knowledge	Gnosis	Wissen	*Jnana* (often pronounced *gyana*)
Sister	Soror	Schwester	Swasr
Daughter	Filia	Tochter	Duhitr
Son	Filius	Sohn	Suunu
Mouse	Mus	Maus	Muushaka

Figure 2. A short list of common words and their equivalents in other branches of the Indo-European language family. In some cases, the relationship is obvious, while in others the word has changed beyond recognition.[1]

European scholars were at a loss to explain this eerie concordance. Over the course of the first half of the 19th century, interest in the relationship between ancient European and Indian tongues led to the inescapable conclusion that Sanskrit, Persian, Greek, Latin, German, Gaelic, Russian and a host of other languages sprang from the same primeval Ur-language now called Proto Indo-European or PIE. PIE was the mother tongue of a group of nomads who spread from India to Ireland. Most scholars now agree that sometime in the middle of the second millennium BCE, PIE-speaking tribes from central Asia undertook a multi-directional migration and settled in India, Europe and Persia. PIE-speaking people even make a brief appearance in the Bible as the Hittites. Wherever they went, they never lost their self-confidence, referring to themselves as the "noble people," *Aryan* in Sanskrit, *Iran* in Proto-Iranian, *Erinn* (the root of the name for Ireland) in Celtic.[2]

From whence PIE-speaking people came is unknown. Some scholars guess that they originally inhabited the Caucus region (an idea termed the Kurgan

---

1 Lanman, Charles. *Sanskrit Reader* (Boston: Harvard University Press, 1884). See also Calvert Watkins's essay "Indo-European and the Indo-Europeans" found in *The American Heritage Dictionary* fourth edition (New York: Hughton Mifflin 2000).

2 Lanman, p. 126-127. Watkins offers a different etymology for *erin*, unrelated to the Sanskrit *arya*. See *The American Heritage Dictionary* fourth edition. Watkins, Calvert. "Indo-European and the Indo-Europeans," (New York: Hughton Mifflin 2000), p. 2015. Herodotus mentions that the Medes were formally called *Arians*. See Herodotus. *The Histories* trans. Aubrey de Selincourt (New York: Penguin Books 1980), p. 466.

Model). Another theory, based on the etymology of the word "salmon" and thus called Salmon Theory, placed them in north-central Europe, near Poland.[1] Formerly, scholars dismissed India as a possible site for the original PIE-speakers:

> And indeed if it were a fact that the Harappans did not know the horse, their claim for any kind of "Aryanship" must fall to the ground, since right from the Rigvedic times, the horse played an important role in the life of the Indo-Aryans.[2]

In other words, the archeological record at sites such as Harappa and Mohenjodharo contains no evidence for horses in ancient Indian civilization at the time of the Vedas' composition (the Vedas being one of the earliest surviving texts in a PIE language). Thus, the authors of the Vedas, and by implication the Proto-Indo European peoples themselves, cannot have been living in India in the second millennium BCE, and were most probably living far to the north, closer to the horse's native habitat in central Asia.

Some have argued convincingly, however, that the archeological record is not as clear as scholars once supposed. Bones of horses, horse-like animals, and half-asses appear in several Harappan sites in small numbers.[3] Moreover, horse-like figurines appear in the archeological record of Harappan civilization.[4] Given the ambiguity of the archeological evidence, some Indian historians have taken a new look at the Aryan Invasion and offered an alternate version of events, sometimes called Indian Urheimat Theory (IUT).[5] IUT claims that all Indo-European languages and European people originated in the Indus river valley.

A full discussion of the issues surrounding the Aryan Invasion vs. IUT controversy is beyond the scope of this book and I lack the qualifications to offer an informed opinion. In his book *The Aryan Debate*, Thomas Trautmann sums up the current state of the debate by suggesting that while the standard (Aryan Invasion) view remains intact, it has taken a few lumps, while the alternative view (IUT) awaits new evidence to place it on a firmer footing.

> [W]e find many instances of toy ox-carts with solid wheels and oxen in sites of the Indus Civilization, but we do not find toy chariots with spoked wheels and horses. An argument from absence, of course, is not as strong as an argument from presence, but the burden of proof lies on those who wish to overturn the standard view, and to meet it they need to come up with lots of evidence.[6]

---

1 Trautmann, Thomas, ed. *The Aryan Debate* (New Delhi: Oxford Press, 2005) for Salmon theory, see p. 59.
2 *Ibid.,* Lal, B. B. "The Truant Horse Clears the Hurdles," p. 231.
3 *Ibid.*, Bokonyi, Sandor. "Horse Remains from Surkotaka."
4 *Ibid.,* Lal, B. B. "The Truant Horse Clears the Hurdles," p. 231.
5 IUT dates to the 18th century, when some early Indologists, such as Freidich Schlegel, argued that Sanskrit and PIE were identical. The idea fell out of favor for a good century and a half, until recently revived.
6 *Ibid.*, p. *xli.*

MY FATHER TOLD ME THAT THE IRISH BUILT THE PYRAMIDS. I NOW KNOW THAT THEY PROBABLY HAD SOME HELP.

The communalization of history is a growing danger in India. Nationalist views of ancient history have been seeping into Indian history books since the rise of the right-wing Bharatiya Janata Party in the 1980s. The current Congress-led government is trying to repair the damage by deleting these jingoistic historical myths from school textbooks, but their effort is not without opposition.[1]

However, the manipulation of history is not the exclusive domain of the political right in India. Left wing and progressive groups have added many fantastic chapters of their own to India's history. In August 2005, for example, Suraj Bhan, Chairman of the National Commission for Scheduled Castes, called for the rewriting of Hindu *religious scripture* itself to eradicate demeaning references to low-caste people.[2]

Moreover, medieval histories of India by liberal academics, such as Romila Thapar's *Somanatha*, have come under criticism for disingenuously downplaying the sometimes-violent history of Islam in India.[3] Some of her critics (e.g., Meenakshi Jain) labeled Thapar's work, which investigates the history and historiography surrounding Mahmud of Ghazni's raid on the Somanatha temple in 1026, "Marxist." To be fair, the book represents fastidious research and adheres to the highest standards of scholarship. *Somanatha* is not a thoughtless left-wing rant. On the other hand, the inferences Thapar draws from her research often follow predictable lines that suggest she drew her conclusions before she conducted her research.

In Thapar's hands, the Islamic chronicles of conquest receive a meticulous deconstruction. She suggests that Muslim accounts of raids on Somanatha were formulaic, overblown, and written to show Mahmud in the role of the conquering holy warrior or the righteous Muslim sultan. She may indeed have a point, but she undercuts her case by applying her sharp analytic scalpel selectively and sparing Sanskrit sources a similar analysis. Thapar interprets the dearth of information about the sack of Somanatha in surviving Sanskrit inscriptions as further evidence that the Persian and Turkish accounts are exaggerations, while ignoring other possible causes for the lacuna (e.g., the local Hindu population's reluctance to dwell on an event that undoubtedly dispirited them). After describing an Arabic and Sanskrit inscription from the 13th century that fails to mention Mahmud, Thapar concludes, with little apparent cause, "The raid of Mahmud could not

---

1 "'Updated' history book offends saffronites," *Times of India* Lucknow Edition, 7/12/05, p. 1.
2 "Reform Hinduism for our larger common good," *Times of India*, Lucknow Edition, 8/30/05, p. 8.
3 See Thapar, Romila. *Somanatha: The Many Voices of a History* (London: Verso 2005) and Jain, Meenakshi. *Flawed Narratives: History in the Old NCERT Textbooks* (Delhi: Delhi Historians Forum 2003).

have been forgotten 200 years after the event if it had been as traumatic as it is currently said to be."[1]

ASSAULT ON HISTORY?

At first glance, I thought I saw a snowballing abuse of history from all points on the political spectrum in India. The last 30 years has seen the rise of both manufactured caste histories, like that of the Pasis, and questionable archeological studies contaminated by politics. A feeling that mainstream history has given them the short end of the stick motivates diverse groups. Pasis naturally find it difficult to accept any account of the history of India that is wholly devoid of their community's contribution. Hindu nationalists, on the other hand, seek to emphasize Hindu victimization at the hands of Muslim invaders. Both groups would like to write themselves into the story of the Mutiny of 1857 (now sometimes called The First War of Indian Independence). Meanwhile left wing writers create an imaginary medieval history in which Islam arrives on India's doorstep as politely as a Mormon missionary.

Historical revisionism is a slippery slope. You cannot allow certain communities (e.g., the Pasis, academic circles) to create their own heroes under the heading of history but deny the same right to others (e.g., Hindu fundamentalists). The very same relaxation of historical rigor that allowed Pasi activists to obscure the "un" in the word "unknown" in Sikandarbag Park facilitated the manufacture of the archeological record in Ayodhya and the re-writing of Indian history by overheated nationalists. In regard to history, maybe we should keep the words of George Washington in mind. No matter how grave the crimes of the past, we "cannot tell a lie" — at least if we can help it.

Or at least that was my thinking. As time passed, I became more skeptical about the much-discussed "assault on history." If history was under assault in India, then who was the assailant and what was his motivation? Some authors have focused on the excesses of the political right and imagined that revisionist history is a ploy exclusive to this end of the political spectrum. As I have tried to illustrate here, however, all points of the political, economic and caste continuums were equally capable of creatively editing the historical record. This begged the question whether history was actually under attack or whether the "assault

---

1 *ibid,* p. 94. She emphasizes the syncratic tendencies in Indian religion, particularly in Sufism and certain (obscure) Tantric texts in an attempt to dislodge a "homogenous" reading of Indian history. Only readers who have accepted her initial analysis uncritically will find this convincing. To her credit, she includes an interesting account of the "Proclamation of the Gates" event of 1842. Succinctly, Lord Ellenborough ordered General Nott, commander of the British forces in Afghanistan, to retrieve the gates of Mahmud's tomb from Ghazni, claiming that they were actually the gates of the Somanatha temple. The claim appears to have been entirely spurious and motivated by a desire to curry favor with Ranjit Singh, King of the Punjab. *Ibid.,* pgs. 167-168.

on history" was more a construction of Western intellectuals struggling to understand a deep-seated cultural difference in way South Asians process information. This possibility is the central concern of the following chapter.

THE MOURNING OF CHAINS: MUHARRAM (AND A SUNNI-SHIITE RIOT) IN
LUCKNOW

In the last chapter, I looked at how various communities in India re-imagined
their own histories by creating revisionist histories inspired by caste pride, communalism and political ideology. Here I will consider Islamic religious history
as a further cause for historical disagreement in India. History aroused intense
emotions for Lucknow's Muslim community, and the festival of Muharram in
particular brought differing versions Islamic religious history, Sunni and Shiite,
into sharp relief. While pondering these competing views of religious history and
their affects upon this local festival, I began to question many of the assumptions
I had about historical sensibilities in India, particularly the idea of a contemporary assault on history, as characterized by Western academics.

Shiite Islam is receiving a great deal of attention these days. For the first time
in centuries, the Shiite majority holds the reins of power in Baghdad. This comes
at a time when Iran, the Shiite homeland and a part of President Bush's Axis
of Evil, continues to develop nuclear power and the world debates what to do
about it. Despite all this news, Shiite Islam remains little understood in the West.
Almost any bookstore in America carries a copy or two of the Koran and a selection of books on Islam, but books that focus exclusively on Shiites are few. In my
struggle to understand Shiite Islam, I was lucky enough to find myself in Lucknow, home of one of the largest Shiite community in India, during Muharram,
the most important event on the Shiite religious calendar.

Muharram marks the death of Imam Hussein at the Battle of Karbala in AD
680. The festival is not merely the celebration of the martyrdom of a Muslim saint,
however. Muharram signifies a pivotal moment in world history for the Shiite
community and marks the beginning of Shiite Islam as a distinct religion. The

death of Imam Hussein is thus as significant for Shiites as the Crucifixion is for Christians and the ceremonies that take place during the month of Muharram are as emotionally charged as a medieval passion play.

The strong sentiment that surround Muharram rest on the central importance of Imam Hussein to the Shiite community's conception of history. Following the death of the Prophet Muhammad in AD 632, his successors, or "Caliphs," governed the growing Islamic empire as both political and religious leaders. When the fourth Caliph, Ali, the son-in-law of the Prophet Muhammad, died in 679 AD, his second son, Imam Hussein, was next in line for the throne. By this time, however, many people believed that the Islamic realm would fare better under the leadership of someone outside of the Prophet's family. In the ensuing struggle over succession, Imam Hussein and a small group of friends and relatives died during a skirmish at Karbala, in present day Iraq. Following his death, the Caliphate fell to others who were unrelated to the Prophet, known as the Umayyad Caliphs, and the seat of political power in the Islamic world shifted from Arabia to Damascus.

Some people, however, remained convinced that the Caliphate should have remained in the family of the Prophet and that Islam had taken a wrong turn with the death of Imam Hussein. This difference of opinion over the line of succession would eventually lead to a full-scale schism in Islam between the Sunni mainstream, who accepted the leadership of the Umayyad Caliphs, and the Shiites, who mourned the death of Imam Hussein and the disenfranchisement of the Prophet's family. Over time, Shiite Islam took hold in Persia, with significant minority communities in Egypt and Syria.

Shiites everywhere remember the death of Imam Hussein and re-enact the Battle of Karbala every year during the first ten days of Muharram, a month in the Islamic calendar (which began in late February in 2005). In Lucknow, the festival of Muharram takes on an additional importance because of the large Shiite population in the city. All of the Kings of Lucknow, who ruled the city and the surrounding Kingdom of Oudh in the early 19th century, were Shiite and Lucknow was where the distinctly Indian traditions connected to Muharram first took shape.

The Mourning of Fire

On the fifth night of Muharram, my wife Deborah I arrived at the Shahnajaf Imambara, the 19th century mausoleum of Ghazi-ud-din Haider, King of Oudh, to witness a ceremony call the *Aag par Mataam* or "Mourning of Fire." We did not go without some trepidation. The Urdu-language newspapers were full of angry pronouncements from both Washington and Tehran on the subject of Iran's nuclear program. Many Shiites in Lucknow looked to Iran as the idealized Shiite state, and I was worried that our presence as Americans might anger some people.

The shrine was lit up with hundreds of colored lights. Shortly after we arrived, a procession of shouting men emerged from the shrine's interior. They beat their breasts with their hands and yelled, "Ya Hussein!" The procession included a pure white horse dappled in red paint to indicate the steed and blood of Imam Hussein.

The revelers moved to a pit of glowing coals for the Mourning of Fire, better known as fire walking. Fire walking is often a circus act in the West, but in Lucknow, it is a popular way to mark the death of Imam Hussein. The young men, still shouting and beating their breasts, walked slowly across hot coals, yelling, "*Ya Hussein! Ya Sakhiina* [O Hussein, O daughter of Hussein], *Ya Abbas* [O brother of Hussein]!"

The participants repeated the Mourning of Fire several times. Another procession of young men emerged from the shrine, and then another, until the courtyard was filled with young Shiite men. They jostled each other as they walk over the hot coals and worked themselves into such frenzy that a scuffle broke out between two participants.

In the middle of the chaos, one young Shiite man took a break from beating his breast to ask me, with eyes bulging "Where are you from? What country have you come from?"

"Canada," I said. "We are from Canada."

After the ceremony, a group of young Shiite men and women approached us and invited us to their house for tea. It was obvious from the religious banners and Arabic prayers hanging from their walls that they were devout Shiites. They displayed warm hospitality toward us, insisted that we eat with them and showed us pictures of their family. The young women of the family were excited to hear that Deborah was an artist and asked her to draw a portrait of one of them. They watched, entranced, as Deborah recreated the girl's features on a sheet of paper. One of the girls declared that she would also like to be an artist one day.

"Where do I go to become an artist like you?" she asked.

"For that," Deborah answered, "you will have to come stay with us in New York City."

"New York City?" One of the young men said to me. "We heard you were from Canada."

"It's very near Canada." I said.

The young man laughed and I realized I had nothing to fear. He introduced himself as Zulfiqar (named after Imam Hussein's magic sword — see below), an Urdu teacher and Arabic scholar. He assured us that he was not going to hold our nationality against us.

POETRY AS CURRENT EVENT: THE MARSIYA OF MIR ANIS

When I hired Fauzia, my Urdu teacher, I made one request. I knew that Fauzia, a well-published Urdu poetess, would rather spend her time talking about literature than discussing the news. I was more interested in reading the Urdu newspapers, however. "Let's not talk about poetry," I said to her. "I am only interested in current events."

I had a good reason to say this. As a group, Indian Muslims are a literary bunch. It seems as if every Indian Muslim I meet is writing a novel and has a favorite author whom he (or she) can quote at length. Poetry, in particular, seems to affect them in a powerful way. I had seen even grown men come close to tears while reciting *gazal* (a type of sonnet), and I did not want my Urdu lessons to become maudlin.

Ignoring my request, Fauzia brought books of poetry to my lessons anyway. One day she brought a book by a famous Urdu poet named Ahmed Fayez, and we worked on translating one of his better-known verses.

> The poet writes "peace": the name of your beauty,
>
> It scatters when you stand on terrace in colorful dress,
>
> It is cleansed in the morning, the noon, and some nights,
>
> Wherever the gown covers your beautiful frame,
>
> In the garden each cypress and pine is adorned,
>
> I learn the meaning of *gazal* when my heart dips,
>
> Its wine glass into the shadow of your cheek and lip,
>
> The poet writes "peace:" the name of your beauty.[1]

The extended metaphors, the sensuous language and the mesmerizing meter all worked together to create an intoxicating effect. I found that it was easy to be swept away in the study of Urdu poetry, to spend hours in a timeless world of symbols and innuendo, re-experiencing the dizzying emotional catharsis of the poet over and over again.

We did not stop with love poetry. Fauzia also introduced me to *marsiya*, a genre of poetry dedicated to the subject of martyrdom. *Marsiya* has a special significance in Lucknow, the home of one of South Asia's most famous Urdu poet, Mir Anis (d. 1874). Mir Anis wrote a famous collection of *marsiya* in honor of Imam Hussein and his martyrdom at the Battle of Karbala.

Mir Anis' composed his opus in a literary and somewhat archaic style and I was unable to translate even a single couplet with any confidence. The only English version available to me was not very interesting to read. The verses struck me as "purple" and overblown and Imam Hussein took a very long time to die. Before his martyrdom, he behaves like a type of Islamic Achilles, slaying slews of enemies with Zulfiqar, his magic sword. Extended passages in praise of his horse are ubiquitous. Finally, in verse 176 of the 16th Book, Imam Hussein meets his end:

---

1 Translation (and mistakes) mine. Urdu text from Fayez, Ahmed. *Dast e Sabaa* (Aligarh: Educational Book House 1997), p. 35.

Ten thousands arrows dashed upon his chest;

A hundred at one time sought out their prey.

The spears transfixed his side and pierced his breast;

Ten struck for every four he pulled away.

The Shadow of the Lord [Imam Hussein] was filled with spines,

Like needles in the backs of porcupines.[1]

These poems may have left me cold, but Mir Anis' *marsiya* play a central role in the festival of Muharram and recitations of *marsiya* cause Shiite congregations to break out into tears. If Urdu love poetry transported me, some Shiites in Lucknow experienced a similar effect from *marsiya* — verses whose theme is often martial, and whose imagery is soaked in blood. As I would discover, these poems affect contemporary relations between Sunni and Shiite Muslims in a profound way. I discovered that, in Lucknow, poetry *is* a current event.[2]

THE MOURNING OF CHAINS

One of the most important events of Muharram is the remembrance of the death of Imam Hussein's brother Abbas. The story goes that during the Battle of Karbala, Abbas could not stand to see Imam Hussein's six-year-old daughter Sakiina suffering from thirst. He rode out to find water for the little girl and never returned. The story brings out strong feelings of fraternity among Shiites. Some Shiites choose to simulate the wounds of Abbas in a ritual called the *Zanjeer ki Maatam*, or the "Mourning of Chains," a type of self-flagellation performed in public using a special type of barbed whip.

On the tenth and final day of Muharram, we saw the Mourning of Chains for ourselves. Zulfiqar (the person, not the sword) accompanied us to the neighborhood of Nakhaas Bazaar, where we found thousands of Shiites walking down the street in a long procession towards the Karbala shrine. The real Karbala, the site of the Battle of Karbala where Imam Hussein was martyred, is in Iraq, of course. In lieu of the real thing, people were heading for the local "Karbala." The police had placed a squad of officers in riot gear on each street corner. When I asked Zulfiqar about this, he told me that, in the past, the Muharram festival has sometimes been the occasion for violence between the Sunni and Shiite communities.

As we walked toward "Karbala", we saw young men with *zanjeer*, a type of cat o' nine tails, in their hands. They began to whip themselves, and soak their

---

1 Matthews, David. *The Battle of Karbala: A Marsiya of Anis* (New Delhi: Rupa & Co 1994), p. 82. Full Urdu text available in Hussein, Abid Saliha, ed. *Anees ke Marsiay* (New Delhi: Tariqi Urdu Bureau 1990).

2 As are films. When asked about his support of film censorship, a Punjabi member of the Indian Cinematograph Committee once candidly remarked, "If you want Indian history more modern than 1,000 A.D., it would be difficult to handle the subject." Barnouw, Erik, and Krishnaswamy, S. *Indian Film* (New York, Oxford University Press 1980) p. 53.

clothing with blood. Others cut their own scalps with daggers. We expected this. What surprised us was the age of some of the participants, who looked no older than eight or nine years old.

We tried to remain as inconspicuous as possible. I was dressed in a black shirt and dark pants, while Deborah was dressed in an olive-green Punjabi with a black scarf around her head. Our attempt to mix in with the crowd worked only too well. Several people stopped us to ask if we are Muslims — perhaps Western converts to Shiite Islam.

After my "Canada" experience, I had given up telling white lies. I told them that we were not Muslims and that we came from America. As it turns out, my honesty was equally counter-productive. A few minutes later, a man approached Zulfiqar and pulled him aside. He warned Zulfiqar to be careful, because some people were not happy about our presence. I did not experience any direct hostility, but some men took long, hard looks at us, and I had the feeling that we were not welcome. Moreover, the sight of hundreds of bleeding men with chains, daggers and whips in their hands made me uncomfortable. We returned home without reaching "Karbala."

The next day, the headlines in the newspapers announced that the government of Lucknow had declared a curfew in the wake of a Sunni-Shiite riot. As I read the article, I was surprised to find that the riot took place in a neighborhood very close to the one we had visited, less than an hour after we had returned home.

The exact sequence of events was not clear. The three newspapers that I read differed in all the details except for the body count — three people dead, 18 wounded, four in serious condition.[1] A number of houses also burned to the ground during the disturbance. The riot apparently occurred when Shiite processions passed through a Sunni neighborhood. A fight between Sunni and Shiite gangs broke out, a rooftop sniper created panic and a Shiite mob began setting fire to buildings. *The Times of India* showed a picture of a tourist bus fleeing the area. It was a safe bet that the City of Lucknow's attempt to promote Muharram as a tourist attraction was off to a slow start.

Asking friends in Lucknow about the disturbance did not clarify things. Zulfiqar claimed that Sunni gangs instigated the violence. Fauzia, a Sunni, suggested that the riot was the result of a plot by Hindu extremists. My landlord, a Hindu, declared that the trouble started with the Shiites, who "are unreformed barbarians."

Whoever started the confrontation; this was not the first time that Sunni-Shiite riots have rocked Lucknow. In 1977, a prolonged riot burnt the Nakhaas Bazaar neighborhood to the ground. This year, the creation of a separate personal

---

1 *Times of India*: Lucknow Edition, *Dainik Jaagaran*, and *Rashtriya Sahara*: Urdu Edition, 2/22/05.

law board for Shiites, the All India Shia Personal Law Board (AISPLB), may have sharpened tensions.[1] Some Sunni leaders believe that the creation of an exclusively Shiite legal organization compromises the political power of the Muslim community as a whole. One local Sunni leader had previously suggested that the creation of the Shiite Board was a plot by "[the] U.S. and Israel to divide Muslims."[2]

Neither the alphabet soup of governing boards nor the bumping of shoulders in the bazaar fully explained the violence, however. As I tried to find a reason for the riot, I kept coming back to poetry. Perhaps poetry was the common link between the gentle Muslim intellectuals that I knew in Lucknow and the enraged rioters that I saw in the newspapers. Just as I could read century-old *gazal* and feel the poet's heartbreak as if it were happening at that very moment, some Shiites listened to the recitation of *marsiya* and re-experienced the pain, outrage and bloodlust of the Battle of Karbala. Every year the participants of Muharram mentally unsheath Zulfiqar, the magic sword of Imam Hussein, every year Imam Hussein, the rightful heir of the Prophet, meets his martyrdom in a swarm of arrows, and every year some Shiites spill their own blood — and perhaps the blood of others as well — in his remembrance.

As I saw during Muharram, the *aam aadmii* (common man) of Uttar Pradesh often exists in a timeless "now" in which events of the distant past repeat themselves *ad infinitum*. This raises the question, is history really under attack in India or did it perhaps never exist to begin with? Journalists and academics who write about the assault on history is such dire terms sometimes fail to notice the culturally specific meaning of the word. Europeans brought their ideas about history with them but the idea has not, as of yet, permeated the intellectual life of mainstream India.

Just as we are accustomed to think of lactose intolerance as a disorder and only realize the contrary is true upon reflection, we imagine the discipline of history as an innate characteristic of all people and only realize its anomalous character with difficulty.[3] Historical thinking in the Hellenic sense was an oddity in world literature, and did not develop indigenously in India.[4] Sanskrit literature

---

1 For more on Muslim personal law in India, see the chapter "A Law Unto Themselves" below.

2 *Times of India*: Lucknow Edition, 1/24/05, p. 3.

3 Adult mammals drinking milk is the true biological oddity; most mammals cease drinking milk when weaned. Humans from herding societies — often in Europe — developed the ability to digest milk after they had attained adulthood. Intolerance for milk is thus not an abnormality all but our default state. See www.scienceinafrica.co.za/2002/june/lactose.htm et al.

4 The word "history", originally meaning an inquiry or investigation, acquired its current meaning when Herodotus of Hallicarnassus used it as a title for his 5th century B.C. opus, an account of the Persian invasion of Greece. Counterbalancing his great innovations in historical method are Herodotus's many dubious claims — he is sometimes called "the father of lies" because of a myriad of inaccuracies that his *Histories* contain. One of the most far-fetched episodes in the text is Herodotus's account of India, taken second-

contains no obvious parallels to Herodotus, Thucydides and Edward Gibbon and ancient Indian literature is notoriously ahistorical. Even as sacred history, Hindu myth is notably untethered to verifiable events. Christians may argue whether the crucifixion occurred in 29 or 34 AD, and Jews about the extent of the Davidic kingdom, but Hindu sacred literature often proceeds with no historical anchor whatsoever.

For example, the *Mahabharata*, the *Iliad* of Hinduism, may preserve a dim memory of an ancient dynastic struggle, but then again it may not. Hinduism's second great epic, the *Ramayana*, may likewise depict the historical conquest of Sri Lanka, but dating the event with any certainty is impossible (certainly it is difficult to accept Rama's army of monkeys as a historical reality). Lastly, the *Puranas*, which round out the body of literature called *Itihas* (roughly "sacred history"), contain mythic material for which no sure historical parallels exist.[1] Islam brought a new sense of sacred history to the subcontinent, but one that remained polemic in nature and mingled with theological abstraction.[2]

Today, many Indians still approach history as sacred history. Accounts of both ancient and current events are told to illustrate the power of the supernatural or convey an ethical ideal, not to simply transmit information. History in the narrow sense is often only a thin patina atop a need to mythologize and moralize, a pronounced trait of the Indian psyche. Earnest students, to recall but one example, told me that the stone pillar outside the La Martiniere School on the banks of the Gomti say atop a secret underground passage that reached all the way to Delhi. The same story circulated about Lucknow's Great Imambara. A boatman in Varanasi told me a long story complete with fastidious details about an ancient Hindu king who built a tower so tall that a visitor could see Delhi from the tower's apex. In Kashmir, I heard that Jesus died in Srinagar and even visited his "tomb" (see the next chapter). Everywhere I went, locals repeated tall tales like these as if they were established fact. Political rumors took on an even greater importance. Scandalous stories about politicians, which do not bear retelling here, circulated constantly, especially during elections.

Mentioning this difference is to invite the ire of many contemporary academics. Edward Said, author of the much-discussed book *Orientalism*, bristles at the

---

hand from an unnamed Persian intermediary. Among other tall tales, Herodotus claims that Indians harvested gold dust from dog-sized ants, copulated in the open and practiced cannibalism. His account of India may contain genuine elements, however. *The Histories* includes a description of an Indian "tribe" that avoids killing animals and eats only vegetable food, perhaps a garbled description of Jain ascetics. See Herodotus. *The Histories* (New York: Penguin Books 1980), pgs. 245-6.

1 Dynastic history prior to the Muslim invasions is often the result of painstaking reconstructions from archeological and numismatic evidence. See Keay, John. *India: A History* (New York: Grove-Atlantic 2001).

2 For an account of the difficulty separating sacred from profane history in Islam, see Ibn Warraq. *The Search for the Historical Muhammad* (Amherst: Prometheus Books 2000).

claim that the Islamic and Western worlds treat historical subjects in a different way, calling it "...the culmination of Orientalism as a dogma..."[1] The Indian mythological imagination need not be conceived of negatively, however. While it can fuel caste and communal conflicts, the Indian penchant for creatively connecting the dots has a positive side as well. The mythologizing process, so moribund in the West, is alive and well in India and provides modern and historical events with context and meaning. This is not such a bad thing in a place where people distrust the press (often with good reason), despise the local government, and where illiteracy rates remain high.

In the end, the so-called assault on history is a well-intentioned but misguided attempt to remain willfully blind to cultural difference. The transformation of an anonymous female sniper into a caste hero named Uda Devi Pasi is the result of powerful, and often constructive, cultural force qualitatively at odds with our Western, Hellenic conception of history. Uda Devi, like many myths, is a lie that hints at a deeper truth. Half way down the Pipal tree, as she dove to her death, Uda Devi Pasi became more than a fact; she became part of the living story of India. And India is nothing if not a refuge for every creature — Hindu, Sunni or Shiite — that haunts our imaginations, or, as the author Romain Rolland remarked, "If there is one place on the face of the earth where all the dreams of living men have found a home from the very earliest days...it is India."[2]

---

1 Said, Edward. *Orientalism* (New York: Vintage Books 1978), p.319. I am not the first to note that Said commits every sin of which he accuses Western Orientalists. Several eloquent rebuttals of Said have appeared in recent years, most notably Robert Irwin's *For Lust of Knowing: The Orientalists and Their Enemies* (London: Allen Lane 2006) and Ibn Warraq's *On Defending the West: A Critique of Edward Said's Orientalism* (New York: Prometheus Books 2007). See also Nanda, Meera. *Prophets Facing Backwards: Post-Modern Critiques of Science and Hindu Nationalism* (New Jersey: Rutgers University Press 2004). Nanda illustrates the absurdities that result when the post-Modernist critique of science reaches Asia and renders service to Hindu traditionalists and proponents of "Vedic Science." Lastly, for a close look at the intersection of belief and historical inquiry, see Jha, D. N. *The Myth of the Holy Cow* (New York: Verso Books 2002). Jha argues convincingly that dietary restrictions against eating beef do not date back the Vedic period. Citing copious examples from ancient literature, Jha postulates that Hindus ate beef for both sustenance and as part of religious rituals well into the classical period.

2 Banham, Martin, ed. *The Cambridge Guide to Theater* (Cambridge: Cambridge University Press 1998), p. 980.

A Law unto Themselves: Muslim Personal Law and the Imrana Rape Case

On June 4, 2005, Imrana Ilahi, a young Muslim woman from a small village in Western Uttar Pradesh, survived rape at the hands of her own father-in-law. As a Muslim, Imrana and her husband chose to refer the case to a local council (*panchaayat*) of elders and religious leaders. The village council, after a careful consideration of the evidence in light of Islamic law (or *shari'at*), ruled that Imrana could not prove rape without presenting witnesses. Moreover, as she had now admitted to extra-marital sex, the marriage bonds between her and her husband were no longer valid and she should instead live with the offending father-in-law as husband and wife. When news of the decision reached the nearby Daru'l 'Ulum Islamic seminary of Deoband, the resident *muftis*, or Islamic jurists, apparently issued a legal decision (*fatwa*) agreeing with the *panchaayat*; Imrana should sever all relations to her husband and live with her father-in-law (the alleged rapist) as his wife.[1]

The Imrana rape case caused a furor in India. The newspapers were full of letters from angry and confused readers from every part of political spectrum. How could any sane person come to such a conclusion? Did Islam really condone such behavior or was the Imrana decision the result of some sort of fantastic act of misinterpretation? Many people expressed exasperation with the idea of Islamic

---

1 The content and even the existence of the Imrana *fatwa* is a point of controversy. Certain members of the Deoband ulema, apparently in response to widespread public outrage, later claimed either that no *fatwa* existed or that it applied only to a hypothetical case of rape between father and daughter-in-law, See Burney, Shahid Raza. 'No Fatwa Issued in the Imrana Rape Case,' www.arabnews. For more information on Daru'l 'Ulum and the history of Deobandi thought, see Metcalf, Barbara Daly. *Islamic Revival in British India: Deoband 1860-1900* (New Delhi: Oxford University Press 1982).

---

courts in India itself. Why did a secular nation allow religiously inspired courts to operate within its borders?

The verdict in the Imrana case traces back to the events of AD 627. The Prophet Muhammad, the political and religious leader of the Arabian city of Medina, was returning from battle with the pagan tribes of Mecca. His young bride Ayesha lagged behind during the retreat and had to spend the night in the desert in the company of a young soldier.[1] When the pair returned to Medina, some alleged that the soldier had acted improperly towards Ayesha during their camping trip and urged The Prophet to punish him. Soon thereafter, the Koran records, the archangel Gabriel spoke to Muhammad and revealed the passage found in chapter 24, verse 13 of the Koran. "Why did they not produce four witnesses? Since they produce not witnesses, they verily are liars in the sight of Allah."[2] Some schools of Islamic jurisprudence take this to mean that proving rape requires at least four male witnesses.

Less clear is why the Islamic courts would suggest that Imrana live with her father-in-law as his wife, although the idea of a wife passing from son to father does exist in the Koran and the Hadith.[3] In 628 AD, the Prophet Muhammad fell in love with Zeineb, the wife of his adopted son, Zeid. The obedient Zeid forfeited his wife to Muhammad, who initially refused her, thinking that marrying her would violate an Arabic taboo against marrying your own daughter-in-law. The angel Gabriel again appeared to sort out the confusion, revealing chapter 33 verse 37 of the Koran. "We gave her unto thee in marriage, so that [henceforth] there may be no sin for believers in respect of wives of adopted son..."[4] Some schools of Islamic jurisprudence interpret the story to mean that, under certain circumstances, brides may remarry within the same nuclear family.

Thus, the Imrana decision followed a type of logic, although, significantly, some orthodox schools of Islamic thought probably would not have reached the same conclusions. I still could not fathom how this dated concept of justice could persist in a self-described secular nation like India. The Imrana verdict violated many people's beliefs about the equality of men and women. Moreover, it followed a very different standard of admissible evidence compared to Western and Indian criminal courts. After all, to expect four witnesses to step forward to

---

1 The *hadith* claims that Muhammad married Ayesha when she was six years old and consummated the marriage when she was nine. Notably, these troubling numbers appear in the orthodox *hadith* of Al Bukhari although they are missing from the earliest extant biography of the Prophet, the *Sirat al Rasul* of Ibn Ishaq. See Guilaume, A. *The Life of Muhammad: A Translation of Ibn Ishaq's Sirat Rasul Allah* (Oxford University Press 2002) and Khan, Muhammad Muhshin. *Sahih al Bukhari* (Kazi Publications 1979).

2 Pickthall, Marmaduke, trans. *The Glorious Koran* (New York: New American Library), p. 254.

3 Imrana's father-in-law reportedly proposed marriage to her to allay the shame of adultery. She refused him.

4 See sura xxxiii verse 37 of the Koran. Pickthall, p. 304.

prove a rape ignores the nature of the crime, which usually takes place in secret. Moreover, the requirement discounted the contributions of modern criminal science. The angel Gabriel, I suspect, did not fully understand the value of forensic and DNA evidence when he revealed verse 24:13 of the Koran.

Two Interviews with Islamic Judges

To make sense of the Imrana case, I spoke to the Vice President of the All India Muslim Personal Law Board (AIMPLB), Sayed Kalve Saqid, at his office on the Unity College Campus in Lucknow.[1] The AIMPLB is the supreme authority of the Muslim judicial system in India and oversees both the village *qazi* (Islamic judge) and the decisions of the Deoband seminary. When I interviewed Mr. Saqid, the Imrana case had not reached the AIMPLB — it never would — but the possibility remained that the board would overturn the decision of the *muftis*.

Before I was able to ask about the role of the AIMPLB and the Imrana rape case, however, Mr. Saqid wanted to talk to me about his trouble with the American immigration office. The American government had denied him an entry visa to the United States and Mr. Saqid thought that was terribly unfair. "I have visited America 40 times before," he said, "and I never had any trouble. Why now?"

"Mr. Saqid," I asked, "is it possible that you have said or done something that might have angered the American government?"

"No, impossible," he answered. "In fact one time, just a few years ago, I was at a Shiite conference in America and we were treated very well. The police gave us protection, no matter what we were saying."

I had read about Mr. Saqid's problems with the US government — in fact, so had almost everybody in Lucknow. His woeful account of alleged harassment by US immigration officials had received a great deal of attention in *The Times of India*. In 2002, before the start of the Iraqi War, Mr. Saqid allegedly painted the American, British and Israeli flags on the doorstep of the Great Imamabara, an 18th century Muslim shrine and one of Lucknow's biggest tourist attractions. The flags' position forced everyone entering the Great Imambara, foreigners included, to step upon them. Since that time, the American government had refused to grant him a visa, without saying exactly why.

I did not understand why Mr. Saqid failed to mention the flag incident at this point in our interview. Afraid of raising a possibly touchy subject, I let his comments pass. Instead, I asked him about the Imrana case. Mr. Sadiq told me that the decision of the *muftis* of Deoband rested on the particular school of Islamic jurisprudence, Hanifite, to which the seminary at Deoband, and Imrana's village, subscribed. While, as a Shiite, he found the ruling disturbing and contrary to his interpretation of Islam, he recognized the *mufti's* right to rule according to their

---

1 The interview took place in July 2005.

tradition. "If the case came to us, we would rule on it according to Hanifite juris-prudence, not according to conscience."

His comment raised another confusing aspect of Islamic courts in India. The AIMPLB does not simply oversee a single system of Islamic judicial thought, but rather a number of different ideas of justice, including all the various schools of traditional Islamic law and Shiite thought as well. This judicial chaos has called the system of religiously specific judicial legislation into question. In the wake of the Imrana scandal, many Indians demanded a uniform civil code for all Indians regardless of religion. I asked Mr. Saqid about the impact of the Imrana case on the issue.

"Uniform civil code is in the air!" he exclaimed. "Nobody has ever written a uniform civil code, so how can anybody have an opinion about it?"

"So you are not necessarily opposed to the idea of a uniform civil code?"

"If somebody were to write a uniform civil code and it was logical and made sense then I would have no objection," he said.

"Even if it contradicted *Shari'at* law?" I asked.

"It could not contradict *Shari'at* law," he reasoned. "*Shari'at* law is justice, so no just system could contradict it."

Although this begs the question, Mr. Sadiq did present a cogent argument in favor of Muslim Personal Law in India as a way to circumvent the backlog of cases in civil family court. He noted that the Indian judicial system has too many cases and too few judges. Cases, especially civil cases, can take years, even decades to receive a hearing. The Muslim courts allow divorce and inheritance cases to reach a timely conclusion, usually in months rather than years. Without Islamic courts, many people would never see justice of any variety.

Later, Mr. Sadiq again brought up the US Immigration office and asked me what he should do to get an American visa. I told him that I did not know much about US immigration policy and reiterated that I was only a writer with no con-nection to the American government. He would not let the subject drop, however. I finally mentioned that flags painted on the doorstep of the Great Imambara and wondered aloud if his visa problems might be related.

Mr. Saqid thought for a moment. "Actually, that was my nephew," he said. "When I found out about it, I told him he had made a mistake. The *faces* of George Bush or Ariel Sharon would have been okay, but the flags were a mistake." He then delivered a panegyric on the American people, expressing admiration for their self-control after the attacks of 9/11 and their non-judgmental attitude to-wards Muslims. Unity College receives many donations from America, he told me. "I even have a Jew on my mailing list! He is from California. I can tell by his name that he is a Jew, Solomon something.... I have never met a Jew. Nevertheless he sends us donations!"

Mufti Bashir-ud-din

For another perspective about Muslim personal law, I traveled to Kashmir to interview Mufti Muhammad Bashir-ud-din, the head *mufti* of the Supreme Court of Islamic Shari'at for the states of Jammu and Kashmir.[1] I wanted to talk to a lower-level Islamic judge and Kashmir, India's lone Muslim-majority state, seemed the perfect place to see how Muslim personal law operated among a majority rather than a minority population.

Stepping off the plane in Srinagar was like entering a time warp. The roads were in poor condition, the hotels dingy and cold, and reliable internet connections almost unknown. Srinagar was even more culturally Islamic than Lucknow. At dawn and at four other times throughout the day, verses of the Koran filled the air; women on the streets dressed in the *burqa*, and, except at the largest hotels, it was almost impossible to purchase an alcoholic beverage.

Srinagar has been the site of ongoing communal violence for the last several decades. The city was once a popular tourist destination with romantic houseboats for rent on Srinagar's peaceful Lake Dal. Today the houseboats float vacant, waiting for visitors that never come. Sand bags and soldiers wait on every street corner, and machine gun nests fortify every large intersection. When I visited Kashmir in January 2007, daily demonstrations protested against the execution of Saddam Hussein and the newspapers carried stories about daily violence by Kashmiri separatists and foreign terrorists.

My guide to Srinagar was a one-eyed Pashtun from a remote corner of Kashmir near the Pakistani border named Yusef. Yusef was initially married at 15 to a girl three years his junior. He divorced her in an Islamic court and married another girl, who, as he said repeatedly in broken English, he "*adoors, just adoors.*" The divorce only took a few days and involved some haggling over the return of wedding gifts. Yusef was a Muslim, but not a very devout one; in the jeep, he removed a bottle of beer from under the seat. "Just once in a while I drink," he said. "I don't think it will keep me out of heaven."

On my way to my interview, Yusef took me to see the tomb of Jesus Christ. Jesus appears in the Koran several times, where he is called *Isa*, son of Mariam.[2] Muslims believe that he was fully human and that he escaped his crucifixion by the grace of Allah.[3] A Kashmiri legend claims that he ended his post-passion life

---

1 The interview took place in January 2007.

2 Miriam is probably a reference to the Virgin Mary. The name also occurs in the Koran to refer to Mariam, sister of Aarron (or Aharon, or Aaron), however.

3 A similar idea was the inspiration for the work of Elizabeth Clair Prophet, an American New Age leader, who wrote a series entitled *The Lost Years of Jesus*. Her books postulate that Jesus of Nazareth traveled to the Himalayas between the ages of 12 and 30. Members of Ms. Prophet's organization, The Church Universal and Triumphant, were arrested on weapons violations in 1989 in Montana, where they had allegedly collected firearms and explosives in preparation for the Apocalypse.

in the Srinagar valley. The tomb of Jesus (or *Youza*, in Kashmiri) thus makes a theological statement; Jesus was fully human, died a human death and awaits the final resurrection of the dead like the rest of us.[1]

The tomb itself was a bit of a disappointment. Located down a side street of old Srinagar, the ramshackle building looked to be little more than a century old. Inside, the sarcophagus of *Youza* was almost 16 in length, nearly as long as the building itself. Yusef told me that the Srinagar valley contains two additional tombs of *Youza*, calling at least two thirds of the legend into serious historical question.

If I had trouble believing that Jesus lived in downtown Srinagar, I also doubted Yusef's claim that the Kashmir Valley was safe for Western travelers, even for short trips in Srinagar. Yusef insisted on driving me, explaining that Srinagar was the home of many "wild people" who "were incapable of reasoning." This January 2007, the atmosphere worsened with the execution of Saddam Hussein, which brought people into the streets in protest. Still, Yusef claimed, "Nothing has happened to a tourist in Kashmir in 15 years." A few minutes later, he warned me, "Maybe it is better not to tell people that you are American."

Mufti Muhammad Bashir-ud-din, the head *mufti* of the Supreme Court of Islamic Shari'at for the states of Jammu and Kashmir, shared many of Mr. Saqid's views on Muslim Personal Law. At his office, or *dar-ul-fatwa* (house of decisions) in Srinagar, Mufti Bashar-ud-din, an expert in Hanafite Law, claimed categorically, "Shari'at does not defame women." He defended controversial practices like triple *talaak* divorce, by which a Muslim man may divorce his wife simply by repeating the word *talaak* (divorce) three times. Although he personally found the practice repugnant, he believed that the practice dated back to the first Caliphs and thus stood on unassailable grounds.[2]

In Kashmir, according to Mufti Bashar-ud-din, the Islamic courts issued more than 50,000 decisions per year, most within three to six months after the plaintiff had filed the complaint. Compared with the 10 to 12 years that a divorce or inheritance case often took to pass through the civil courts, the Islamic courts were extremely efficient.

On the subject of a uniform civil code in India, the Mufti complained that all criminal law in India followed the secular Indian Penal Code. "Islam has rules for

---

1 The belief in a tomb of Jesus finds no sure foundation in the Koran, which denies that Jesus was of divine nature but also seems to makes an ambiguous reference to the Ascension; "...they slew him not for certain. But Allah took him up unto himself." (4:157-158). Trans. Pickthall.

2 Under Hanifite law, a Muslim man who pronounces triple *talak* may not re-marry his wife until she has married another man, consummated the union and divorced the second husband. The injunction rests on verse 2:230 of the Koran "And if he hath divorced her (the third time), then she is not lawful unto him thereafter until she hath wedded another husband. Then if he (the other husband) divorce her it is no sin for both of them if they come together...." trans. Pickthall.

murder and theft as well, but still Muslims in India follow the Indian Penal Code in criminal law. Cannot they let us even have our own rules and customs for civil matters?"

"But isn't that the problem with the Imrana case?" I asked. "It would have been a criminal case under the Indian Penal Code, but the Islamic judges considered it a matter of adultery — a marriage problem — because she did not produce witnesses."

Mr. Bashar-ud-din immediately distanced himself from the Imrana decision, saying that he did not understand the case. "She was either compelled against her will, or she was agreeable to her father-in-law," he said. "In the former instance she should have been allowed to stay with her husband; in the latter, both were guilty of sin. But without evidence admissible by *shari'at* law, how can you convict her father-in-law of such a terrible crime?"

Later, the *mufti's* aide brought us tea. Mufti Bashar-ud-din, a kindly old man with a close-trimmed beard, asked me about my life in America, my family, and my education. He then asked me if I had read the Koran.

"Cover to cover," I said.

"Then why have you not accepted Islam?" he asked. "It is the final revelation of God."

"Sure," I said. "Jeez, I'm not sure what's holding me back."

THE FUTURE OF ISLAMIC LAW IN INDIA

On August 16, 2005 the Indian Supreme Court agreed to hear a challenge to the constitutionality of the "parallel judiciary system" represented by the AIM-PLB.[1] Those in favor of a uniform civil code face an uphill battle, however. The ruling left-center Congress Party has tolerated and even defended the retention of separate judicial systems since Independence and even the BJP-lead government, which had adopted the cause of a uniform civil code, was unable to make any headway towards its creation during its 1998-2004 tenure.[2]

The positions of national-level political parties on this issue are counterintuitive. The Congress Party leadership often claims to champion secularism, while many people think of the BJP (Bharatiya Janata Party) as a party inspired by Hindu ideology. On this issue, however, the roles are reversed. As an anonymous on-line commentator remarked, "Thus, in India, there exists a peculiar situation where the opponents of a secular law are called 'Secularists' while those in favour of a secular law are termed 'communalists' or even 'fascists'".[3]

The Imrana case is not the first time that a jarringly unjust decision from Islamic clerics has raised eyebrows. In the 1980s, the Shah Bano case, in which a

---

1 "SC Alarmed by Shariat courts," *Times of India: Lucknow Edition*, 8/17/05, p. 1.

2 Brass, Paul. *The Politics of India Since Independence* (Cambridge: Cambridge University Press, 2004).

3 http://en.wikipedia.org/wiki/Uniform_Civil_Code.

wealthy Muslim man attempted to deny his wife of 45 years alimony after he had married a second wife, created a crisis for the Congress-led government of Rajiv Gandhi. When the Supreme Court insisted that a woman's right to alimony applied to all Indians regardless of religion, the AIMPLB kicked off a nation-wide agitation or "Shari'at protection week" in October 1985. The Gandhi government's introduction of the Muslim Woman's Bill the following February, which exempted Muslim men from any alimony payments beyond a short initial period as required by Shari'at law, was widely perceived as capitulation to conservative Muslim leaders.[1]

Many Indians I have spoken to who still favor communal law courts often cite the positive aspects of Muslim Personal Law. The *muftis* of Deoband and the AIMPLB, after all, do not always reach such jarring conclusions as they did in the Imrana rape case. In some instances, Muslim Personal Law can appear progressive.

> It might be relevant to point out that the limits of legal and judicial discourse on UCC [uniform civil code] become apparent when one recognizes that there is hardly ever any discussion or debate on those areas of MPL [Muslim Personal Law] that might be considered progressive such as the proviso on inheritance. A Muslim woman has the right to parental property. A married woman inherits her husband's property in its entirety in the absence of children; otherwise she shares it with her children.[2]

I wonder at this author's definition of progressive, however. Muslim Personal Law rests on certain medieval texts of Islamic jurisprudence. These, in turn, stand on older texts, which rest on injunctions in the Koran and the Hadith. While, in theory, Islamic legal thought could adapt to modern social conditions, in practice, this is extremely rare:

> There is nothing...in the theory of Islam to force the principle of blind imitation on the Muslims. In fact, it is only due to political and other causes that they still consider themselves bound by older views, while the letter of the law allows them liberty to develop their system of jurisprudence. Therefore, to say that legally no one can have the rank of *mujtahid* [law reformer] at present is wrong; the practical difficulty, however, that there is no chance of anybody being recognized as such today, remains. Unless a bold step is taken....the *shari'at* will remain a fossil.[3]

As characterized by this author, Islamic courts are an ossified institution, bound to tradition and incapable of reform. In fact, Islamic courts were never

---

1 Jaffrelot characterizes the early 80s as a time when a "reversal of roles" occurred in Indian politics, with the Congress party (and its offshoots, e.g. Congress (I)) exploiting communal differences for political gain and the Hindu right championing secular courts and stepping away from its more radical fringe. See Jaffrelot, Christophe. *The Hindu Nationalist Movement in India* (New York: Columbia University Press 1993), p. 336.

2 Gangoli, Geetanjanli. "Muslim Divorce and Discourse around Muslim Personal Law," *Divorce and Remarriage among Muslims in India*, Imtiaz Ahmad ed. (Delhi: Manohar 2003), p. 384.

3 Fyzee, Asaf A. A. *Outlines of Muhammadan Law* (Delhi: Oxford University Press 2003), p. 38.

supposed to survive into the 21st century in India in the first place. At the time of independence, Muslim courts remained as a temporary institution until a uniform civil code became available. Article 44 of the Indian constitution lists a uniform civil code as one of the goals of the new Indian government. "The State shall endeavor to secure for the citizens a uniform civil code throughout the territory of India."[1] Since Independence, however, progress is scant, despite the popularity of the idea. Some polls show as many as 84% of Indians support the adoption of a uniform civil code.[2]

Islamic courts will not disappear anytime soon, however. A functioning uniform civil code would require, first, that some group of brilliant jurists author a law code agreeable to every religious group on the subcontinent, a gargantuan and difficult task. Secondly, it would require an overall retooling of the civil courts, such that family law cases reached a conclusion within a reasonable timespan. As long as divorces continue to take a decade or more to wind their way through the Indian court system, lawmakers may hesitate to approve a uniform civil code in the Indian legislature.

Many writers on the subject of religious courts in India would object at this point that Islam is not the only religion with its own personal law codes — Hindu, Christians, and Parsees law code also exist — and that I have unfairly focused on Islamic personal law in this book without considering the others. The term "Hindu" in this context, however, refers not only to those usually termed Hindu, but also Jains, Buddhists and Sikhs. "Hindu" in this sense represents widely disparate groups of beliefs and cultures. Moreover, Christians and Parsees represent small and localized sections of Indian society. Thus, in places like Uttar Pradesh and most of north India, the current system of personal law means two different courts, one for Muslims, and one for everybody else. This, in turn, strikes many Hindus as everything that is wrong with the Congress Party's stewardship of India — good intentions morphed into injustice.

Although defended on the grounds of tolerance, Muslim courts arguably worsened communal relations rather than improved them. Hindus (which for the purposes of Indian personal law includes Buddhists, Jains and Sikhs), Muslims and Christians followed different legal customs and strictures related to inheritance, marriage and divorce. This inevitably caused friction between communities. Sonu, a Hindu business owner in Goa, remarked, "If I want a divorce I have to go through years of annoyances. If a Muslim wants to get a divorce then he gets one in a month. How is this fair?"

---

1 Jain, M.P. *Outlines of Indian Legal History* (Delhi: Wadhwa 2005), p. 645.
2 "Public Opinion Favors a Uniform Civil Code," *Times of India*, 6/2395.

I can best describe Narahi Bazaar, my favorite place to shop in Lucknow, as a riot with vegetables. While arguing over the price of tomatoes, I simultaneously needed to dodge rickshaws, dogs and motorcycles. As I shopped, children harassed me, vendors cheated me and goats tried to bite me. Narahi had no apparent organization or plan to it and simple errands sometimes lasted entire afternoons as I wandered lost in the bazaar's twisted alleyways. Still, everything imaginable was available there, if you knew where to look.[1] Narahi Bazaar even had a *Sarakar Theka Bhang Bhandar* (Government-Contracted Hashish Shop) where, for about two dollars, customers could buy enough cannabis to induce catatonia for a month.[2]

---

1 Purveyors of similar goods often cluster together in Indian marketplaces. Thus, all the fishmongers and the spice-sellers lined up in Narahi Bazaar, one after the other. This seems counter-intuitive; I expected that, as in Western cities, storeowners would eschew a neighborhood with too many stores selling similar wares. In India, however, a store's clientele is often the result not of random foot-traffic, but of long-standing patronage. A person may go to the fishmonger that his family has frequented for years, rather than chase a bargain at another store. Storeowners thus cluster for convenience; if something is out of stock they can arrange to have it brought from a neighboring store.

2 The government *bhang* stores mystified me. Often located in undesirable neighborhoods, they offered powerful *golis* (balls) of *bhang* for a few rupees each as well as hashish candies and packets of low-quality marijuana. The signs were inevitably written only in Hindi and they did not advertise. I remain unclear how government *bhang* stores fit in with the somewhat Byzantine drug laws in India. The UP government offers a license "...for the retail sale of Bhang Under tender cum auction system" (see www. upexcise.in). The contractor must restrict his merchandise to *bhang* "obtained from any Government Bonded Warehouse," to sell only to those over 18 years of age, to sell no more than 120 grams of bhang at one time (a very strong cup of coffee), and to remain closed on state holidays *et al.*" From whence the government acquires the stores of *bhang*

Over time, I came to know the stores, where to get the best cheese and the sweetest *lassi* (sour milkshake), as well as the storeowners. The latter could be a contentious lot. Each day I had to negotiate a maze of petty grievances, the cheese-wallah was rude, the vegetable-wallah sold me a fermented squash and regularly overcharged me, the boys at the corner had called me a *laal bandar* (red monkey, a derisive name for often sunburned foreigners of northern European origin). I would plan my visit according to which vendors I was avoiding or hoping to meet on any particular day.

On the other hand, the sellers at Narahi patiently answered my endless questions about the bewildering variety of their produce. Corporate farming had never gained a foothold in India and most fruits and vegetables still came from family-owned farms. Diffuse ownership of the land meant disparate growing practices and hybridization and endless varieties of fruits and vegetables. What we call heirloom vegetables in America were the rule in Uttar Pradesh and I could never learn the names for all the sub-varieties of squashes, tomatoes, mangoes, jackfruits and apples at Narahi Bazaar.

Narahi Bazaar was the only place to buy vegetables in my neighborhood until the Sahara Corporation (owners of Sahara Airlines and the *Sahara* newspaper) opened the Sahara Ganj Shopping Mall a few hundred yards down the road. With the mall came Big Bazaar, a Western-style supermarket with all the charm of a Wal-Mart outlet. All the prices were fixed, all the produce was neatly lined up from floor to ceiling, and all the usual produce was available under the same roof — except hashish. Like any large retail outlet, Big Bazaar bought in bulk; the vegetables were those that could survive long hauls over bumpy roads or those that could endure refrigeration. The produce might have been cheap, but it lacked the wild variety of Narahi Bazaar.

Big Bazaar seemed like an alien presence in India, a redefinition of shopping culture. Remove the people from Big Bazaar and it looked like any retail chain in any part of America. Oversized and unfailingly convenient, Big Bazaar offered Lucknow shoppers something new, commerce without hassle, without argument and without disorder. The store, like all stores of its kind, was designed to distill shopping into a straightforward exchange of currency for goods and services that required no conversation or meaningful social contact of any kind. If shopping at Narahi Bazaar was sometimes akin to playing rugby, Big Bazaar was like a trip to

---

in its warehouses is a perplexing question, as cultivation is apparently illegal by my reading of article 20 of the Narcotic Drugs and Psychotropic Substances Act of 1985. A September 28, 2001, article in the *Times of India* claims that UP earns up to "15 crore" (150 million) rupees from the sale of "wild" bhang sold to contractors (see http://timesofindia. indiatimes.com/articleshow/1066045124.cms). My best guess is that "wild" is a relative term in this context. I have seen cannabis growing rampantly in India on land that was obviously cultivated to a greater or lesser extent. The UP government apparently pays private contractors to collect "wild" cannabis, then, in turn, sells these items to licensed bhang contractors.

the dentist's office, sterile, efficient and deadening. The cashier smiled, took my money and then, occasionally, even thanked me for coming.

As my apartment sat between Narahi Bazaar and Big Bazaar, I spent much of my time considering the differences between the two. Each day I would decide which culture I wished to inhabit, which set of social mannerisms I wanted to experience, and their respective charms and shortcomings. One bazaar respected my space; the other deliberately violated it at every opportunity.[1] Each one represented a distinct and competing sense of manners, one uniquely Indian, and one I saw as a symbol of an encroaching Western consumer culture.

My attempts to negotiate between these competing notions of courtesy often led to misunderstandings. Indians and Americans share many things — both nations are democracies, both had to fight the British Empire for their independence, both cultures prize civil liberties like freedom of expression and freedom of religion, and both Indians and Americans make fun of their politicians and gripe about taxes — but we still manage to drive each other crazy with our respective ideas of manners, ideas as different as Narahi and Big Bazaar. In Lucknow, the home of *tameez aur tahazeeb*, these differences became pronounced at times.

In 2006, the British edition of *Reader's Digest* quantified politeness, sending undercover investigators to 35 different nations to find the most polite and the rudest cities on earth.[2] The *Reader's Digest* moles reported how often residents of these places held doors for women, picked up documents dropped on the ground and said "thank you" to customers. Asian cities did not do well; as a group, they gravitated towards the bottom along with Bucharest, the rudest European city on the list. The survey found New York City the most civil, and Bombay the rudest, cities on their list.

Lucknow was not included in the *Reader's Digest* survey, but I am sure that it would have done little better than Bombay. Saying "thank you," holding the door and spontaneous acts of trash collection were uncommon there and on some days I could have agreed with the results of the *Reader's Digest* survey. I found Indian's reluctance to stand in queues infuriating and their seeming inability to understand that I sometimes wanted to be left alone completely maddening. It seemed as if the entire nation needed to attend finishing school, an impression writer Sarah MacDonald shares in her chatty travel log, *Holy Cow: An Indian Adventure*,

> India is like Wonderland. In this other universe everyone seems mad and everything is upside-down, back to front and infuriatingly bizarre. I'm Alice: fuzzy with feelings about my previous trip down the rabbit hole, I'm now flying straight back through the looking glass to a place where

---

1 Author David Korten, author of *Agenda for a New Economy: From Phantom Wealth to Real Wealth* (San Francisco, Barrett-Koehler Publishers 2009), notes during an interview on www.democracynow.org that he finds American farmers' markets similarly sociable. He claims that hard data backs up his claim, but does not name his source.

2 For full complete results see http://www.rd.com/content/openContent.do?contentId=2 7599&pageIndex=2.

women are blamed for sleazy men and planes are sprayed when they fly from a clean city to a dirty one. In this world we applaud a dreadful landing that's as fast and steep as a takeoff, we jump up and tackle fellow passengers in a crush at the door while the plane is still moving, and the air hostess gets off first.[1]

Furthermore, when I turned on the TV, I noticed that Indian broadcasting companies did not adhere to our American ideal of political correctness. Television advertising sometimes reveled in racial and sexual stereotypes; an ad campaign for *White Mischief* whiskey, for example, depicted a vapid blonde woman enduring various acts of harassment with a wide, brainless smile, almost as if she were enjoying it. On television, a *Coca-Cola* ad gave the same treatment to the Japanese. An Indian actor (Amir Khan) played a Japanese tourist buying lunch at an Indian restaurant. His squinty eyes and the camera around his neck were accompanied by a poorly rendered Japanese accent. The result is something that would never appear on TV in America, a type of East Asian "Amos and Andy." While advertisers were careful not to antagonize Muslim or Hindu sensibilities, underrepresented groups (e.g., white women and Japanese people) were fair game.

Yet, I could not forget that the people of Lucknow surprised me with their friendliness as often as they disturbed me with their insensitivity. Lucknow in particular and India as a whole did not lack manners; they simply had a different — sometimes perplexing — conception of appropriate behavior. Over time their sense of manners made more sense and eventually some of the behavior that *Reader's Digest* took as polite was difficult to justify. In the end, I had serious questions about the magazine's claim that their investigation represented "...a reasonable real-world test of good manners around the globe."[2]

Take the phrase "thank you" for example. Our culture demands its use at every juncture. Thank you for passing the salt, thank you for bringing me a glass of water, thank you for being my friend. We thank a waiter for bringing us our lunch and a sales person for selling us something. Our "thank you" is like a hiccup, flowing almost involuntarily from our lips, and rarely an expression of genuine gratitude. Perhaps we are more motivated by fear as by feelings of thankfulness; we are afraid that somebody might notice is we *didn't* say "thank you." They might think we are rude.

The Hindi equivalent for thank you, *dhanyavaad*, is used sparingly, in instances where somebody has truly done more than is required by duty or custom. In Lucknow, you neither thanked the waiter nor the shopkeeper. In fact, saying *dhanyavaad* too much, or at the wrong time, was in itself rude. I once visited the city of Varanasi with an Indian friend whose brother had once lived there. One of his former co-workers arraigned for a company car to drive us around, free of charge, for

---

1 MacDonald, Sarah. *Holy Cow: An Indian Adventure* (New York, Broadway Books 2002) p. 7.

2 http://www.rd.com/content/openContent.do;jsessionid=F1F87A1960E9602FEA02005E FC478764.appl_rd1?contentId=27599&pageIndex=1

three full days. This man was a virtual stranger to me, so before I left I expressed my gratitude for what I perceived as uncommon generosity.

"*Dhanyavaad*," I said.

"*Yeh, dhanyavaad hain kya?*" 'What is this thank you?' he asked, with an offended tone in his voice. To him, I was the friend of the sister of a friend; *of course* he would provide me with free transportation while I was in town. So while you might not get a "thank you" when you leave the corner store in India, neither do you need to express thanks as often as you do in the West. Which convention is more polite depends on which culture you begin with.

Similar objections hold for *Reader's Digest's* selection of picking up trash as a criterion for politeness. Picking up trash only makes sense if you have somewhere to put it. New York City has no shortage of public trash receptacles and some forms of waste removal (e.g., picking up dog droppings) are not the result of personal initiative but rather are enforced by law. Lucknow, on the other hand, has few public trashcans. This does not mean that Indians have no concern for their environment or the common good; it simply means that sanitation in large Indian cities has not reached the same point as in Western cities. Moreover, the Indian conception of cleanliness has a powerful effect on people's behavior. Papers lying on the ground are considered dirty and few self-respecting Indians would stoop to pick them up. This may seem self-centered to us, but Indians have a rational aversion to any activity that could put them in danger of contracting any one of India's myriad contagious diseases.

Lastly, the idea of holding doors for people when they enter or leave a building is also somewhat unfair as a test of politeness. In Lucknow, any unwanted communication between unrelated men and women in public is bad manners. Holding the door for a lady, far from being considered polite, might be seen as an attempt to initiate unwanted contact with a woman who was neither your wife nor your sister. If some of the *Reader's Digest* reporters were female, this may have skewed the scores against the residents of Mumbai.

The editors of *Reader's Digest* could easily have created a survey in which India excelled. For example, if one of the tests was the number of times people invited the researcher over to their house for dinner, I have no doubt that Bombay would have topped the list and New York would be near the bottom. This may be simply the result of different social realities. In India, many families have a stay-at-home mother or wife who prepares meals daily. One more mouth to feed is usually not a problem. In New York, on the other hand, many people live alone and often have neither the time nor the inclination to prepare a meal for a visitor.

The same goes for showing interest in the details of others' lives. The same New Yorker who might open the door for you and say thank you repeatedly, might never ask you where you come from, how many siblings you have or the ages of your children.

Indians on the other hand will immediately pepper you with questions about your family, your education and your employment. For them this is simply a normal expression of curiosity. For us, this can go too far, especially when a stranger inquires about our annual salary — a taboo question in polite Western society. Although this line of questioning may seem invasive to us, at least visitors to India never feel ignored.

We hold our own ideas of politeness so dear that we often cannot perceive the cultural relativity of them. For example, I always say "God Bless You" after somebody sneezes and expect the same from others. If someone fails to bless me, I automatically assume that they would prefer me dead. The irrationality of this belief rarely occurs to me. No matter that the habit is a vestige of a medieval superstition identifying the breath with the soul, no matter that I am almost an atheist; a sneeze requires the invocation of the Supreme Being and that's all there is too it. Similarly, it is impolite to place your elbows on the table although there is no rational reason for it as far as I know.

Indians adhere to a wholly different, but equally irrational, set of mannerisms. Summoning a person with the palm turned upwards is a *faux pas*, as is whistling, giving gifts with the left hand and opening gifts in front of guests. Beeping the car horn, on the other hand, even when you are the only car on the road, is expected. Offering an extra rupee upon paying a bill and touching a person's feet are common signs of respect. Eating with your hands is normal, as is sitting on the floor and two men holding hands in public — a good way to keep track of your friend in a chaotic marketplace.

Occasionally, eastern and western ideas of social propriety clash directly. This is the case with staring. Most Americans learn early that it is impolite to stare but this rule is unknown in India. When I walked down the street, people looked at me as if I were an animal escaped from the Lucknow Zoo. Initially, this bothered me deeply. Then, one day, I was walking down the street, the object of intense scrutiny by hundreds of complete strangers. I was just thinking how annoying this was when a rickshaw full of beautiful Lucknowi women drove by. They all swiveled their heads 180 degrees to take a second look at me, their large brown eyes sparkling with curiosity. Maybe staring isn't all *that* bad, I thought to myself.

The summer after I moved to Lucknow, two nearly simultaneous events made me wonder further about the relative values of Indian and American manners in times of crisis. When monsoon rains flooded downtown Bombay in 2005, numerous storeowners distributed free food to stranded commuters and the city itself survived the deluge with a notable amount of stoicism and self-control. By comparison, New Orleans' inundation at about the same time resulted in widespread looting and general civic chaos. Oddly, although Indians had a difficult time following the rules, they maintained order and social cohesion in the midst of a serious emergency. Americans, on the other hand, seemed to become unhinged and violent when an ill wind blew.

In the end, I was skeptical of any claim that a city or particular ethnicity was rude. In all cultures, people form social bonds, engage in the rituals of commerce, and — given enough time — warm to strangers. When I first moved to New York City from New England friends and relatives often asked me if I "liked the people down there." NYC once had a long-standing reputation as a rude place and they couldn't imagine living among them. Now Gotham has become some sort of Mecca of meticulous manners, or at least *Reader's Digest's* version of them. I think I liked it better when everybody thought New Yorkers were rude, however; people had lower expectations of us.

Maybe what Rudyard Kipling once wrote is true: "East is east and west is west and never the twain shall meet." But if they ever do bump into each other, West will probably apologize for his clumsiness. East, not understanding why West is apologizing, will ask West about his family and invite him over for dinner, whereupon West, thinking East is being disingenuous, will refuse his invitation, leading East to conclude that West is a humorless knob. They will part with a mutual huff of disapproval.

Swimming in the Existential Baptismal Font: Tourists and Tourism in India

Anthropologists sometimes describe a phenomenon called "going native" that affects those on extended stays in foreign countries. Going native causes some travelers to lose their cultural bearings and to see the world in the same way as members of their host culture. In some instances, going native can help the visitor to understanding foreign social customs and outlooks. In other cases, however, the experience of going native can be problematic. In the 1950s, for example, a New Yorker named Tobias Schneebaum took the idea of cultural immersion too far. Living among an isolated group of hunter-gatherers in Peru, Schneebaum participated in a tribal war and even dined at one of his tribe's cannibalistic feasts.[1]

While I did not do anything as extreme, I sometimes feared that I was going native during my time in Lucknow. Whenever this happened, I would head to one of the tourist spots to talk to any Europeans (or, rarely Americans) who happened to be wandering through India. I came to look at tourists in a wholly different way, not as fellow travelers, but in the way that Indians see them, as exotic, somewhat naïve vagabonds. As I traveled to some of the most popular tourist spots in India, such as Benares, Khajaraho and Goa I often wondered what drove so many Westerners to India. What do we expect to find?

Tourism in Asia is much more than just a business; it is a raw, unrehearsed interface between radically different worlds. Tourism is non-experts meeting non-experts, Delhi shopkeepers meeting retired attorneys from Pittsburgh, Nepali rickshaw drivers encountering vacationing ski instructors from Colorado,

---

1 For more on Schneebaum's adventures, see his 1969 memoir *Keep the River on Your Right* or the recently released film of the same name.

housewives from Kansas in conversation with orthodox Muslim imams. It is the confluence of two populations, not in the marketplace or across a bargaining table but face-to-face, without a script and without a net. The results are sometimes humorous, sometimes tragic and often exasperating.

Bleeding Hearts

In India, even the price of a 10 Rs. (about 25¢) rickshaw ride can be the subject of a long and impassioned debate. The rickshaw driver might mention that he has six children — three of which are half-naked — and complain that I am larger and heavier than the average Indian. If an auto rickshaw, the driver would gripe about the price of gasoline and the unfair traffic ticket he was required to pay. I would respond that I may be a *gora* (white man) but I was not a *crorepati* (millionaire), that the distance was quite short, that gasoline prices would inevitably fall the next day, and that I may look large, but am actually quite light.

These exchanges were simply part of everyday life in India, and neither the rickshaw driver nor I intended any real malice. To my European friends, Judith and Urs, it looked like a shouting match, however. I worried that they saw me as ill tempered and tight fisted. Westerners are not accustomed to arguing like this in public and they often consider bargaining distasteful. Many tourists arrive in Asia with the idea that, given currency exchange rates, there is no reason why they should have to argue about prices at all. Most will happily pay four times the going rate for transportation, souvenirs and museum admissions as long as they do not have to raise their voice. Over the next week, I caught our European friends handing over excessive amounts of cash to rickshaw drivers and storeowners without complaint.

Perhaps they imagined that Indians perceived their over-compensations as generosity. They would have been dismayed to hear what their rickshaw driver or shop owner said about them once they were out of earshot. Giving 100 rupees for a 10-rupee rickshaw ride is not necessarily considered generosity; it is often derided as idiocy. Excessive liberality makes prices rise further for subsequent travelers and reinforces the impression that Westerners are little more than ATM machines with legs. When traveling in India, you can contribute towards many worthy causes. Scattering money indiscriminately to taxi drivers and beggars has little effect on poverty, however, and it makes you look foolish.

At a hotel outside of the city of Benares, Judith, a conceptual artist from Switzerland, explained why she had come to India. Like thousands of other European and Americans, she had come to India to twist herself into pretzel-like poses in one of Benares' myriad yoga ashrams. Equally important for Judith was that her visit to India offered an opportunity to purchase a particular type of yoga pants that were much in demand in Switzerland. She explained that in her yoga class in Zurich, wearing yoga pants from India was a mark of distinction.

Yoga, one of the six classical *darshana*, or schools, of Hindu philosophy, is a complex religio-philosophical ideology that professes to free the human soul (*atman*) from the unending cycle of birth and death (*samsaara*) through a series of ascetic mental and physical practices.[1] Belief in the benefits of the latter for human health is widespread among Westerners. Some of the more extravagant claims (e.g., yoga is good for the complexion or boosts the immune system) receive no support from medical science. Other benefits, such as weight loss and muscle toning, are similar to the effects of regular exercise and calisthenics. Yoga does seem to reduce stress. Then again, so do listening to music, moderate drinking and sex.

Despite the scarcity of hard evidence supporting yoga's reputed miraculous health benefits, Judith had no doubt that practicing yoga improved her constitution. She claimed that yoga "massaged her inner organs." When asked which organs in particular, she answered that she had a distinct feeling that her kidneys worked better after her yoga class. As strange as it sounds, she is not alone in holding beliefs like this; millions of Westerners like Judith remain convinced that yoga can accomplish anything from curing baldness to increasing IQ.[2] Despite increasingly inane developments such as Bikram Yoga studios — heated to 105° and 40% humidity — and an attempt to include "competitive yoga" as an Olympic event, the yoga craze stubbornly refuses to jump the shark.[3]

This Western obsession with yoga sometimes strikes Indians as comical. For them, yoga is a part of their religious life and the term carries connotations of devotion and asceticism. Until recently, Western yoga enthusiasts, who hold that the outward postures of yoga (*asana*) alone bring some sort of medical benefit and who have little interest in yoga's religious or philosophical foundations, were puzzling to many traditional Indians. We would perhaps find it similarly odd if Indians arrived in America and began praying the rosary out of conviction that it was good for their fingers.

If Judith was obsessed with yoga pants, however, at least she wanted to wear something. Oddly, while many tourists are fixated on certain, de-contextualized practices of the Hindu religion, they seem oblivious to contemporary social mores. Many women — usually European women — that I saw traveling in India remained particularly stubborn about their wardrobe. On many occasions, I noticed foreign ladies in miniskirts and tank tops even in remote and rural areas of India. At one hotel in Rajasthan, a French woman showed up at the pool top-

---

1 For a clear introduction to Samkya-Yoga philosophy see Eliade, Mircea. *Yoga: Immortality and Freedom* (New Jersey: Princeton University Press 1969).

2 See www.myhealthsense.com/F040629_yoga.html.

3 I assumed that the uncomfortable temperature in Bikram or "hot" yoga was an attempt to recreate the conditions of the Indian monsoon. The Bikram Yoga website, www.bikramyoga.org, claims that the heat aids the practitioner is "detoxification."

less. This was embarrassing to the hotel staff, who attempted to hide themselves rather than be caught staring at her.

My friend Scott was equally disconcerting — although not nearly as interesting — to watch. Scott wore a pair of shorts when we visited Delhi's Jama Masjid, a large Mughal-era mosque in the city's old section. The doormen insisted that he cover himself with skirt-like garment called a *lungii*. For the locals, the sight of a white man wearing a *lungii* was cause for convulsions of laughter. Scott took umbrage at the attention. Who was at fault here, though, I wondered. Arriving under-dressed at a place of worship, particularly when it is sacred to a religion that is not your own, is a major *faux pas*. I wanted to ask him how my friend would feel were an Indian man to arrive at Christmas Mass wearing a loincloth.

As far as I am aware, every guidebook for travel on the Indian subcontinent contains a section on appropriate dress and individual state governments have even published recommendations for traveler's attire.[1] Thus, tourists cannot claim ignorance about wardrobe in India. Most of them are aware that their appearance is occasion for both embarrassment and mirth. For some, realizing that they will be in the country only for a few weeks drives their dare-to-bare behavior. Others probably hold some sort of absolutist view of clothing ethics; if it is appropriate in Milan, Paris or Berlin, it must be okay in India as well. Some Western women that I have met see wearing skimpy clothing as a right akin to freedom of speech and regard any compromise with local custom as a betrayal of feminist ideals.

As with their misplaced donatives to rickshaw drivers, however, inappropriate dress makes life more difficult for foreigners who live in India and reinforces Indian people's most persistent myth about Westerners, that we are all sexual libertines. Moreover, the "if you've got it, flaunt it" approach to female apparel simply does not make any sense in India. Many Indians do not see suggestively dressed tourists as liberated women but as sexual objects deliberately seeking the amorous attentions of young men. In a country where rape is all too common and sexual crime widespread, letting it all hang out is not only culturally insensitive but also dangerous.

No News is Good News

Some Western tourists remain unaware of Asian culture willfully. On the Nepali border in West Bengal, on the other hand, the locals pitch in to keep visitors in the dark. In May 2005, I trekked along the popular Singalila ridge in West Bengal and crossed the Nepali border at Tumling and Kala Pakhora. The area was under the effective control of the Nepali Maoist insurgency and I saw no evidence of the Royal Nepali Army or the Nepali government. In many villages a

---

1 "Decent Exposure," *Times of India: Lucknow Edition*, 12/8/05, p. 8.

hammer and sickle flag graced the door of every household and Maoist and anti-American graffiti covered the walls.

The Nepali village of Tumling, (elevation 10,164 ft.) had no electricity, so guests at the Shikar Guest House gathered around the wood-burning stove as the sun dropped behind the hills and the temperature fell below zero. While warming myself over a bowl of glowing embers I met Nira, the owner of the guesthouse and a local schoolteacher. When asked, Nira denied that there was any Maoist activity in the Tumling area. I asked about the graffiti and the communist flags; surely, they were there for a reason. Still, Nira would not admit to a Maoist presence in her village.

All along the Singalila ridge, the people I spoke to denied that the Maoist insurgency had caused any violence in the area. At one inn on the Indian side, I met a member of the SSB (Shastra Sena Bal or Indian Border Security Forces) who assured me that there had been no conflicts along the Indo-Nepali border in the Darjeeling district. The innkeeper of the same inn became incensed when I asked about trouble with Maoists along the Singalila ridge.

"Lies!" she said. "It is all lies! None of it is true!"

The innkeeper's response reflected the dearly held hope of local business owners that news of the Maoist insurgency will remain a closely guarded secret. The truth, however, is that in April 2004, Maoists attacked the Nepali village of Pashupatinagar about 36 kilometers from Darjeeling. Several Nepali police officers died and many shops in the village's bazaar burned to the ground. The lull in violence since this incident was probably the result of the Royal Nepali Army's withdrawal from the district.

Thus far, violence in this area has affected only Nepali police and security forces. Even a single stray bullet striking a foreign backpacker could be disastrous for the local tourist industry. North of the Singalila ridge, the Sikkim Tourist Ministry has already drawn up plans to alter hiking routes so that they do not stray over the Nepali border and the Darjeeling district planned similar changes in the near future.[1] This would hurt the tenuous recovery of tourism in Nepal, which fell precipitously in 2001 and 2002.[2] Thus, the reluctance of people along the Singalila ridge to talk openly about the current civil war is understandable. The less the tourists know the better.

MY LIFE AS A GOA FREAK

I put off going to Goa for years because I was sure that once I arrived, I would have a difficult time leaving. I was correct; I originally planned to stay for four days and ended up staying for three months. I became accustomed to watching the sunset over the Arabian Sea, *Kingfisher* beer in hand, and my trip back

1 "New trek routes to keep off Nepal border," *The Statesman, North Bengal & Sikkim Plus Section*, 5/25/05, p. 1.
2 See http://www.expresstravelandtourism.com/200509/spotlight04.shtml.

to Lucknow kept slipping my mind. I made friends quickly in Goa and became inextricably entangled in their lives. My editor at the time threatened to cut off my funding if I did not rise from my beach chair and start writing about what he considered more newsworthy regions like Kashmir. I eventually left, but only because I risked total professional and economic ruin by remaining.

I was not the first person to willingly lose himself in Goa and refuse to return home. In the 1960s, hippies and free spirits from Europe and America saw Goa as a perfect place to drop out of society. Goans were reputed to have a laid-back *laissez-faire* attitude; life was cheap and hashish plentiful. As chronicled in Cleo Odzer's book *Goa Freaks: My Hippie Years in India*, by the 1970s Goa had attracted a semi-permanent population the West's wildest characters.[1] Hippies created their own weekly markets in Baga and Anjuna where they peddled everything from smoking paraphernalia and jewelry to tarot card readings and holistic massages. In the 1990s, Goa became the Mecca of the Rave and Trance scenes, and many aspiring DJs made the pilgrimage to places like Disco Valley and Paradise Beach where they spawned their own sub genre of music called Goan Trance, a fast-paced, head-numbing mix of electronic sounds and exotic sound samples.

By the time I reached Goa, the party was winding down. The local population had tired of the craziness and the police had outlawed Raves and other spontaneous celebrations. Parties had become underground affairs, advertised clandestinely by word of mouth. Still, when one did occur, the unrestrained spirit of Goa could still emerge — at least for a short time. One bacchanal I attended at Morjim Beach lasted three days and ended only when the police arrived and beat the stereo system with bamboo sticks until it ceased to function. They then arrested the DJ and whisked him away to the local police station.

The unrestrained sexual and pharmaceutical misbehavior of Westerners had pushed the famously laid-back Goans to the breaking point. I witnessed many instances of violence against foreigners in Goa. A European friend reported that the staff of a nightclub in Calungate attacked him when he questioned his bill. On another occasion, I witnessed a group of Goans beating a Swedish tourist into unconsciousness with a brick. Goa was the only place in India where being an American elicited few feelings of tolerance or respect. *Farangii* (foreigner) had become just another caste in Goa, and not a very well-respected one.[2]

This intolerance for Westerners — especially hirsute, hashish-smoking ones — coincided with the advent of Indian tourism. Until recently, few Indians came to Goa. Few people had enough disposable income for a weekend at the beach before the sudden growth of the Indian middle class over the last decade. Even

1 Odzer, Cleo. *Goa Freaks: My Hippie Years in India* (Blue Moon Books 1995).

2 Violence against foreigners reached a tragic climax in the spring of 2008, when the body of a 15-year-old British girl was found floating in the Arabian Sea near Anjuna Beach. Buncombe, Andrew. "Britons in Goa: Death, Drugs, and Extortion," *The Independent*, 3/9/08.

when they did arrive, they rarely made their way to the beaches. Sunbathing was not a popular Indian pastime and even today most Indians arrive at the beach fully clothed.

Today the growing Indian middle comes to Goa by the busload. Numerically, they now outnumber European and American travelers by a considerable margin. The hospitality industry in Goa continues to cater to foreigners because they spend much more per head than Indian tourists, who tend to travel in large, family groups and stay *en masse* in as few rooms as possible. Still, many Goans were beginning to understand that the future of Goan tourism was in domestic travelers from within India.

Despite all these changes, a few holdouts of the old Hippie guard remain on the north shore of Goa. At the Sunrise Café in Chapora the last smoldering remnants from the glory days of Goa — withered old German junkies with pincushion arms, tattooed freaks, hash-eaters, a head case from Melbourne and an androgynous young person who locals referred to as Crazy Annie — gathered for their morning coffee and *chillum* (hashish pipe). While eating breakfast there one morning, I met Diotima and Christo (not their real names), long-time residents of Goa from Greece. Diotima made jewelry and gave tarot card readings for tourists. She was one of those remarkable people you meet in India who throw themselves at the mercy of the world and survive to tell about it. She had wandered through Bihar by herself on foot, witnessed left-handed Tantric rituals in Bengal, and worked as a tattoo artist in French Polynesia.[1]

Diotima and Christo invited me over to their room for tea. I followed them through terraced farming land to their small hovel. Outside their window, a bright blue kingfisher hovered in the air and dove for insects. Diotima showed me her jewelry and offered to do a tarot reading for me. The tea was strong and Diotima became verbose. She told me that monkeys had been breaking into their house while she was out.

"If they find something to eat, they are happy," she told me. "But if they find nothing, they get angry and [defile] my Kali shrine!"

On further visits to the Sunrise Cafe, I gave some of the people I met my e-mail address and phone number but I never received any contact information in return. Over time I learned that many of them were running from something — a broken family, a failed marriage, drug addiction, a criminal past — and nobody

---

1 *Tantra*, roughly translated as Hindu occultism, entails numerous esoteric rituals. The *panchamakara* (Five M's) rite, for example, entails the use of *mans* (meat) and *maithuna* (ritualized sexual intercourse) as well as intoxicants (usually alcohol and some form of cannabis). Tantric ceremonies exist in right-handed and left-handed varieties. In right-handed *tantra* some of the elements of the ritual are replaced with symbols (e.g. a coconut for meat) while in left-handed *tantra* the constituents of the ritual are taken literally; thus the ceremony is necessarily performed clandestinely late at night. For more information on Tantra, see Woodroffe, John. *Principles of Tantra* (Kessinger Publishing, 2003). Published under the name Arthur Avalon.

had an e-mail address or a phone. Chapora was a place for people who did not want to be found; it was off the grid.

In Chapora, everybody talked endlessly about his or her "visa time." The Indian government only gave six-month tourist visas to most travelers.[1] That meant that every 180 days a traveler had to jump the border to a nearby country, apply for a new visa and re-enter the country. Among travelers in Chapora, "visa time" had a more sinister meaning as well. Many people did not survive on selling jewelry alone; their trips across the border often entailed drug smuggling. Although the work was dangerous, a person could survive for an entire year from of a few runs to Pakistan, Nepal Thailand, or Europe. Contraband moved in both directions; heroin and opium came in from Pakistan and marijuana from Nepal, while Ecstasy and other synthetic narcotics went from Goa to a half-dozen cities, especially Bangkok. Reportedly, blood diamonds from Africa also passed through Goa on their way to Singapore and Taiwan.[2]

Thus, conversations about "Louis' trip to Pakistan," superficially a casual conversations about a friend's sightseeing tour, were actually a means of sharing information about clandestine activities. This lent an undercurrent of tension in the laid-back atmosphere on Goa's north shore. Everybody knew somebody whose "visa time" did not go well, and everybody knew who had done time in a jail in Thailand or Singapore.

Christo had many stories of narrow escapes at a number of Asia's airports. On one occasion, earnest but poorly trained narcotics officers confronted him about a piece of rose quartz they found in his luggage. Diotima had given it to him for good luck, but the airport authorities were convinced it was a form of crystallized cocaine. They sent it to a lab for analysis, failing to notice the actual narcotics hidden in Christo's other bag. When the test came back negative, the guards released him, rose quartz in hand and contraband in tow.

Friends such as Diotima and Christo, and a host of other "hardcore" Goan residents, introduced me to an entirely new culture, one to which I had little previous exposure. Like Judith, my Swiss friend obsessed with yoga pants, my Goan friends also looked to Hinduism for religious inspiration. Experience tempered their enthusiasm, however. They had seen unscrupulous holy men take advantage of Western travelers, Tibetan rimpoches who trades spiritual insight for sexual favors, wandering yogis with a repertoire of mystic razzmatazz they used to separate the *gora* (white man) from his money. Nevertheless, all of them viewed India as a place worth traveling to or living in, even if funding their spiritual journey required criminal activity.

---

1 The Indian government now offers five-year visas to some nationalities.
2 Blood diamonds are diamonds from Western Africa used to finance violent insurgencies in countries such as Angola and Sierra Leone.

INDIA: THE EXISTENTIAL BAPTISMAL FONT

Walter Kirn wrote in the *New York Times Review of Books* (November 11, 2007) as part of a review of Paul Theroux's latest travel memoir:

> One of Theroux's running themes about India is that it punishes those who stand apart from it but transfigures those who fully submit to it. What looks like a cesspool of concentrated misery can be, for those who bravely bathe in it, an existential baptismal font. India doesn't cleanse people of their sins so much as revive their elemental humanity.

I liked to think that I was now hard-boiled about India and that the childish wonder I felt when I first traveled to India when I was a 19-year-old undergraduate had passed into a more mature appreciation of the culture. Then, inevitably, some new sight, idea, taste or sensation befuddled me and I realized that I was still a babe in the woods in this part of the world. This may be what drove my fellow travelers and me to India; we all wanted to be in a place where everything was new and people expected little more than wide-eyed wonder from us. In this sense, perhaps India was a type of baptismal font; it re-created psychological states that normally occurred only in childhood.

A type of caste system existed among my friends and associates who lived in India long-term. We looked down on tourists because, unlike researchers and relief workers, they did not seem to be doing anything important. Maybe we were wrong in this assumption, however. Tourists did have an important job, even if they were unaware of it and sometimes did it badly — they give many Indians their first impression of Europe and America. Air travel had made Indians and Westerners neighbors. But culturally insensitive tourists, who arrived half-dressed with overflowing wallets, for whom every other word was "Om" and who arrived with an inaccurate set of preconceptions about Indian culture, made jarringly *annoying* neighbors.

Sometimes, other Western travelers embarrassed me and I wanted to disassociate myself from them. Then I reproached myself. Stop it, I thought, you are becoming like Tobias Schneebaum — so engrossed in an alien culture that you are figuratively eating your own kind. After all, tourism is neither good nor bad in itself; it is what individual travelers make of it. It can bring alien peoples closer together and foster understanding or, alternatively, it can erode cultures and engender xenophobia. What differentiates good tourism from bad tourism can be as simple as taking a trip to the library to read a book or two about local customs. It is a small world, but it is not a mono-cultural one, at least not yet. Future tourists to India please take note — and pass the salt; this shrunken head needs some zing.

PORTRAIT OF A DANCER: TRADITIONAL PERFORMING ARTS IN LUCKNOW

"The Indians are the Italians of Asia....It can be said, certainly, with equal justice, that the Italians are the Indians of Europe, but you understand me, I think. There is so much Italian in the Indians, and so much Indian in the Italians. They are both people of the Madonna — they demand a goddess, even if the religion does not provide one. Every man in both countries is a singer when he is happy, and every woman is a dancer when she walks to the shop at the corner. For them, food is music inside the body, and music is food inside the heart. The language of India and the language of Italy, they make every man a poet, and make something beautiful from every *banalité*. These are nations where love — *amore, pyaar* — makes a cavalier of a Borsalino on a street corner, and makes a princess of a peasant girl, if only for the second that her eyes meet yours. It is the secret of my love for India...that my first great love was Italian."[1]

In his role as *nataraja*, or King of the Dance, the Hindu god Shiva dances so wildly that the universe trembles.[2] The first time I saw Rosella Fanelli and Anuj Mishra's Kathak performance, I was similarly shaken. As they danced, they brought the Hindu pantheon to life. Rosella successively adopted the roles of Radha, the consort of Krishna, anxiously waiting for the arrival of her divine lover, then Sita, the long-suffering mate of the god Rama, and then the vengeful goddess Durga, glaring in holy rage at the audience. In another number, the dancers lined up behind her and imitated Hindu temple sculpture by approximating a multi-armed deity. Meanwhile, Anuj, her partner, spun with astounding speed, stopped on a dime, then spun again. His physical endurance, flexibility and split-second timing drew gasps from the audience. Their fast-paced, kinetic perfor-

---

1 Roberts, Gregory David. *Shantaram*. (New York: St. Martin's Press 2005).
2 Pavitrananda, Swami trans. *Siva-Mahimnah Stotra* (Pithoragarh: Advaita Ashrama 1976), p. 32.

mance displayed both technical mastery and an emotional authenticity that was nothing short of transcendent.

Kathak, a classical Indian style of dance, literally means "storytelling" and Kathak performances include historical or mythological narrative. Watching Rosella and Anuj get into character was almost like watching a type of spirit possession. When Rosella danced she underwent an astounding transformation. Before the music started, she seemed nervous but when the first note sounded all fear vanished. Every turn of her foot, every motion of her hand and every expression on her face followed the dictates of the Kathak tradition. Alternately vulnerable and unapproachable, Rosella drew the audience to her with a come-hither smile and then put them off with a dismissive gesture. While in character, she became something ethereal, a conduit for the full range of human (and superhuman) emotions. When she had finished, I was almost afraid to speak to her and was surprised to find that in conversation she was again a flesh-and-blood woman, speaking Hindi with an Italian accent.

As it turned out, among all the stories of Kathak dance, Rosella's own story was also worth telling. A native of Italy, she moved to India in her 20s and took up the study of dance. Settling in Lucknow, one of the centers of Kathak dance, she became the student of a well-known Kathak guru, Pandit Arjun Mishra. Over the last 15 years, Rosella has brought this unique Asian art form to audiences in Europe, America and Israel. She has become one of the few Westerners (and perhaps the only one alive today) to earn critical and popular acclaim in Kathak dance, and she is a passionate advocate for the modernization and globalization of the art form.

Deceptively thin, her svelte exterior hid the coiled, iron-hard muscles of a professional dancer. She explained that the ankle bells that Kathak performers wear are quite heavy and performers must develop exceptionally strong calves and thighs. The most difficult obstacle to learning Kathak, however, was cultural rather than physical. In India, a dancing guru is not simply a teacher but an all-controlling influence in a student's life. Rosella's guru demanded total devotion and wanted complete control over all aspects of her life. As her ability began to rival his own, their relationship soured and they parted acrimoniously.

As a *farangii* (foreigner) Rosella had to combat deep-seated feeling among many Indians that classical Hindustani dance is *their* art, an expression of *their* souls and could not be mastered by an outsider. Rosella sometimes used a stage name when she performed in America because the audiences wanted to see Indian dances performed by an Indian woman. As with Western classical music, however, classical Indian art forms have become international and some of Kathak's freshest faces are from Europe and America. I wondered what the world of Western music would have missed if they had adopted a similarly xenophobic attitude toward Asian virtuosos of classical music like cellist Yo Yo Ma.

This wariness of innovation and outsiders is exactly what ails Kathak dance, in Rosella's opinion. Kathak has taken a back seat to its South-Indian cousin Bharatiya Natyam on the international circuit. This is partly the fault of Kathak gurus, who do not understand the necessities of promotion and western-style professionalism. If Kathak is in need of renaissance, Rosella may be exactly what the doctor ordered. She is not adverse to innovation, but at the same time possesses a firm grip on traditional technique. At one point in the performance she had choreographed, Rosella and the other dancers gathered in a circle and begin chatting like women at a village well. Their "chatter" was not in any ordinary language, but rather consisted of complex *tukra*, or rhythmic recitations articulated in rapid-fire unison, that almost recalled scat of the be-bop era. "*Taa Theii tata theii, aa theii tata theii, taa theii tata theii...*"

Not only is the world of Kathak dance reluctantly accepting foreigners and foreign influences, it is moving abroad and finding an international audience as well. Both Anuj and Rosella have performed overseas, and Rosella danced at New York City's Lincoln Center in 1997, an experience she looked back at with fondness. On these trips abroad they sometimes mix Kathak with European styles such as Flamenco, a style of dance at which Rosella is also proficient. She explained that Flamenco is familiar to Western audiences and prepares them for the Kathak performances.

When asked whether the resulting style is "fusion," Rosella gave an interesting reply. She did not consider the performances fusion because Flamenco and Kathak are historically related. Flamenco grew out of gypsy folk dancing, and, she explained, the Gypsies are refugees from India.[1] Thus, the two styles are intimately related, particularly the footwork. Far from being fusion, a flamenco/ Kathak performance reunites branches from the same tree. It is less modern innovation than a type of hyper-traditionalism that rediscovers the Ur-style in both Spanish and Indian art forms. Anuj, when asked the same question, responded that he is not opposed to such experimentation within certain limits. "If a Kathak dancer wears a mini-skirt, then this is too much," he said.

The Eight Stages of a Woman in Love

In the days before Christmas 2005, Rosella and some friends threw a party at the nearby Carlton Hotel. By the time I arrived sometime after midnight, Rosella had taken to the dance floor with a fury. Released from the constraints of tradition, she danced a wild, wine-inspired tarantella to the sound of Bombay film music. Also full of holiday cheer, I joined in but could not keep up with her. By

---

1 The Gypsy language, Romani, appears related to certain tribal languages of northwest India and Pakistan. For reasons that are not clear, the Gypsy people apparently left India about AD 1000. See Fonesca, Isabel. *Bury me Standing: The Gypsies and their History* (New York: Knopf 1995).

2 AM, we were unable to continue and the staff of the hotel hinted that it was time for us to leave.

Accompanying me on this evening was Apurva the jeweler. A member of a wealthy, gem-trading family, Apurva had a well-studied knack for flattering and cajoling local women into buying a wide array of glittering, glowing, extravagant, and wholly unnecessary jewel-laden accessories. The ladies of Lucknow brought their husband's weekly wages to his shop and left with enough gems to make a geologist jealous.

Twenty-four years old, Apurva was to be married in just a few short weeks, but the sight of Rosella dancing made him want to reconsider. At the end of the party, Rosella refused to leave with her date, who was tipsy and could not drive. Instead she asked Apurva (who owned the car) and myself (whose job was to keep Apurva in line) to drive her home. When we reached her apartment, Apurva insisted on walking her to the door, despite the fact that it was only ten feet from the road. After a failed attempt at a goodnight kiss, Apurva climbed back into the car. Unrepentant, he blew kisses at her from the front seat; "I love you Rosella!" he called out to her. "Rick loves you too! We all love you!" Rosella gave us both a doubtful look over her shoulder and then disappeared through the door.

A week later I watched Rosella and her dancing partner Anuj film a promotional video for an Israeli arts council. Between takes, they choreographed their routines, using a type of code. Many Kathak moves have names, like "peacock" or "horse," and they work out the details of in a peculiar theatrical argot. "We will go from peacock, to horse, and then lots of flowers," said Rosella. Between numbers, the performers bickered about lighting and amplifiers, just like any modern performers. At other times they called out rhythms to each other, "Try this," said the tabla (drum) player, "*Dhin dhin daage trike tu na kat ta daage trike dhin na, Dhin dhin...*" or asked the vocalist for a devotional riff from a traditional hymn (*bhajan*).

Between shots, Rosella was a bit of a tyrant. When the tabla player made a mistake in the rhythm at the end of a scene she launched into him, "You have ruined the scene and you think it is funny? That is what is wrong with you. For you, this is a job, for me this is about enjoyment. If I do not enjoy, I do not dance. You, as soon as you think you can stop, you stop. It is ridiculous."

Later, over pizza and beer, Anuj and Rosella admitted that all the international attention Kathak attracts comes with a cost. While discussing *taal* (rhythm), they agreed that recent years have seen a simplification of the beats used at Kathak performances. Traditionally, Kathak, like all Indian classical music, has a wide array of time signatures, anything from the 4/4-like *teentaal* to truly odd rhythms like a nine-and-a-half beat cycle of *sarenau taal*. In the past, many of these unique rhythmic patterns appeared in Kathak performances. Old-school audiences could appreciate the technical difficulty of dancing, for example, to a 17-beat time signature. These days, lament Anuj and Rosella, the international audience and even many audiences in Bombay understand little of *taal*. Only in tradition-steeped places like Lucknow, Patna, Benares and Allahabad are audiences able to appreciate oddball rhythms.

Kathak requires a sense of balance between the masculine and the feminine. Both male and female dancers must exhibit *laasya* and *taandav*, the womanly and manly modes respectively. Depending on the particular dance, a male dancer may need to display the feminine mode and a female dancer the male mode. To err on one side or the other is to invite the wrath of critics. One Western Kathak dancer, they told me, displays so much *laasya* and so little *taandav* that the Indian dance community universally eschews him despite his considerable physical abilities. Dancers of the Jaipur Kathak tradition, on the other hand, dance with such *taandav* that Lucknowi dancers consider them one-dimensional.

Aesthetics also reveals itself in the way Kathak performers depict romantic love. Rosella explained that she sometimes portrays the Eight Stages of a Woman in Love, a traditional theme in Indian art. This theory holds that a woman in love moves through eight successive stages beginning with the woman's total infatuation, in which the lover can do no wrong, and moving through the inevitable disappointment, feelings of betrayal and, finally, resignation to the inconstancy of men. These eight stages include one stage in which the woman verbally and physically abuses her faithless lover.

"Do you know what I am talking about, *Reek*?" Rosella asked me.

"Yes," I said, "In fact, I think I have known some women who got stuck in that stage."

THE GURU

Anuj invited me to visit his father — and Rosella's guru — Pandit Arjun Mishra. Mr. Mishra, one of India's most respected names in Kathak, lives in a modest house in the neighborhood of Nishatganj. Knowing that Rosella and her guru were now working separately, I tried to avoid mentioning her name. Instead, I simply said that I was writing an article on Kathak and had seen his son dance on several occasions.

"Then I am sure you have seen Rosella dance, too," he remarked sourly.

When I admitted that I had, Pandit Mishra launched into a diatribe on the value of the guru / student relationship. "You must study at least 25 or 30 years before you call yourself an artist," he said. "Fifteen years is not enough." When I asked how long his son had been dancing, he admitted only four years, but claimed, "When you are living in the guru's house you learn faster. So my daughter, for example, has only been learning for a few years, but it is equivalent to 14 years."

This respect for experience in Kathak means that some dancers perform long past their physical peak. Although Pandit Mishra looks to be in his 50s, he continues to headline at many festivals in India. Still spry, his limbs have nevertheless acquired the unavoidable heaviness and stiffness of middle age. While it is interesting to watch an old master at work, certain moves that Kathak dancers execute, such as acrobatic spins, require the flexibility and reflexes of the young. Pandit Mishra did not concede this, however. He denied that a dancer in her prime can counterbalance lack of experience with physical prowess.

In fact, for Pandit Mishra, the older something was, the better — not only for the individual but also for the tradition itself. He told me that he is a 10th-generation dancer and that his *gharaanaa* (dancing tradition) stretches back into the 17th century, or "some 300 years." Pandit Mishra's family had been involved in the Lucknow Kathak tradition for centuries and he hopes to pass on the tradition to his son and daughters. This long tradition makes him wary of any innovation. "*Bevkuufi!* [This is silliness!]" he exclaimed. "If I am dancing Kathak and using Western drums, how rotten!"

In the afternoon, Pandit Mishra's students arrived for their daily *riyaaz* (practice). As he called out the rhythm, three young girls, ages 9–12, danced a complicated and prolonged dance number. Their dexterity impressed me and when their dance ended, I applauded enthusiastically. Pandit Mishra shot me a disapproving look. He called one of the girls over to him. "Hold out your hand," he said to her. Obediently, she held out her forearm. Pandit Mishra grabbed her arm and slapped her forcefully on the wrist. He repeated this with the two other girls. "They have not been practicing so I have given them this punishment," he explained. "It will make them tough."

According to Anuj, what I witnessed in the dancing studio was only a mild taste of his father's strictness. He told me that, in the course of his education, his father "broke many sticks on me." Once, when he was particularly slow in his progress, his father woke him up and 3:00 AM and demanded that he dance. At another time, after one of his trips to Europe on which he had been dancing flamenco, his father noticed his stiff flamenco-like upper body posture and beat him. Still, Anuj had nothing but respect for his father. Only corporal punishment, in his opinion, can instill the necessary discipline and motivation to learn Kathak.

A Quick Note

Several days later, I went to visit Rosella at a digital lab in the neighborhood of Indranagar, where she was editing her promotional video for an Israeli arts council. When I arrived, she showed me the footage, and, with the help of several harried assistants, proceeded to edit it down to ten minutes of her best material.

"*Reek,*" she said quietly, "the video will have to be accompanied by promotional brochure. You are a writer, yes?"

I nodded my head.

"You can write some promotional material for me, I think?"

When I agreed, Rosella requested a document containing a history of Indian classical music, an explanation of Kathak technique, a brief biography of the 16th century poetess Mira Bai, a concise summary of relevant Hindu mythology, an elucidation of the tenets of Yogic philosophy — all in understandable language — along with a panegyric of her dance troupe.

"That's sort of a tall order," I said. "When will you need this?"

"What time is it now?" She asked.

"Six-thirty."

Rosella thought for a moment. "I will need the promotional material by 8 o'clock, yes?"

"Rosella," I said, "I can't do that."

"Why?" she asked, "You know these things from school."

"Not off the top of my head, I don't." I said.

Rosella's eyes hardened and for a moment and I feared I would witness an un-rehearsed imitation of Durga the fierce goddess. "You will not help me, *Reek?*" she said, "I thought you were a writer. Okay, forget it then, if you will not help me!"

"Well, I didn't say that exactly," I said.

A few hours later, I returned with the most hastily written document I have ever authored. Luckily, Rosella did not know much English and she could not perceive my essay's many shortcomings. Now appeased, she thanked me warmly. Holding the CD in her hand, she said, "This will be perfect, I know it will be."

I sat with her far into the night as she worked. Rosella told me that, after some 15 years in India, she was ready to return to Europe. She would like to take Kathak back with her and start a school in Italy, but needs to find the right lo-cation and adequate sponsorship. She expressed exasperation at the constant struggle for recognition and funding.

"Sometimes I just think I will quit and just commit suicide," she told me.

"C'mon," I said, "don't talk like that."

"Then I will quit and work at McDonald's," she said, perhaps imagining the only thing she could think of that was worse than suicide.

At midnight, Rosella guessed that she would be working for another three hours. She wanted to go home but she could not; the next morning she was flying to Rajasthan for the King of Udaipur's New Years Eve party and she needed to finish her video editing that night. I stayed with her as long as I could but, as on the dance floor, I could not keep up with her and headed home to bed.

As I left, I turned around and took one last look at her, bent over a computer monitor, splicing digital images of herself together, her eyes heavy with exhaus-tion, her patience at an end. This scene was emblematic of the challenges of Kath-ak in the 21st century. In the past, all dancers had to learn was dancing. Today, to make it as a Kathak dancer on the international stage, performers like Rosella also need to understand promotional videos, brochures and arts councils.

This tension between tradition and modernity sometimes seems to be tearing Kathak apart at the seams. Rosella, Anuj and Pandit Mishra must play to two different audiences. In Lucknow, Jaipur and Benares, the cognoscenti demand total adherence to the traditions of the past. The rest of the world, however, wants dance that is flexible, fast-paced and open to innovations. Satisfying both audiences simultaneously is almost impossible. The rift between Rosella and Pandit Mishra is the same growing chasm between the ways of the past and the necessities of the present that has opened in all the traditional performing arts of India. On one hand is the modern world of European tours and recording contracts, on the other, the half-millennium of tradition.

Throughout it all, Rosella maintains her poise and a laser-sharp focus. Every dancer knows that success in dance is not a matter of education alone; it is the conjunction of training, circumstance and genetics. A great dancer requires certain traits that cannot be taught: grace, beauty and unflagging self-confidence. Rosella has all these traits in abundance. All she needs now is a few production assistants — and a copywriter who knows something about dance.

While My Sitar Gently Weeps

To be honest, my interest in Rosella was more than professional. I not only wanted to write about her, I also hoped that she would use her connections in the Lucknow music scene to find a respectable sitar teacher for me. I first began to study sitar when I was nineteen and have continued to play sporadically over the last decade and a half. I am still only a novice. Although my digital dexterity easily impresses untrained ears in America, I am nothing special in India, where aspiring musicians often begin to play at the age of five.

That is fine by me. I am only a passionate amateur and have no pretensions of performing professionally or even publicly. For me, playing the sitar is a private aesthetic adventure. In the chaos of India, the few hours I could devote to music were sometimes the best part of the day. Although I occasionally entertained (or annoyed) my guests with an informal recital, I was usually content to strum my instrument alone in the privacy of my own study.

When I moved to Lucknow, I hoped to find a teacher quickly and begin to study music again. Unfortunately, it was not that easy. Most reputable teachers from the Lucknow *gharaanaa* (tradition) had moved to either Delhi or Calcutta. Lucknow does have a school of classical music, the Bhatkhande School. When I visited, however, the faculty seemed unsure what to do with a foreigner. Luckily Rosella knew all the musicians in Lucknow and introduced me to Sibte Hassan, who she recommended as the best sitar player in the city. Over the next ten months, I visited Sibte regularly and made some progress in my playing. More importantly, I learned about a tradition of sitar music rarely heard in the West and gained a wider understanding of Indian music theory.

James Baldwin once wrote, "All I know about music is that not many people ever really hear it."[1] Although he was referring to experimental jazz, his observation holds for Hindustani Classical music as well. Westerners, if they know anything about the genre, often dismiss it as a bohemian craze. This is partly an accident of history. Ravi Shankar, the famous sitar maestro, first brought the art form to the attention of mainstream America when he played at Woodstock in 1968, and Beatle George Harrison took up the study of the instrument soon thereafter. This created a popular association between Indian classical music and some of the worst aspects of the 1960s counterculture. Even today, many Americans consider the sitar as musical accompaniment for an LSD trip.

Our associations with Hindustani music are unfair to the art form, however. Indian classical music is a tradition-bound and demanding discipline governed by complex systems of melody and rhythm and requires a lifetime of study to master.

Playing the sitar requires an understanding of melodic modes called *ragas*. Neither a scale nor a key, *ragas* are more accurately defined as acoustic patterns that govern a musician's composition and improvisation. Each raga has a proper season and a proper time of day when a musician should play them, and each raga should evoke a certain feeling or *rasa*. Ragas may convey a feeling of peace (*shantirasa*), devotion (*bhaktirasa*), erotic excitement (*shringararasa*) or heroic chutzpah (*virarasa*).

Ragas have a magical effect on my mood. Some ragas calm me; others excite me or induce a profound sense of melancholy. Playing certain ragas is like opening an attic window to let the fresh spring air in. Others are like chilly, gray days in November. Some are sophisticated, evening ragas that dazzle me with sweeping phrasing and intricate hooks. On the other hand, certain ragas can give the listener the feeling of having his heart broken.

A few ragas have such a bent sound and melodic structures so twisted, they initially sound like poison to my ear. Rag Purvi, the Eastern Raga, is one of these. Traditionally played at sunset, its many sharps and flats add up to a sound akin to the buzz of a mosquito, the Muslim call to prayer and the sounds of a cat in heat all sounding at once. Strangely, at the point of Rag Purvi's most convoluted progression, just when I decide that I cannot listen to such a misshapen piece of music, the sitar wrings an extraordinary, bittersweet elixir from its tortured tones, like the distilled regrets of an entire world mourning the loss of another day.

Sibte Hassan

Sibte Hassan lived in a one-room flat in an alleyway not far from Meera Bazaar, a depressed area across the river from my apartment. During our first lesson,

---

1 See Baldwin, James. *Going to Meet the Man* (New York: Knopf Publishing 1995).

I tried to follow him as he played Rag Bhageshri but I could not. I feared I had simply become ambisinister until I realized that his sitar had fewer frets than mine did. He explained that his *gharaanaa* (tradition) habitually removes several frets to enhance the flow of the bent notes. His tradition (sometimes called the 17-fret tradition) not only altered the number and position of the frets, but also required that some strings be tuned to different notes.[1]

The differences did not stop there. Formerly, I learned from teachers schooled in the same tradition as Ravi Shankar and thus learned to play in a similar way. Sibte's *Senia Gharaanaa* takes a different stylistic approach to music.[2] He found my playing cluttered and full of unnecessary grace notes and fancy digital acrobatics. His tradition, he explained, prefers the clear, simple development of melodic lines without extraneous finger hammering (*zamazama*), warbling (*gamak*) or set chords (*chikari*). In this, the *Senia Gharaanaa* is closer to the traditional Dhrupad style of medieval music from which all Hindustani classical music developed.

Much Indian classical music is fantastically ornate, such that the listener is lost in an almost infinite tangle of notes. In contradistinction to this baroque style, Sibte's tradition offers something less esoteric and more sonorous; a style in which the infinite variety of a single, unadorned riff can be appreciated to its fullest extent, and where melodic smoke-and-mirror tricks do not overwhelm or purposely perplex the listener. Strangely, I found playing in Sibte's style more difficult than in the style I first learned. Previously, complexity sometimes masked flaws in my technique. In the *Senia Gharaanaa's* sparse style, however, I could not hide; if I played something incorrectly, my mistake was clearly audible.

Under Sibte's tutelage, I made slow progress. He corrected certain bad habits that I had picked up from playing alone in America for so many years. For example, he made me change the way I held my left hand, which caused me terrible agony at first because my fingers had to develop new calluses. Sitar strings are no different from piano wire and handling them requires that the tips of the index and middle finger become wholly insensitive. This is a painful process. When I complained, Sibte lit a cigarette and grabbed my hand. He then placed the glowing tip of the cigarette over my fingers tips, without touching them, until I felt an intense burning sensation.

"Here," he told me, "burn your fingers with a cigarette every day, and then you will feel nothing, you will see."

The cigarette trick helped and my fingers began to toughen up. The only problem was typing; I felt nothing in my fingertips after a time, but, while I built up my calluses, it was almost impossible to type without pain. Sibte next suggested

---

1 The convention of removing certain frets is apparently a 20th century innovation. Today, some members of the Senia Gharaanaa still play with a full set of 20 frets.

2 The Senia Gharaanaa dates from the 16th century when Tanzin Senia (or Taansena) played in the court of Akbar the Great. See Garg, Lakshminarayan. *Sangiita Vishaarad* (Hathras: Sangeet Karyalaya 2004), p. 23.

covering the tips of my fingers with henna. This turned my fingers an orange color, and I am not sure that it had any beneficial effect, but I followed Sibte's advice anyway. Sibte had a hundred tricks to keep my fingers working. He rarely talked about theory or acoustics, but rather focused on the practical, the angle of my fingers, the bend in my wrist, how it is better to secure the frets with plastic rather than string (it prevents collateral noise caused by sliding the hand along the neck).

The traditional method of learning sitar starts with fixed compositions and ends with improvisational riffs that adhere to a strict rhythmic and melodic framework. Improvisation in Hindustani classical music is somewhat similar to playing riffs in certain types of jazz; it requires both technical understanding and momentary inspiration.[1] I was adept enough at memorizing Sibte's off-the-cuff compositions when he wrote them in my notebook. I found it much more difficult, however, when he told me to "go for it" and improvise while he played the *tabla* (hand drums). I could either play something that was melodically interesting, in which case I lost the beat, or I could follow the beat by playing something pathetically simplistic. Doing both at the same time was beyond me.

To practice with me, I hired a young tabla player from Rai Baraeli who had been playing the drums since he was four years old. I paid him well, but my lack of experience and limited ability meant that he could only play the most basic rhythms and he soon got bored with me. Sibte took up the slack and began accompanying me on the tabla himself. Slowly, I made progress. Starting with shorter rhythmic cycles (e.g., the 10-beat *jhap taal* or the 7-beat *ruupak taal*) I eventually gained the ability to follow a rhythm while composing interesting riffs according to the rules of the *raga*.

Sibte also taught me how to play fast. With his help, my hand speed increased rapidly. He showed me how to play by never letting my left hand leave the frets. By applying constant pressure on the strings, keeping the left arm loose so that it could swing up and down the neck with ease, and altering the angle of my finger picking, I was able to play riffs much faster than I ever could before. One day a houseguest noticed my newfound dexterity. Proud of myself, I improvised an Asian approximation of "The Devil Went Down to Georgia."

"The Devil bowed his head 'cuz he knew that he'd been beat," I sang. "And he laid that golden sitar on the ground at Johnny's feet."

I wished that the devil would do the same to me. Finding a good sitar was almost as difficult to learning to play one. Most sitars in stores were virtually useless except as display pieces and dealers asked for as much as $1500 for a professional-quality instrument. Luckily, Sibte knew the location of the work-

---

1 Improvisational riffs or *taan*, are not a part of all types of Indian classical music. Dhrupad music, a forerunner of modern Hindustani music still performed in India, has much less opportunity for improvisation than later *Khyaal* and *Thumri* styles. The latter is an innovation of the courts of Lucknow's Nawabs. See Garg, pgs. 232-240.

shop of Muhammad Alam Khan, a master sitar maker. Out of his eight-by-four foot workshop deep in the alleys of Lucknow, Muhammad and his associate Zafar Khan make top-notch products for discount prices. Muhammad ordered sitar parts from Calcutta and then assembled them at his workshop. When it was finally ready, he showed it to me with evident pride. The workmanship was breathtaking, the neck consisted of rose wood framed with inlaid bone, the gourd (really a pumpkin-like vegetable treated and faced with wood) was decorated with curved wooden faux leaves and vines, and the tuning pegs were carved to look like rose buds. Muhammad strummed it for a few minutes before handing it to me. He promised that the bridge (*jalwari*) would "open up," or improve in sound, over the next few years. He was right; over the next year or so, the sweetness and resonance of my sitar increased.

Although Sibte was married and had six children, he rarely saw his family. They lived in Bombay and he had a bachelor's life. Predictably, his home was usually in a state of complete disarray and he was often unshaven and disheveled when I arrived. He was not much of a socialite either. When I invited him to meet my editor, who was in town, Sibte disappeared without a trace for a week. Neither did he seem to show much interest in the money I paid him; on most months he was unsure if I had paid him or not.

In short, Sibte seemed to have few interests other than music. He did not let religion get in the way of his playing either. Sibte had a small picture of Saraswati, the Hindu goddess of learning and music, on the neck of his sitar. I asked him about this, pointing out that he was a Muslim and that the worship of Hindu deities was taboo for him. "In art there are no Muslims or Hindus," he replied.

He expected me to have an equivalent commitment to music. We scheduled our lessons to last an hour, but they often went for over two. After such a long session, my hands were often aching and I could not manage another note. Sibte would continue anyway, oblivious to my discomfort. "One more variation (*tan*)!" he would insist and start playing before I had a chance to object.

Traditionally, the relationship between Guru and student (*shishya*) is laden with rituals and responsibilities. Upon mentioning the name of your guru, a student should to touch his earlobes as a sign of respect. The student must touch the guru's feet when meeting him and to tie a string around his own wrist indicating that he is bound exclusively to his teacher. As a foreigner, I avoided these formalities — just as well; touching other people's feet gives me the willies.

As time went by, however, I could understand the overwhelming feeling of respect that students have for their gurus. Playing with Sibte had a remarkable effect on my own ability. When I was sitting next to him and under his guidance, I was able to play even complex variations with comparative ease. When I was alone, on the other hand, my fingers sometimes stiffened and I could not manage even simple pieces. Perhaps it was a matter of confidence or a desire to please my teacher, but it sometimes felt almost as if his presence alone was enough to lift me from my usual confusion into his world of musical mastery.

Nevertheless, over time I discovered that certain aspects of my personality keep me from being a great musician. This epiphany occurred while playing Rag Shivaranjini. Shivaranjini has a flattened note (*ga*), except on occasion when the piece requires *ga* natural. Exactly when the musician should play *ga* natural is a mystery to me. I wanted Sibte to give me some sort of inviolate rule for this note, as in "play ga natural every 36 beats." Sibte could not give me a straight answer. "When it feels right, then you play it," he would say. I liked *ga* natural so I began to play it often. Sibte's nose wrinkled in disgust. "You are playing *ga* natural too often," he complained. "You must stop."

Sibte plays on All-India Radio several nights a week. He has also toured Australia, Singapore, and the central Asian republics (Uzbekistan, Kyrgyzstan). He is not a big name in Indian classical music, however. Lucknow was once a center for Hindustani music and sitar music in particular. These days, other cities eclipse it and most of the maestros have moved to Delhi. When I visited the All-India Radio studio in Lucknow, I saw many more like Sibte, masters of traditions little known outside of India making weekly performances on the radio for modest wages.

Indian classical music is changing. Some complain that the traditional methods of instruction in which a student learned from one *gharaanaa* for his entire life have given way to fusion, not only between *gharaanaas* but also between Hindustani classical music, jazz and world music. In today's Indian music scene, young musicians focus as much on marketing and self-promotion as on practice and showing respect to their tradition. Pandit Ravi Shankar griped about young Indian musicians in *India Today*, saying, "A young lad who has just taken a few lessons wants to be like me."[1]

Perhaps "old-school" stars like Pandit Shankar are inadvertently responsible for the current crisis in Indian classical music, however. In India today, centuries-old musical traditions are fast disappearing. On the international stage, a handful of big names (e.g., Shankar, the late Villayat Khan, Ali Akbar Khan, and the late Nikhil Banerjee) have broken into the mainstream and monopolized the market. Without a trip to India, the Western listener often ends up with an artificially narrow view of the stylistic variety in Hindustani Classical music. Recordings from the 17-fret tradition, for example, are almost impossible to find in America. Many other *gharaanaas* are in the same predicament. To emerge from the shadow of big stars like Ravi Shankar, young artists must peddle novelty and ever-more-extravagant hybrid styles.

True masters of traditional *gharaanaas*, like Sibte, become wards of the state, eking a living out of state-sponsored radio programs. Younger Indian musicians

---

1 Ranjit, S. Sahaya. "Striking a New Note," *India Today*, 11/28/05, p. 61.

are not lazy; they lack opportunity. "The problem perhaps lies in the fact that while the number of classical musicians has grown manifold in the past decade or so, the number of classical venues has not risen correspondingly."[1] If, as Baldwin said, most people are not hearing the music; it may have more to do with the recording industry than our own ears.

Post Script

In October 2007, I attended a performance of the Boston Philharmonic at Harvard University. Between compositions by Ginastera and Mussorgsky, the orchestra played *Svara-Yantra*, a piece by the contemporary Indian-American composer Shirish Korde. *Svara-Yantra* (which means, roughly, "mandala of notes") required a tabla drum, played by the able Samir Chatterjee. Korde's work is a melding of a symphony orchestra with Indian music theory and extended improvisational sections (*taans*). The piece started out with an *alaap*, a rhythm-less improvisation, and then continued on through adaptations of Rag Mishra Pilu and Rag Kirwani, in which the main themes of these ragas were transformed into overwhelmingly complex symphonic phrases. In the final movement, a talented Polish violinist (Joanna Kurkowicz) provided an interpretation of a piece from the 70s jazz-Hindustani fusion innovator John McLaughlin.

The performance was not without a glitch or two. Hindustani music is not easy for a full symphony orchestra. The musical theories that govern the separate musical traditions are not easily married. The result was a piece of music that did not sit easily in any tradition. Western classical music has often turned to outside influences for inspiration, but in this case, it was not only the music but also a complex music theory that required adaptation.

Nevertheless, the challenges of an East-west musical experiment invigorated the performers and the *jaldi* (final, fast tempo movement) brought the appreciative audience to its feet. As I watched a full symphony orchestra struggle to make melodic sense out of Rag Mishra Pilu, it occurred to me that I was watching a significant moment in the cultural development of India. The world had finally started listening.

---

1 *ibid*, p. 62.

RINKY'S DREAM: CONTEMPORARY ART IN INDIA

I did not initially miss the New York City art scene when I moved to India. After living for eight years married to a sculptor, I would have died happy had I never attended another gallery opening for another *avant-garde* artist. I never acquired much of a taste for many forms of contemporary art. Whenever my wife Deborah dragged me to gallery openings, museum exhibitions, open-studio events or art performances, I spent most of the night trying not to insult the artists and the subway ride back to Brooklyn railing against what I perceived as pretentious buffoonery.[1]

To be fair, I did appreciate the free glasses of champagne served at openings, and, on rare occasion, I imagined I saw true artistic genius hanging on the walls of some Williamsburg gallery. Moreover, I did attend some lively parties and meet some interesting people. I am not much of an aesthete, however. I prefer Andrew Wyeth to Andy Warhol and I find today's cutting-edge art superstars either exasperating (e.g., Matthew Barney) or revolting (e.g., Damian Hirst). Deborah patiently explained the significance of these artists, how they are valuable by virtue of the ideas they represent and the response (including my rants) they elicit. Still, I could not help wondering whether all these video, installation and performance artists who comprised the contemporary fine-arts world in New York City could successfully represent a bowl of fruit.

---

1 Deborah Simon studied at the San Francisco Art Institute and the Repin Art Institute in Leningrad before earning her MFA from the School of Visual Arts in Manhattan in 1998. She has shown in galleries from California to New York and currently works in the displays division of the Bronx Zoo in New York City.

It took moving to India to realize that, without an *avant-garde* to inflame me, art was dull.[1] The Lalit Art Academy Annual Art Exhibition in Lucknow certainly could have used a Warhol or two. The show was a collection of rehashed 19th-century art styles, occasionally mixed with Mughal influence. This hodge-podge of aesthetics meshed with varying degrees of success; some work looked as if it were copied out of an art history textbook. Deborah was even more negative than I was. She noted that more recent art movements, such as Pop art, installation, mixed media, video and photography, were missing. In short, the show contained none of the major influences that have informed fine arts over the last 40 years.

The other lacuna at Lalit Art Academy was irony. The work suffered from an earnestness that was exhausting. A precious few works managed to lighten the mood, but the work never lost an atmosphere of overblown self-importance. This miasma of pretentiousness parted briefly for the small, playful sculptures of Lucknow-based artist Manishaa Singh. His swine-like creatures showed such an intoxication of emotion that they momentarily dissipated the oppressive cloud of gravitas that hung over the gallery.

As I visited other art galleries and openings in Lucknow, I noticed an interesting trend — a gaggle of Ganeshas. His elephant-headed form was everywhere and in every imaginable style. The popularity of the elephant-headed god as a subject of contemporary art probably stemmed from the unique position he holds in the Hindu pantheon. Ganesha is a worldly god who offers his devotees neither eternal salvation nor everlasting grace, but only success in business and auspicious beginnings. Displayed on countertops and painted above doorways, Ganesha is accessible and earthy, literally — one myth claims that Ganesha was formed from the filth of a goddess' body.[2] Artists felt free to depict Ganesha in any imaginable way without offending Indian religious sensibilities.

A few weeks later, we attended another art opening at Lal Baradaari, a publicly funded gallery, in which the artist had covered the walls with portraits of a famous Bombay film star. I took this as an attempt at humor, but Deborah was not so sure. Perhaps, as the artist claimed in his statement, he simply "liked his [the actor's] face." While there, a photographer from the *Times of India* approached us, asked us a few questions and snapped a photo. Two days later, our picture appeared on page 3 of the Lucknow version of the *Times of India* under the caption

---

1 For an exhaustive consideration of the missing avant-garde in India, see Kapur, Geeta. *When was Modernism? Essays on Contemporary Culture Practice in India* (New Delhi: Tulrika Press 2000). Kapur suggests that cultural forces that might have constituted an Indian avant-garde found expression in national political movements.

2 The story comes from the *Shiva Purana*. Parvati, Shiva's consort took a bath and formed a figure from the filth of her body. Shiva returns and, enraged at the presence of another in the goddess's bath, cuts off the figure's head. Parvati, distraught, insists that Shiva find her creation another head. Shiva, in haste, returns with the head of an elephant. The depiction of Shiva, Parvati and Ganesha as a divine family is a common motif in Indian iconography.

"Art Attack." The accompanying article claimed that Deborah "found the mixed usage of charcoal and pencil colours interesting."[1] Although she did not remember saying this, we did not demand a retraction.

THE MOCKTAIL CULTURE?

If the art scene in Lucknow lacks something today, it was not always so. From the 15th to the 19th centuries, India was home to a vibrant and lively tradition of miniature painting that lasted until the dissolution of the Mughal dynasty. As the Mughal Empire dissolved, the breakaway kingdom of Oudh, centered in Lucknow, attracted many painters seeking patronage and developed its own unique style of painting.[2] After the Mutiny of 1857, the British made little effort to preserve existing artistic traditions in India and, without court patronage, Indian fine arts went into eclipse. Since Independence, Indian art has struggled to reform itself. Attempts to bring Indian art into the 21st century have, until the last decade, met with limited success.

Celebrated author V. S. Naipaul characterized the state of contemporary Indian art in his 1979 book, *India: A Wounded Civilization*:

> The Indian past can no longer provide inspiration for the Indian present. In this matter of artistic vision the West is too dominant, and too varied; and India continues imitative and insecure, as a glance at the advertisements and illustrations of any Indian magazine will show. India, without its own living traditions, has lost the ability to incorporate and adapt; what it borrows it seeks to swallow whole.[3]

For Naipaul, Indian artists have done little in the decades since Independence except imitate the West. Like somebody decorating a Christmas tree, Indian artists reach into the box of the Western art world, select certain ornaments, and arrange them into a disconnected mishmash of influences. What is missing is something distinctly Deccan. Like the non-alcoholic mocktails that Indians are fond of drinking at weddings, Indian art may look potable but lacks an authentic spirit.[4]

Naipaul's comments may no longer be up to date, however. Today, pieces of Indian art are selling for unprecedented amounts.[5] A painting by M.F. Hussain sold for about half a million dollars at a Sotheby's auction in 2006, while a canvas

---

1 "As Big as it Gets," *Times of India*: Lucknow Edition, 4/14/05, p. 3.

2 See Chakraverty, Anjan. *Indian Miniature Painting* (Roli Books 1990).

3 Naipaul, V. S. *India: A Wounded Civilization* (London: Penguin 1979), p. 113.

4 *New York Times* critic Holland Cotter, inspired by the work of early-20th-century modernist Nandalal Bose, takes an alternate view, "...modernism wasn't a purely Western product sent out like so many CARE packages to a hungry and waiting world. It was a phenomenon that unfolded everywhere, in different forms, at different speeds, for different reasons..." Carter, Holland. "Indian Modernism via an Eclectic and Elusive Artist," www.nytimes.com/2008/08/20/arts.

5 A 2006 article in *The Hindu* claimed "Contemporary Indian art is gaining fresh acceptance in Western art circles" and described a group of NRIs (non-resident Indians) discussing

by Tyeb Mehta went for $1.6 million at Christie's in 2005. These prices reflect a dramatic increase in the recent cost of Indian art; until 2000, Hussein's art sold for about $16,000 a canvas.[1] Although the price of an object at Sotheby's may be unrelated to its critical acclaim — the doodles of John Lennon have also sold for high prices at auction but few would claim that they were great works of art — this does suggest that Indian art has at least gained unprecedented attention on the world art market.

Contrary to Naipaul's conclusions, I found much art in India that struck me as original. In fact, creativity took root in the Rock Garden of Nek Chand, in the city of Chandigarh, just a few short years after Independence. Chandigarh is a modern Punjabi city, built in the 1950s and designed by a European architect, Le Corbusier. Organized into a grid, each city block is a "sector." Wide, featureless avenues separate the sectors with predictable regularity. No ancient temples or ruins disturb the tedium. A product of Nehru's India, the metropolis is a deliberate break with the past, a socialist fantasy where there are no Upper East Sides or Brooklyn Heights, no Spanish Harlems or Brownsvilles — just Sectors 1-61. The good restaurants are in Sector 17, the artificial lake, near Sector 6.

Such a bleak, self-consciously egalitarian city is the last place you would expect to find original modern art. It is here, however, in the northern tip of Chandigarh (Sector 4), that an untrained and unheralded artist named Nek Chand gave India one of its most striking works of post-Independence sculpture. Working in an undeveloped sector of the city, Mr. Chand began to collect discarded items and to arrange them into a type of *ad-hoc* sculpture garden. At first, this was simply for his own enjoyment; he had never taken an art class and had no pretensions of creating a lasting work of art. As time went on, however, his creations became more elaborate. Walls made of broken dishes and electrical appliances, trees made from wires and ranks of imaginative, sometimes unidentifiable creatures give the Rock Garden a fantastical, otherworldly ambiance.

In 1972, the city of Chandigarh slated Sector 4 for development and was on the verge of landscaping Nek Chand's garden into oblivion. By this time, however, word had leaked out that the area was the home of a strange, secret garden. Public outcry stayed the wrecking ball and city authorities, realizing that Nek Chand's Rock Garden had potential as a tourist attraction, declared the site sacrosanct. Today thousands of visitors wander through Nek Chand's labyrinth and look in wonder at his creations.

---

art as a lucrative investment. Gathani, Butak. "Indian Art Gains Serious Investors," *The Hindu*, 5/28/2006.

1 A closer look at big-bucks art deals like this revealed that most of the collectors involved were of Indian origin. One Delhi gallery manager estimated that Indians made 85 percent of art purchases, a seismic shift from just a few years ago (Kolesnikov-Jessop, Sonia. "India's art market booming,"*Herald Tribune*, 1/25/2007). This begs the question, have Hussein and other Indian artists been discovered by the critics or the *crorepatis* (millionaires)?

Before I visited Nek Chand's Rock garden a friend told me "the art is really disappointing." I strongly disagreed. Nek Chand rearranged the banality of urban life into something beautiful and haunting. Notably, the Rock Garden lacked any clear influence from traditional Indian culture. Like the city of Chandigarh itself, Mr. Chand was unencumbered by the countless millennia of Indian history, free to make something that reflects the brave new world of modern India.

IMMERSION #39

My tour of the Delhi art scene began at Anant, a chic gallery in the neighborhood of Defense Colony, where we viewed a show entitled *Immersions*, by Delhi artist Atul Bhalla. While there, I found myself in conversation with Nuzhat Kazmi, a lecturer on art history at Jamiya Miliya Islamiya, a prestigious Delhi university. As often happens to me in these situations, I was unable to think of anything insightful to say about the show, which mostly consisted of simple cement objects immersed in square glass tanks of water. I considered suggesting the addition of a few goldfish to the work but managed to hold my tongue. Instead I parroted Naipaul's complaint that Indian contemporary art is largely derivative. "It could be found in any gallery in New York City or London," I said to her, gesturing towards one of the artist's pieces. "There is nothing distinctively Indian about any of it."

Nuzhat proved both Naipaul and me wrong, however. She led me to Immersion #39, which, to my eye, looked like another large rock in a fish tank. I had missed something however. The large, oddly shaped rock was actually the artist's representation of *mushk*, a traditional means of transporting water made from the hide of a sheep. A sharp-eyed visitor can still spot *mushk* vendors in the bazaar outside Delhi's Jama Masjid. The water from a *mushk* skin is supposed to possess magical and medicinal qualities and the water from a *mushk* remains remarkably cool, even on the hottest day. In Immersion #39, what looked like uneven lumps were actually the stumps of the sheep's legs, and what appeared as a crack in the rock was the seam from which the *mushk's* water flows. The piece contained any number of political or social subtexts invisible to the untrained, or culturally naïve, eye. Immersion #39 was both distinctly Indian and undeniably contemporary.

When Deborah spoke to Nuzhat's 4th-year BFA students a few days later, the question of Indian art's derivative nature again arose. When Deborah asked the students about the relationship between Western and Indian art, she received curiously contradictory answers. On the one hand, the students insisted that their work was uniquely Indian and objected to the idea that they were simply imitating the West. On the other hand they accepted as fact that if "you want to be a part of the international art world, you must speak its language, which is Western."

If these students were confused over the relationship of Indian art to Western art, they were not alone — I was too. Western intellectuals (among whom I number V. S. Naipaul) often unfairly damn Indian artists from two different directions; they either imitate the West too closely, or they do not imitate the West *well enough*. If they copy Western styles, they are rip-off artists; if they ignore Western influences, they are uneducated rustics. Indian artists thus find themselves in an impossible position.

Contrary to Naipaul's dated observations, the Indian artists I met in Delhi (if not Lucknow) did not lack for originality. Moreover, I did not get the sense that they suffered from an aesthetic wound that lingered from the British Raj. Many Asian cities, including Tokyo and Seoul, have emerged from periods of foreign occupation similar to India's British-era with vibrant fine arts scenes that are able to hold their own with London or New York. I doubted that Indian art's main problem is really a slavish submission the "dominant" aesthetic of the West.

To my eye, the shortcoming of the Indian art scene was less style than content. Some galleries in Delhi exhibited talented artists but the subject of their art seemed genteel. Nowhere did we find any work akin to Damian Hirst's infamous bovine vivisection or Annie Sprinkle's display of her own inner organs. No South Asian Christo had wrapped islands in pink plastic, and no Asian Serrano had photographed a Hindu version of *Piss Christ*. I looked in vain for a depiction the cruelty of everyday life, the banality of modern urban culture, or the spiritual nausea of a commodity-driven world.

In short, Indian art, despite its stylistic sophistication, struck me as fatally *polite*. I saw no attempt to awaken the viewer with the grotesque or the obscene, no exploration of the human misery so abundantly available in India and no honest depiction of India's toiling, rural masses. Indian artists often passed on social protest in favor of postcard-ish depictions of village life.[1] The exploitive dimension of sexuality remained unexplored, violence remained below the surface and most conceptual pieces struck me as timid and often nerdy. Most art shows I attended in India had all the pretentiousness of the New York galleries without any of the outrageous concepts, the provocative attitude or the wicked fun.

I suspect that this conservatism in Indian art is a symptom of the underlying social and economic conditions in which Indian artists live. Contemporary fine art is neither the court art of royalty nor the folk art of the masses; it arises from the urban middle-class. In India, the middle-class is still growing, however. Among the bourgeoisie that does exist here, the hegemony of the Indian family often stifles artistic ambition before it reaches maturity. Young people, even

---

1 New York performance artist Pat Oleszko objects that political art is also largely missing from the 21st-century New York art scene. In her opinion, the ability for artists to act as social critics and provocateurs has diminished over the last several decades with the retraction of government support of political art and the restrictive atmosphere of the post-9/11 world.

those with the economic means to do otherwise, often live with their parents until marriage and few Indians at any age live apart from close relatives. In such an environment, art may naturally tend towards the innocuous.

RINKY'S DREAM

In fact, many Indian artists work under such adverse conditions it is a wonder that they produce art at all. I first met Rinky in her family's comfortable two-story house in the village of Manupura outside of Benares.[1] She had recently married a man who she had first met on her wedding day. In her wedding pictures, a stunningly beautiful Rinky stood next to her short, bespectacled husband. Immediately following the wedding, her husband returned to his parents' house to await Rinky's arrival. Five months later, Rinky was still procrastinating. She did not want to leave the village of her birth for an unknown family in a city she did not know, to live with a man she was not sure she liked.

Instead, Rinky wanted to be an artist. In her small studio behind her parent's house, she had covered the walls with her latest work. They were folksy compositions chronicling life in Benares and historical themes. In one oil painting, a woman stood on the banks of the Ganges River and stared down an aggressive monkey. In another, the Queen of Jhansi rode out against her British foe during the Mutiny of 1857.[2] Rinky's work was not sophisticated. She had not mastered perspective or anatomical accuracy — her monkeys looked like balls of yarn, her horses like barrels on legs. Despite all this, there was a playful exuberance to them and an earnestness that made them endearing.

A few weeks later, after we have returned to Lucknow, Rinky called me from her friend's cell phone. She said she wanted to see Deborah's portfolio. I explained that most of her work was in America and was not available for viewing. She stayed on the line anyway, asking innumerable questions about what it was like to be an artist in America. After a time, it became apparent to me that Rinky did not really call about Deborah's portfolio. I wondered whether she simply wanted to talk to somebody who was not from her village. She was looking for an escape from her life, her family and the husband she did not know a way to live as an artist independent of spouse and family.

Rinky's story lays bare the challenges of developing a successful fine-arts scene in India. For financial and social reasons, young artists do not often run away from home to live in the big city and pursue a "life less ordinary." Even if they did, there is nowhere for them to go. India, to my knowledge, lacks anything resembling a true artists' ghetto. For the last half-century or more, the New York art scene has germinated in bohemian enclaves where young artists gather, live and learn their trade. Places like Soho in the 1970s and 80s, Williamsburg

---

1 Both the name of the village and the name of the artist have been changed.
2 The Queen of Jhansi was a rebel leader and hero of the Mutiny of 1857. She died in battle with the British at Gwalior. See Mahasweta, Devi. *Queen of Jhansi* (Seagull Books 2000).

and Dumbo in the 1990s, and Hoboken and the South Bronx today define and shape the development of modern art in America. Characterized by cheap rent and vacant industrial buildings, artists' ghettos provide a geographical locus for experimental art, an alternative social milieu from whence artists may critique and react to mainstream society.

Neither artist's ghettos nor the idea of an artistic subculture exists here in any recognizable form. It begs the question; could Pollack have been Pollack if his parents had successfully badgered him into studying engineering? Because of these financial and social realities, artists in India do not resemble our mental image of an artist. They are often not the alienated, bohemian wild men of our imaginations. Rather, young artists are too often persons like Rinky — working from home, precariously perched between college and marriage, and bullied by their parents into renouncing their artistic aspirations in favor of something less risky.

THE FOUNTAIN

In many ways, modern art as we know it started with a urinal. Marcel Duchamp's "Fountain," — essentially a disconnected commode on a pedestal — created a storm of controversy in Europe when first shown in 1917. The debate that "Fountain" inspired on the definition and meaning of art itself is ongoing some 90 years later. Most art critics consider Duchamp's creation as a pivotal moment in the history of art and a recent survey of 500 critics, curators and artists earned Fountain the distinction of Most Influential Work of Modern Art.[1] *New York Times* art critic Michael Kimmelman remarked on the subject:

> If there was no difference between Duchamp's urinal and an ordinary urinal (plumbing aside) and an art show could consist of nothing, then art no longer necessarily resided in the thing itself but in those who interpreted the thing. Meaning it resided in what you aptly call the in-group. This by definition created an out-group, a majority, whose alienation greases the exclusionary system. The art market depends on this — the spectacle of rich people paying obscene amounts for somebody else's underpants or similar objects....[2]

It is the existence of an exclusionary in-group, the fracturing of society into an artistic coven and the mainstream society it mirrors, that creates the environment in which contemporary art flourishes. This necessary split between artistic in-groups and out-groups has yet to occur here. Before Indian artists can fulfill their roles as gadflies, pranksters, social critics and Sibyls, they must have the economic and social conditions to create a viable artistic subculture. Only then will they be able to undertake the bold creative experiments that contemporary fine arts demands. India does not lack the underpants; it simply requires the audacity to call them art and the vision to believe it.

---

1 See "World's Best Piece of Art?: A Urinal," www.cnn.com, 12/2/04.
2 Kimmelman, Michael. "The Accidental Masterpiece," www.slate.com, 10/4/05.

FAMILY MATTERS

A friend once claimed that she could introduce me to "Lucknow's biggest gangster." Thinking that this sounded like an interesting story, I attended a party at the Carlton Hotel down the street from my apartment to meet this Lucknowi Al Capone. We will call him Ahmed but, of course, this is not his real name. He was an obese man who drove a Sumo (a large SUV) and wore a sparkling shirt with a giant collar. He seemed normal enough, if somewhat arrogant, but my attempts to elicit underworld stories from him were fruitless; he just wanted to dance.

While Ahmed was shaking his (considerably large) thing, somebody made the unfortunate mistake of stepping on his foot. Suddenly, Ahmed removed a small caliber pistol from his pant leg and began waving it in the face of the left-footed offender. Getting no immediate apology from the stunned young man, Ahmed hit him over the head several time with his pistol. I was afraid that Ahmed was going to commit murder in front of my eyes.

Then a buzz sounded from Ahmed's pocket. He grabbed his cell phone and answered softly, "Hi Mom....yes I know....okay, okay...it's not really my fault.... okay, okay..." He then said a quick good-bye, jumped into his SUV and sped away. Later somebody explained to me that when Ahmed flew into a rage, a quick-thinking bystander called his mother and told her that her son was causing a scene. She called her son and insisted he return home, which he did immediately. In India, even among the criminal element, family reigns supreme.

Both Indians and Westerners have difficulty thinking clearly about the subject of family. The word itself calls up powerful emotions about people about whom we care deeply. Often, we imagine that all families must be essentially similar to our own and that all cultures must value families to the same extent.

When Ahmed's mother cut short his homicidal rage by maternal diktat, however, I realized that family in India meant something different from what it means in my own culture. In India, families have a powerful influence over each member's life, even into adulthood. Families can decide whom a person will marry, what profession they will pursue and which schools they will attend. The tolerance young Indians showed towards meddling parents intent on micromanaging their lives repeatedly astounded me. I wondered whether some sort of essential psychological difference was behind this cultural difference.

As it turns out, I was not the first person to ask this question. Some thinkers (namely classicist E.R. Dodds and anthropologist Ruth Benedict) have argued that each society falls into one of two possible categories, guilt culture and shame culture. The way members of each society make ethical decisions differentiate the two.[1] In our own culture, a guilt culture according to this theory, many of our decisions rest on feelings of guilt. Guilt is a private experience in which a person's internalized personal sense of justice is at odds with his behavior. In a guilt society we are just as likely to feel that we have "failed ourselves" as anybody else.

In shame cultures, however, ethical life is a public affair, a matter decided by the group, the caste, the religion or more often than not, the family. Bad behavior elicits a feeling of societal shame, a fear that one's community may suffer from of a person's behavior. As writer Ruth Vanita wrote "In India, reputation is familial rather than individual."[2] Although it is difficult to make blanket statements about the ethical lives of more than a billion people, India, according to this scheme, seems to fall squarely in the shame culture camp.

This "rule of the family" has an indirect impact on population issues. Young Indian newlyweds feel a tremendous pressure to provide their parents with grandchildren, especially male grandchildren. Despite the widespread understanding that India has an immense population control problem, young people continue to marry at an early age and beget relatively large families because this is the will of their parents. Hindus also struggle with a religious belief that each individual is born with a debt to their parents that they can only pay by having male children. This leads couples to seek *in utero* investigations into their child's gender — sonograms — followed often by the abortion of the female fetuses. The result of this is a gender ratio that is off kilter, with fewer than 900 women for every 1000 men in the Punjab according to 2001 census figures.[3]

---

1 Classics scholar E. R. Dodds first postulated this theory in his landmark book *The Greeks and the Irrational*. Anthropologist Ruth Benedict first applied the idea to contemporary Asian cultures. See Dodds, E. R. The Greeks and the Irrational (California: University of California Press 2004) and Benedict, Ruth. *The Chrysanthemum and the Sword: Patterns of Japanese Culture* (New York: Houghton Mifflin 2006).

2 Vanita, Ruth and Kidwai Saleem. *Same-Sex Love in India* (Delhi: MacMillan India 2000), p. 198.

3 "Male to Female Ratio in the country alarming," *The Hindu*, 10/21/03.

The resilience of large families in India receives rationalization from a school of thought called "Saffron Demography." Certain right wing Hindu groups accuse Muslims of deliberately having large families in an attempt to increase their political clout.[1] Whether deliberate or not, the Muslim population is growing faster than the population as a whole. Some scholars (e.g., Patricia Jeffery) have argued that this is probably due to as much to the poverty endemic to the Muslim population as to any deliberate attempt to alter the electoral balance. Intentional or not, a larger Muslim population seems threatening to many Hindus who look Indian politics through a communal lens.

The Hindu right is not the only group second-guessing the value of population control, however. Oddly, Western economists have further confused the issue with loose talk about a "demographic dividend" by which India's "dependency ration" (the ratio of working age people to non-working-age people) continues to improve against India's primary regional competitor, China for the next thirty years.[2] Although the idea of an improving dependency ratio is intended as a description of India's demographic growth pattern rather than a prescription for family planning, it can and often is misinterpreted to mean that continued population growth is desirable.[3] Consider, for example, writer S. A. Aiyar defense of the Indian railway minister, Laloo Prasad Yadav, against criticism that he has fathered an irresponsibly large family in an overpopulated country.

> ....while much of India has taken to contraception and the birth rate has fallen below replacement level in states like Kerala and Tamil Nadu, it remains high in the backward states of Bihar and Uttar Pradesh. China's population will stop growing by 2030, and so will that of some Indian states, but India's overall population is projected to keep rising till 2100 or longer, thanks to UP and Bihar. Many Indians regard this as a curse. But another way of looking at it is that Uttar Pradesh and Bihar will keep giving India a demographic dividend long after other states have ceased to... So, don't laugh at Lalloo Yadav for having nine children. If each of his children in turn has nine kids, that will greatly increase India's demographic dividend. It is said that God works in mysterious ways. So does Laloo.[4]

All this adds up to a place that is soon to become the most populous nation on earth. Family pressure provides the proximate cause for large families, while saffron demographics and common misconceptions about the demographic dividend create the widespread impression that a few million more babies is not such a bad thing.

---

1 See Jeffery, Patricia and Jeffery, Roger. *Confronting Saffron Demography: Religion, Fertility and Women's Status in India* (Gurgaon: Three Essay Collective 2006).

2 Luce, p. 351.

3 See http://news.bbc.co.uk/2/hi/South_asia/6911544.stm and http://www.thehindubusinessline.com/2006/01/17/stories/2006011701531100.htm.

4 http://www.swaminomics.org/articles/20060929_lalu.htm.

A Visit with the Singhs

One summer, I made a memorable visit to the Punjab with an old friend from graduate school named Munna Singh.[1] She took me to visit her family in the city of Chandagarh. The Singh family included Munna's brothers, sisters, in-laws, cousins and friends of the family who all came over to see the arrival of the foreigner. In the evenings, the extended Singh family would pile into their very small car and drive to Chandigarh's artificial lake. In that car, with cousins and siblings piled up on my lap, there was little room for myself. My sense of individuality seemed, at times, in danger of flickering out.

Munna Singh was 39 and unmarried, a rare and undesirable circumstance for a traditional Indian family. My first impression upon visiting her family was that they had accepted Munna's anomalous lifestyle. They teased her about her lack of a husband and her general lack of interest in finding one but it sounded to my ear like harmless ribbing.

Then one day, while I was sitting on their back porch, Munna's father, a retired circuit judge with a Rhadamanthine demeanor, asked me some uncomfortable questions.

"Please tell me," he said. "Why is my daughter such a rolling stone?"

I tried to explain that she had lived in America for a long time, that life was different in America, especially on the West Coast where Munna lived. I put a positive spin on Munna's choices. "Lots of people in America are rolling stones; we like rolling stones in my country. Munna is in the right place." His skeptical expression told me that he did not think much of my answer.

As time went on, the Singh family became more curious about my presence. Explaining to them that I was just an old friend who had met Munna in graduate school did not satisfy them. One night, apropos to nothing, Mr. Singh began to tell a story about the son of a former colleague. "He met a young woman and got her in trouble," he said, looking directly at me. "When his father found out, he thrashed the boy until he cried. He had to, otherwise how would he know never to do it again?" He delivered the story with a smile, but the message was clear; I left the next morning on the early train.

After my visit, I perceived the Indian family as insidious. In the usual lists of threats to the subcontinent's development — environmental collapse, political instability, growing economic disparity — I wondered whether the more dangerous challenge to India's future was social rather than environmental or political. More specifically, I wondered whether the immense power that the Indian nuclear family wields in the lives of most Indians and the lack of any strong sense of generational identity, or generation gaps, makes Indian society unable to deal effectively with changing times.

---

1 Not her real name.

In America, the generation gap, the idea that each generation has a unique identity and a responsibility to break with the traditions of the past, may have a beneficial effect on society. Richard Croker and Ken Dychtwald, authors of *The Boomer Century*, characterizes the post War generation that came of age in the 1960s as one with an openness to new ideas, the quest for innovation and the will to experiment.[1] As a member of a subsequent generation, sometimes called Generation X, I developed certain ideas that were the result of my identity with people my own age. As a group, we tended to reject the economic liberalism of our parents and shifted right politically. On the other hand, Generation X shifted left on social issues by embracing gay rights, gay marriage and pro-choice in greater numbers than my parent's generation. Generations younger than my own will undoubtedly develop their own political and social tendencies and my own outlook will one day seem as outdated as that adopted by the flower power generation of the 1960s.

In India, this type of generational identification and has yet to occur. There is little generation gap between the old and young in the sense described above. Young people may adopt different haircuts and wear jeans in India, but they are rarely willing to reject outright the ideas they inherit from their families and their castes. When I considered Indian fine arts (see "Rinky's Dream" above) I saw that the Indian arts lack a bohemian counter culture, an ability to run away and live a life less ordinary in a counter cultural enclave. While looking at death rituals (See "In Search of Flesh Eating Turtles" above), I noticed a similar trend, young, intelligent Indians, aware of the negative environmental impact of certain traditions nevertheless refuse to reject them in deference to the family. This problem is widespread across Indian society as a whole. Author David Mandelbaum writes in his book *Society in India*:

> Parental authority is unceasing as an ideal and is sustained in fact, though the actual duration and degree of this authority are affected by economic circumstance and *jati* [caste] tradition. Within a household a son or daughter must not flout a parent's will, especially not the father's. If grown sons do not wish to follow a parental mandate, they usually find ways to circumvent rather than to contradict it.[2]

This is not to say that young Indians, if asked, will not complain about the strangeness of some of their parent's behavior. None of the deeply divisive rifts between generations that occurred in the late 1960s in America, however, appears in India in any recognizable form. In India, the generation gap is a fad, a reason for young people to imitate Western fashion. Rarely does it coincide with generation-wide political beliefs, popular movements or radical changes in life-

---

1   Crocker, Richard and Dychtwald, Ken. *The Boomer Century: How America's Most Influential Generation Changed Everything* (Springboard Press 2007).
2   Mandelbaum, David. *Society in India* (Berkeley: University of Chicago Press 1970), p. 39.

style in deliberate and even perverse contra-distinction with the previous gen-eration (e.g., the love children of the 1960s).

In all my time in India, I can remember many instances in which the students at the local university protested for more government funds for comput-ers or university supplies. I can remember numerous protests related to caste politics and reservations for low-caste members. Often the participants were, overwhelmingly, members of the castes directly affected by the policies they pro-tested. On the other hand, I cannot recall a single instance of students protesting for world peace, environmental responsibility or the future of people other than themselves. Rarely did protests occur when the *fayadaa* (benefit) was not directly advantageous to the participants.

Many of the prerequisites for the type of social evolution that occurred in the 1960s and 1970s are missing in India. In America and Europe, industrialization meant that women could also work in factories, something that became impor-tant in the World War II era when much of the male population was engaged on the battlefield. Rosie the Riveter was the first sign of the massive changes in gender relations that were to occur over the next thirty years.

These changes did not occur in India in the same way. While contemporary call center work offers some young women a new role in society with a degree of financial independence to middle class, urban women, the long-term effects of this work on gender roles as a whole does not seem pervasive or seismic. In her independent film *India Calling* (2009), filmmaker Sonal Chawla follows the professional domestic life of a young call center worker in Gurgaon. In a revealing scene, the young woman's seemingly supportive parents say that their daughter's career must end with her marriage. She must "settle in" says her father.[1] For this young woman, and, we can presume for many others, the new economy in South Asia does not seriously challenge traditional gender roles. Similarly, demographic realities — the average age of Indians will remain under 30 for some time to come — do not seem to translate into generational rifts. India remains a nation with a pre-industrial family structure facing problems of the 21ˢᵗ century.

> ...little Kumar or Madhu is at the same time trapped in a web of family relationships and duties. These can limit social and intellectual freedom, atrophy an analytical mind, and curtail the development of a wider civic culture by encouraging commitment and loyalty only to the extended family, clan, or caste.[2]

Indian "family values" could have a detrimental effect on India's future. A rigid loyalty to family and tradition could mean that Indian society in the 21ˢᵗ

---

1 *India Calling* was part of the NewDocs 2009 film festival presented by the NYU Arthur L. Carter Journalism Institute on 31 January 2009 at New York University.

2 Crossette, Barbara. *India: Facing the Twenty-first Century* (Bloomington: Indiana University Press, 1993), p. 6.

century will promote outdated societal forms and practices in an age that can no longer tolerate them. The familial, shame culture-based, identity of the Indian individual might not fit in an age and an economy in which independent entrepreneurship is a necessary precondition for success. In India, a person too often becomes the sum total of their family connections. In such an environment, it is difficult or impossible to create the types of merit-based systems upon which a modern society depends.

OH BROTHERS, WHERE ART THOU?

As the reader can tell, I have highly ambivalent feelings towards Indian family life. To be honest, confusion and misunderstanding characterized many of my experiences with Indian families. As a graduate student in Varanasi, I once lived for a semester with an Indian family. Their hospitality was unceasing, but they could not understand why I required a door with a functioning lock, and took the request as a personal slight. The loss of personal space was unbearable and I vowed never to live with an Indian family again.

I have maintained that pledge to this day, but my friend Biloo almost made me change my mind. Biloo was my driver in Lucknow. His name means "bear" and, with his stout, powerful physique, he physically fit the moniker. Biloo always told me that his wife made the best chicken kababs in Lucknow, and when I showed up for dinner she proved him right. Biloo's five daughters and one son were a pleasure to spend time with, and no evening was complete until Biloo's nine-year-old daughter performed a Bollywood-inspired dance in my honor.

One autumn night Biloo loaded all his daughters, his wife and me into his Ambassador sedan for a trip to the Barabanki Horse Fair, an annual livestock festival in the village of Deva Sharif.[1] Arriving late at night, we soon found ourselves walking through an endless field of sleeping horses and into the midst of a wildly chaotic celebration that included magic shows, one-ring circuses, burlesque shows, death-defying motorcycle stunts *sans* safety equipment, death-defying food in every imaginable variety and enough jostling humanity to rival downtown Calcutta. I found the experience dizzying and feared for the safety of Biloo's young daughters in the surging crowd. My concern was lost on them however; one complained that this year's festival had been dull in comparison to years past.

At Biloo's house, I saw the positive side of Indian family life. His children called me *chaa chaa* (uncle) and I, in turn, called them by their family identifications (*bhai*, brother, *behain*, sister etc.). I am a loner by disposition, but without families like Biloo's, who were willing to accept a *farangii* as their own, if only for an evening or two, life in Lucknow would have been unbearable.

---

1   Deva Sharif is the site of the famous and beautiful *dargah*, or tomb, of Sufi saint Haji Wari Ali Shah (d. 1905). Among many great feats of learning and piety claimed by his devotees is Ali Shah's meeting with Otto von Bismarck in the late 19th century.

Indians often use terms of family relation when addressing strangers. For example, I called Biloo's wife *Bhaabhii*, sister-in-law. This made me Biloo's brother. The practice also served a secondary purpose; it de-sexualized relationships between unrelated adults of different genders. When meeting the daughter of a friend, for example, I would refer to her as "sister" and accept the responsibilities of a relationship between siblings. If a new female acquaintance was considerably older than I was, propriety dictated that I call her *diidii*, or older sister.

As time went by, these off-the-cuff families came to mean something more to me. I liked calling the taxi driver "brother" and my landlord's wife "auntie." When I returned to America, I missed having so many brothers, sisters, aunts and uncles. My biological family, as large as it is, could not replace the thousands of instant "brothers" and "sisters" I could find in any Indian town. For all my griping about the iron grip of the Indian family and its potentially retarding effect on progress, I grew accustomed to the familial character of Indian life. To this day, America can feel like a collection of strangers accidentally contained within an international border. As the next chapter begins by noting, I am not the first person to find isolation one of the greatest shortcomings of American social life.

Caste and Communal Politics: Or Lonesome No More!

In Kurt Vonnegut's futuristic novel *Slapstick or Lonesome No More!* Wilbur Daffodil-11 Swain, the last president of the United States, devises a system for preventing loneliness, which he sees as America's most pressing problem. A government computer randomly assigns all citizens a middle name and number (e.g., Horetense Muskellunge-13 McBundy, Edward Strawberry-4 Kleindienst or Mildred Helium-20 Theodorides). In this new system of social organization, people with similar names became cousins and those with the same name and number are siblings. If approached by a cousin or brother, citizens have an obligation to assist in any way possible. If approached by a person with a dissimilar moniker to whom you had no relationship, however, the proper response is to say to them (with as much civility as possible) "Go take a flying [leap] at a rolling doughnut! Go take a flying [leap] at the mooooooooooooooon!"[1]

Vonnegut's *Slapstick*, makes an important point about human social behavior. We have an innate desire to organize ourselves into distinct groups, even if no obvious reason exists for their creation. Different societies accomplish this in different ways. Citizens of the Byzantine Empire, for example, would declare themselves members of either the Blue Faction or the Green Faction.[2] These identifications were unrelated to ethnicity, religion or family and originally denoted a preference for one chariot racing team over another. Despite the *ad hoc* nature of the Green / Blue split, the distinction became so important that successive emperors would identify themselves as a member of one or the other and civil dis-

---

1 Vonnegut, Kurt. *Slapstick or Lonesome No More!* (New York City: Delacorte Press 1976).

2 See Gibbon, Edward. *The Decline and Fall of the Roman Empire: Volume 2* (New York: Penguin 1996).

turbances and palace intrigue would sometimes revolve around this chromatic dichotomy.

The same tribalism manifests itself in our own culture in a thousand different ways, from our choice of baseball team to our brand of soda. Although politicians often glorify unity, we have a deep-seated human need to differentiate ourselves from others by identifying with a group, no matter how arbitrary that group's *raison d'être*. To be a featureless face in an expansive crowd is unbearably lonely. In a place like India where the crowd seems endless and competition for resources fierce, identification with a social group such as caste is of paramount importance.

Caste has received a great deal of bad press in both the West and in India. Whenever the subject arises, it seems, caste appears as something society must eradicate, or transcend, or at least hide as much as possible.[1] However, given our propensity to vivisect populations into competing groups on our own volition, caste in India may rest on psychological imperatives that people have little control over. Caste is central to most Indians' very sense of self; if caste did not exist, somebody, like Vonnegut's President Wilbur Daffodil-11 Swain, would have to invent it.

India, of course, did not have Wilbur Daffodil-11 Swain. The inventor or inventors of the caste system are lost in history. Historically, Proto-Indo-European invaders from central Asia may have brought the idea of caste with them when they invaded the subcontinent in the second millennium BCE. Equally plausibly, the invaders created the caste system after their migration to impose order on a subjected population (See the chapter "Uda Devi Zindabad"). However it happened, Sanskrit texts such as the *Manusmrti* (or Laws of Manu) were soon speaking of castes and their associated duties with the same love of rigid and fastidious rules apparent in the Book of Leviticus.

Of course, caste has always been more than simply an arbitrary differentiation of one group of people from another; it is also a hierarchy. Unlike the system in Vonnegut's novel, castes exist along a vertical continuum that includes high-caste, low-caste, outcaste, and a thousand variations in between. The Laws of Manu explains that the caste system arises from the sacrificial vivisection of a primeval man, *Parusha*. High-caste people like Brahmin priests came from Parusha's mouth and warriors (*kshaitriya*) from his torso. The lowest castes, according to Manu, came from Parusha's feet. The social hierarchy was thus a natural and divinely ordained division of labor. A healthy society thinks with its head and walks with its feet, Manu suggests; you would not really want it any other way.

---

1 For one example of a typical plea for the "end of the caste system" see Sengupta, S. "Crusader Sees Wealth as Cure for Caste Bias," www.nytimes.com 8/29/08.

Over the centuries, caste became much more complicated. Each of the four-fold divisions of labor (called *varna*) established in the Laws of Manu (priest, warrior, craftsman, and laborer) fractured into hundreds of smaller groupings, each with a hereditary occupational association. Today, one caste is traditionally responsible for a certain type of ritual (e.g., Mahabrahmins — see "In Search of Flesh-Eating Turtles" above), or a narrowly defined task (e.g., the Chamars, or leather-workers). The variety of castes and sub-castes is almost endless. I was surprised to discover a caste, Rustogi, whose hereditary occupation was money lending, often at high rates of interest.[1] In the modern age, the professional connotations of caste have weakened, such that an outcaste Chamar is as likely to work in a government office as tan leather, but traditional occupations are still integral to each caste group's identity.

Over the centuries, caste divisions sometimes became an excuse for horrific acts of social injustice. Caste distinctions connote relative states of religious grace and orthodox Brahmins must maintain a state of ritual purity in order to perform their religious duties. This precludes their sharing meals with members of some castes, whose hereditary occupations carry the stigma of ritual impurity, (e.g., the Chamars). Not surprisingly, a person's place in the caste system often suggests the level of financial affluence and political power he or she enjoys.

It is a cliché to say about Indian politics that a person does not cast their vote; they vote their caste. This simply means that members of the same caste are likely to vote for the same candidate. In Uttar Pradesh, voting blocks, cobbled together from caste groups, form the corner stone of state-level politics. The Bahu Samaj Party (BSP) appeals to low caste and outcastes (*dalits*) while the BJP (or Bharatiya Janata Party) appeals to high-caste Hindus. The Samajwadi Party appeals to mid-caste Hindus and Muslims, the Congress Party appeals to almost nobody these days.

Each party seems to offer a thin ideological patina to underlying communal or caste conflicts. In the last two years as I attempted to make sense of politics in Uttar Pradesh I never saw any sort of debate about issues, nor were elections often the occasion for discussing substantial matters of policy. Similarly, protests at Lucknow University often centered on caste quotas. I waited in vain to see students protest, as they do in America, against a war, or for an environmental concern. India is a pluralist democracy, although at times it seems like a plurality of castes and communities, rather than a plurality of competing political visions.

Many commentators and writers look upon caste politics with a skeptical eye. Kuldip Nayar, a former minister in the Rajya Sabha (the upper house in New Delhi) wrote on gulfnews.com regarding state elections in Uttar Pradesh:

> My worry is that the voter is succumbing to appeals in the name of caste and religion and not assessing the merits and demerits of candidates. As

---

1 See Banerjee, Abhijit V. "Inequality and Investment," www.globetrotter.berkeley.edu.

the nation goes from one election to the other, whether it is for parliament, the state legislature or the local body, it appears that criminals, casteists and money bags are gaining ground.[1]

The influence of caste on local governance can be unfortunate. During the summer of 2006, Sona arrived in tears to tell me that the city government had decided to knock down her *bastii* (illegal settlement). She lived down by the Gomti River, where the poorest people in Lucknow live — the river is highly polluted and nobody actually wants to live next to it. On the day that the bulldozers arrived to knock down the huts in her shantytown, I went with her to witness the event. I noticed that although illegal settlements lined the river on both banks, the city was only obliterating her *bastii*. Residents always gave me the same answer when I asked them why this was so; Sona's settlement voted Congress, and the ruling party, the Samajwadi or Socialist Party, was making an example of them. Settlements that voted for the Samajwadi remained standing. In effect, the city had said to Sona's caste "Go take a flying [leap] at a rolling doughnut..."

If caste affects politics, politics, in turn, affects the caste system in profound ways as well. Over the last fifty years, the Hindu right and regional caste organizations have re-imagined of the very idea of caste. They have reconceived the historical origins of the institution, which they depict as a benign, religiously inspired, division of labor perverted by later conquerors such as the Mughals and the British.[2]

Although suspect from a purely historical angle, this reinterpretation of caste is also a constructive effort to enlist the support of traditionally disadvantaged groups in the political process and defend caste from the vilification it receives from the political left. Outsiders might not realize how condescending it may sound to conservative Hindus when PM Singh, or Sardar-ji (roughly "Mr. Sikh") as he is called in Lucknow, a non-Hindu, calls Untouchability a "blot on humanity" as he did in December 2006.[3] Caste determines an individual's very concept of self, and while most low-caste Hindus desire freedom from excessive prejudice and unfair economic treatment, they do not necessarily desire freedom from the caste system itself.

The last statement constitutes a common misperception. Journalist Nick Schmidle wrote in an article on Slate.com on April 16, 2007, upon encountering low-caste Hindus in Bangladesh, "If your Hindu faith considered you Untouchable, wouldn't you consider conversion?" The most common answer to this question over the last 2,500 years, however, has been "No." Despite centuries of

---

1 See www.gulfnews.com.
2 See Jaffrelot, Christophe. "The Sangh Parivar Between Sanskritization and Social Engineering," *The BJP and the Compulsions of Politics in India* Hansen, Thomas and Jaffrelot, Christophe eds. (Delhi: Oxford University Press 1998).
3 PM Singh used the phrase at the Dalit-Minority International Conference in New Delhi on December 27, 2006.

Muslim domination and a century of British (Christian) domination and, in the Middle Ages, wide spread Buddhist and Jain domination, the subcontinent remains a largely Hindu nation. One reason for the resilience of Hinduism in the face of contrary religio-political hierarchies is the stubborn persistence of caste identity. Conversion often does not erase caste distinctions at all. Members of other religious communities in South Asia, such as Sikhs and Muslims (and even the Buddhists) often maintain caste-like distinctions, making conversion much less attractive to low-caste Hindus than it would seem.

Perhaps a more important reason low-caste Hindus do not convert in large numbers to Buddhism or Islam (with the occasional exception) is that blood *is* thicker than water. Hinduism is as much an ethnicity as a religion and caste in an essential part of that identity. Most low caste and outcaste Indians that I know are no more likely to renounce their caste because of its historic disadvantages than an Irish person is likely to renounce his Irish ancestry because his ancestors historically got the short end of the stick.

Moreover, membership in particular castes has even become a political asset in India. Members of low castes reap the benefits of government quotas and political parties that recognize the strength of their numbers. In some cases, having one's caste included in a list of Scheduled or "Backward" castes is a sought-after political goal. In the winter of 2008, the Gajjar caste of Rajasthan led a statewide agitation to pressure the central government to degrade the classification of the Gajjar caste, thus making them eligible for coveted quotas for government jobs and university enrollment.[1]

State level politics in India is often a perplexing dance of caste, community and policy, with the latter taking a backseat to the former. In the statewide elections in Uttar Pradesh in the spring of 2007, the Bahu Samaj Party (or BSP), a party dominated by *dalits* or Untouchables, the lowest rung of the caste ladder, swept away the other parties and received enough seats to form a government. The BSP's main opposition in the election was the BJP or Bharatiya Janata Party, a national-level political party that appeals primarily to upper-caste Hindus. In this election, the BJP succeeded in capturing two important caste blocks of untouchable voters but it was not enough. The BSP attracted Muslims voters from their support of the incumbent Samajwadi (or Socialist Party) and caste-ism mixed with class-ism trumped communalism at the ballot box.

Despite the results of this election, communalism continues to inspire and direct national-level politics in India. How this happened, and what qualitative judgments (if any) we can make the rise of the Hindu right wing is the subject of the next section.

---

1 "Group in India Ends Protests," *The New York Times*, 6/19/08, p. A12.

AYODHYA CHALE! THE RISE OF THE HINDU RIGHT

I arrived in Delhi for the first time in the summer of 1990 as a nineteen-year-old exchange student from the University of Wisconsin. I had never before left America and had rarely ventured beyond my native New England. With youthful bravado, I decided that Delhi did not scare me. The palm trees and steamy weather gave me the impression that India was like Florida, where I had gone as a child on a trip to Disney World, the only differences being that India had more people and countless free-range cows. The full force of culture shock did not hit me until a few days later when I stepped out of the Kashi Vishvanath Express onto the platform of the train station in Varanasi in eastern Uttar Pradesh — swarming with travelers, beggars, monkeys and lepers — and I realized with sudden clarity that India was not like Florida at all.[1]

My teenaged mind was blown further by subsequent developments in late 1990 and early 1991. That fall, the streets of Varanasi filled with young men and *saadhus*, holy men, wearing orange scarves. *Ayodhya chale!* Let's go to Ayodhya! They yelled, surging through the narrow alleyways of Bengali Tola, where I lived in a cold-water flat. Police in riot gear followed. The government imposed a curfew on the city and the university in which I was enrolled canceled classes. A group of young, orange-scarved men stopped me in the alley one day to explain to me that they were on their way to build a temple to their god Ram in the nearby city of Ayodhya, but that the government was trying to stop them. They struck me as a likable group of young men, passionate about their cause and intent on explaining their motivations to me. What a nasty government India must have, I thought, to stop these nice young men from building their temple.

The young men had failed to mention that they did not own the land on which they wanted to build their temple, nor had they told me that a large 16th century mosque, called the Babri Masjid (Mosque of Babar), stood on the spot, nor that they would have to destroy it (much to the anger of the Indian Muslim community) before construction of the proposed temple could begin. I was unaware that their effort to build a temple in the city of Ayodhya would set off a series of events that would forever change the political landscape of the nation.

As the days of military-imposed curfew stretched into weeks, the young political activists running amok in the alleys of Varanasi became much less attractive. Trapped in my neighborhood, I caught the news on a jumpy black and white

---

1   The teeming masses of India also unhinged Dr. Paul Erlich, author of the Malthusian doomsday manifesto *The Population Bomb*. Erlich claims to have first realized the apocalyptic threat of population growth during a visit to Delhi. "The streets seemed alive with people. People eating, people washing, people sleeping. People visiting, arguing, and screaming. People thrusting their hands through the taxi window, begging. People defecating and urinating. People clinging to buses. People herding animals. People, people, people, people....Would we ever get to our hotel?" Erlich, Paul. *The Population Bomb* (New York: Ballantine 1972), p. 1.

television in the back room of a local tea stall. As far as I could tell from watching Doordarshan (one of the few television channels on the air in the early 1990s) the entire nation of India had gone mad. Nightly images of Hindu-Muslim violence, marches and street battles convinced me that I had landed in the middle of an Asian version of Kristallnacht.

The young men in orange scarves that I had initially found so charming were part of a nation-wide agitation instigated by right-wing Hindu organizations, led by the Bharatiya Janata Party (BJP), who were challenging the power of the central government. Mobilizing Hindus over the issue of the Babri Masjid in Ayodhya, where traditions of uncertain origin places the birth place of the god Rama, BJP leader L. K. Advani decorated a Maruti van as a primeval war chariot and rolled across India on a nation-wide *rath yaatraa* (chariot journey) accompanied by surging crowds.

Political conditions had created a perfect storm for the rise of the Hindu right wing in 1990. Prime Minister V.P. Singh's Janata Dal-led coalition government required the support of parties, including the BJP, to stay in power. In August 1990, the Singh administration unwisely released the results of a the Mandal Commission, a new scheme for caste quotas in India that reserved over a quarter of government jobs in some sectors for members of low castes. High and middle caste Hindus throughout India felt their government was ruining India with a misguided program of social engineering and misadministration. The Mandal Commission precipitated a weakening of support for the Janata Dal government and, eventually, its fall from power.[1]

The BJP capitalized on this political crisis by organizing the *Rath Yaatraa*. Advani's "chariot journey" left from Somanath on September 25, intending to reach Ayodhya by late October. Although authorities arrested Advani in Bihar and the *Rath Yaatraa* never arrived at the Babri Masjid, the agitation was a political *tour de force*. In the wake of Advani's arrest, thousands of *kaar sevaks* (those dedicated to the reconstruction of the temple), Hindu holy men, disgruntled middle-class Indians and radicalized students converged on the city of Ayodhya intending to destroy the mosque with or without Advani.

> At dawn on 30 October, about 40,000 *kaar sevaks* arrived at the entrance to the bridge leading to the old town of Ayodhya. The police were forced on to the defensive by the ever-growing crowd of militants...a *naga saadhu* [naked holy man] seized control of a police bus to breach the front ranks of the security cordon. About mid-day, the gate to the Babri Masjid / Ramjanambhoomi was forced open... allowing dozens of *kaar sevaks* to enter the precinct. They began to attack the mosque and a saffron flag was placed on one of its domes.[2]

---

1 See Jaffrelot, Christophe. *The Hindu Nationalist Movement in India* (New York: Columbia University Press 1993), pgs. 411-424.
2 *ibid*, p. 421.

Security forces eventually restrained the crowds and the Babri Mosque would stand for another year. On December 6, 1992, another swarm of *kaar sevaks* descended on Ayodhya, this time breaking through the security perimeter (some claim that the security forces were complicit in the attack) and tearing the Babri Masjid apart with pickaxes and shovels. In the years following the destruction of the Mosque in Ayodhya, the BJP gained ground politically, finally winning enough seats in the Indian legislature to form a government — first briefly in 1996 and again in 1998. The 1998 BJP-lead government ruled India until its ouster in 2004.

Today, despite the BJP's loss in the general elections of 2004, they remain a powerful force in national-level politics. The right wing coalition led by the BJP is resurgent in some states — including Karnataka where they won state-wide elections in the Spring of 2008 — and still threatens to take the center in New Delhi by playing on pan-Hindu pride, cultural issues and anti-incumbency (an important factor in all Indian elections).

Since the *Rath Yaatraa* and the Ayodhya conflict, scholars and pundits have tried to make sense of the emergence of the Hindu right wing. Many have echoed the fear I had as a student that the Hindu right was a militant organization made up of Hindu storm troopers attempting to establish a totalitarian regime. In her recent book *The Clash Within: Democracy, Religious Violence, and India's Future*, Martha Craven-Nussbaum, for example, characterizes the Hindu right as fascist. Nussbaum sees the BJP as a party inspired by Nazi-ism, led by fast-talking ideologues, and menacing democracy itself. "[D]emocracy has been under siege from religious extremism in another critical part of the world," Nussbaum's book proclaims. "[T]he forces of the Hindu right pose a disturbing threat to its democratic traditions and secular state." Nussbaum is not alone in holding these views. Writer Edmund Luce expresses a similar alarmism in his book *In Spite of the Gods: The Strange Rise of Modern India*, stating, "The most coherent threat to India's liberal democracy is Hindu nationalism." Luce also promotes the Nazi-BJP connection, even noting that the date of the Godhra fire, which preceded the anti-Muslim Gujarat riots of 2002, fell on the anniversary of the burning of the Reichstag in Germany in 1933.[1] Indian intellectuals have made similar accusations; famed In-

---

1 Luce, Edward. *In Spite of the Gods: The Strange Rise of Modern India* (New York: Doubleday, 2007), p. 159. In summary, the events of the Godhra fire are as follows; on February 27, 2002, a train packed with Hindu pilgrims returning from Ayodhya stopped at the Godhra train station. A confrontation ensued between the pilgrims and Godhra's Muslim inhabitants. As the train pulled away from the station, the S6 car suddenly caught fire killing fifty-nine passengers. Many Hindus assumed that the fire was the result of a firebomb or Molotov cocktail thrown from the platform onto the train and anger over the incident fueled the communal riots that followed. The official government investigation of January 2005 (The Banerjee Panel) concluded that the Godhra fire originated from a cooking fire inside the S6 car. While this may be true, it strains credulity to imagine that the incident was wholly accidental and unrelated to the preceding confrontation.

dian writer Arundhati Roy used the term 'fascist' eleven times to describe the BJP government in a recent speech in Aligarh.[1]

The idea that fanatical Hindus are trying to turn India into a theocracy or a Hindu-Nazi state makes for dramatic reading and it falls in line with my initial assumptions about the Hindu right as a student. Upon closer examination, however, any actual connection between the BJP and fascism is difficult to establish. The RSS, a militant forerunner organization to the BJP, probably did take cues from European fascist movements when it formed in the 1920s. Years later, the RSS aided the BJP as it rose to prominence.

However, both the RSS and the BJP leadership have always been clear about their differences; the RSS is a primarily a social movement, while the BJP strives to become a mainstream political party. Their aims are neither identical nor always in agreement.[2]

Nussbaum and others make a long leap of logic when they then characterize the contemporary BJP as fascist. The BJPs connection to European fascism is historical and indirect. Claiming that this makes the modern BJP fascist is analogous to, say, claiming that the Volkswagen car company is as fascist organization because the first Volkswagens rolled off the assembly line in Nazi Germany.

More importantly, the BJP party does not behave like a fascist organization. When voted out of office in 2004, they went far more peacefully than you would expect any truly fascist or anti-democratic movement. As writer Ramachandra Guha notes in relation to the 2004 general election, "When was the last time a "fascist" regime permitted such an orderly transfer of power?"[3] None of this prevented Nussbaum from claiming that a "quasi-fascist takeover of the Indian government seemed possible, and at times even imminent" during the time she was writing *The Clash Within*. Without further qualification, the claim seems to have little or no basis in reality.

The second common critique of the BJP is that it seeks to expand the role of the Hindu religion in government. The BJP has used Hindu symbols and language to fashion its political rhetoric. The emblem for the BJP, for example, is a lotus, a central motif in Hindu mythology and iconography. Moreover, they have sometimes used terms (e.g., *Raam Raajya* or Rule of Ram) that might suggest theocratic aims. In the field of education reform, the BJP promoted the use of school textbooks that included some dubious theories on Indian history and even allowed instruction in Hindu astrology for credit at certain public universities.

But democracy did not give way to theocracy any more than it gave way to fascism during the BJP administration. Rather, some of the BJP's pet causes seem to champion secularism. The existence of religious courts in India, for example,

---

1 Guha, Ramachandra. *India After Gandhi* (New York: Harper Collins 2007), p. 743.
2 See Jaffrelot, Christophe. *The Hindu Nationalist Movement in India* (New York: Columbia University Press 1993), pgs. 314-338.
3 Guha, p. 744.

is an ongoing source of judicial chaos. The laws of divorce or inheritance differ depending on the religious community to which an individual belongs. The result is a wide array of communal civil courts promoting a number of different legal standards. The existence of religious courts in India, for example, is more the result of the Congress Party's complicity than the BJP, which officially encourages a uniform civil code for all Indians regardless of religion.[1]

If the Hindu right is neither fascist nor theocratic in nature, however, many commentators have tried to brand the movement as pathological. Christophe Jaffrelot suggests, in his otherwise excellent study of Indian politics, that members of the Hindu right suffer from a mass inferiority complex. For the contributors to *Creating a Nationality: The Ramjanambhumi Movement and the Fear of the Self*, the communal tensions surrounding the Ayodhya rest on "the disowned other self of South Asia's modernized middle class."[2] Nussbaum goes even further, suggesting that members of the *Sangh Parivaar* (an umbrella term for right-wing or Hindu nationalist organizations) suffer from some sort of mass psychosexual dysfunction.[3]

> We see the psychological origins of violence most clearly, perhaps in the preoccupation of the Hindu right with purity and respectability, a preoccupation that involves them in a repudiation of sensuousness and sexual vulnerability.[4]

Claims like this are impossible to prove or disprove and for that reason alone have questionable value.[5] Notwithstanding the viability of placing hundreds of millions of Indian voters on the psychoanalytic couch *en masse*, these claims belittle legitimate political and historical gripes that BJP supporters have about the Congress Party's steward ship of India over the last 60 years. Moreover, having known many BJP supporters personally, claiming that they are all suffering from an irrational "repudiation of sensuousness" is simply insulting.

BJP voters display all the diversity of the Republican Party in America. Cultural bigotry motivates some of them, but most seem animated by a reasonable skepticism towards left wing ideology and policy. Many of the rank-and-file BJP supporters I have met were well-educated professionals and did not act or speak like fanatics or neurotics. As a group, they shared doubts about the government's policies towards minorities and a strong sense of identity as Hindus. They were neither more violent than members of other parties were nor more antagonistic towards democracy as a form of government. Most had little sympathy for or

---

1 See the chapter "A Law unto Themselves".

2 Nandy, A. with A. Trivedy, S. Mayaram, S. Yagnik, eds. *Creating A Nationality: The Ramjanambhumi Movement and the Fear of Self* (Delhi: Oxford Press 1995), p. viii.

3 See Nussbaum, p. 330 and Jaffrelot, Christophe. *The Hindu Nationalist Movement in India* (New York, Columbia University Press, 1993), pgs. 19-25.

4 Nussbaum, p. 334.

5 Diagnosing political opponents is also common in American politics. Professor Jonathan Haidt of the University of Virginia argues in "What Makes People Vote Republican?," www.edge.org, that rightwingers suffer from ethical "rigidity."

interest in fringe organizations like the RSS or the Shiv Sena, which they often viewed with bemusement.

They often shared ambiguous feelings about Congress leader Sonia Gandhi. Sonia, the Italian-born wife of Rajiv Gandhi, entered Indian politics reluctantly after the assassination of her husband in 1991. She remains a central figure in the Congress Party, and turned down the post of prime minister after the Congress's victory in the 2004 general election. One Indian friend, a widely respected scientist with a PhD from an American university, asked me how I would feel had a foreigner ended up as a kingmaker in American politics by an accident of marriage — a question for which I did not have a good answer.

The list of further complaints against the Hindu right and the BJP — inciting riots, intimidation, and revisionist history[1] — could be leveled against many groups in India across the political spectrum.[2] Even the reclamation of holy sites is not exclusive to the Hindu right. Ayodhya was not the first place in which Indian political parties used the promise of rebuilding a temple for political profit. A similar scenario played itself out at the Somanath temple on India's northwest coast. One of the Congress Party's founding fathers, Vallabhbhai Patel, made a vow to rebuild the temple, which Mahmud of Ghazni razed in 1026.[3] Construction on the current Somanath began under the direction of Congress minister K.M. Munshi and came to completion in the 1990s.[4]

The last oft-repeated charge against the BJP is that the party is anti-Muslim. This is also difficult to deny or to prove. For some, plainly, the Hindu right represents an opportunity to throw off centuries of perceived victimization at the hands of an alien Muslim culture and assert Hindu identity. Many BJP supporters, if asked, would object that they are not anti-Muslim, rather the Congress

---

1 On recent example would include the ransacking of the offices of the right-wing Bombay newspaper Navakal by hired political thugs (The Hindu "Rane 'supporters' attack Marathi daily office over editorial." 1/22/09). In the wake of the attack, the 75-year-old editor of Navakal defiantly called the attackers and their employer, local Congress politician Narayan Rane, "goons." This is not the first time that Khadikar, who aligns his paper with the right-wing Maharashtra party Shiv Sena, has appeared in the center of controversy. In 1993, Khadikar spent time in prison for three articles printed in the wake of the Ayodhya riots faulting the central government with mismanaging communal tensions. (see http://cscsarchive.org). Narayan Rane began his political career in the Shiv Sena and then switched his allegiance to the Congress Party. His family launched a new Marathi-language newspaper, Prahar is 2008.

2 The events of the Gujarat riot recall the Calcutta riots of 1946, when horrific violence occurred under the nose and perhaps with the encouragement of Muslim League minister H.S. Suhrawardy. For a contemporary account of the origins and effects of the carnage see Talbot, Phillips. An American Witness to Indian Partition (New Delhi: Sage 2007), pgs. 184-194.

3 Thapar, Romila. Somanatha — The Many Voices of a History (London: Verso 2005), pgs. 181-191. Thapar notes that the Congress Party did not uniformly support rebuilding the Somanath temple. Some, including Nehru himself, hoped to distance the government from the project.

4 Ibid., p. 181.

Party is irresponsibly pro-Muslim and has unfairly favored Muslim causes in an attempt to woo a traditionally large and monolithic voting bloc.

Before we can reasonably condemn the entire movement as bunch of bigots, the history of Hindu-Muslim relations in South Asia must be taken into account. If America's problem with Islamic terrorism began in earnest with the 1993 World Trade Center bombing, India's equivalent problem began in the 11th century. Even excepting ongoing violence in Kashmir, the litany of savagery committed in the name of Islam in contemporary India is long and ugly. Most recently, the list would have to include the 1993 serial bombings in Mumbai, the Delhi bombings of October 2005, the SIMI bombings in 2007-2008 and the attack on Mumbai in November 2008.[1] The latter created such a media storm that India's unique problem as a neighbor of a tottering Pakistan became impossible to ignore. According to a study by the National Counterterrorism Center in Washington, the death toll from terrorist attacks in India between January 2004 and March 2007 alone topped 3,674.[2] Were all the casualties incurred in the general Indian population and in the Indian armed forces at the hands of Islamic extremists over the last 30 years tallied together, it would dwarf t he number killed in the tragedy of September 11, 2001 by a wide margin.

Naturally, this ongoing violence chips away at many Indians' proverbial tolerance, as it would at any Americans' had they lived through violence of similar duration and intensity. This does not excuse horrific acts of communal retribution — such as occurred during the anti-Muslim riots in Gujarat in 2002 under the nose of BJP minister Narendra Modi — but such facts should make Western commentators reluctant to climb atop their politically correct soapboxes on the subject of anti-Islamic sentiment in India.[3]

The particular zeal with which Western writers attack the BJP often seems more a projection of their personal ideological biases onto Indian politics than

---

1 SIMI refers to Students Islamic Movement of India, a militant organization banned in India since 2001.

2 See Sengupta, Somini. "India, Facing a New Wave of Violence, is Rattled by the Randomness," *The New York Times*, 7/29/08. Not all of these casualties were necessarily the result of Muslim-on-Hindu violence, a point not lost on the Indian newsmedia following the Megalgaon blasts blast of September 9th, 2008. In this event a small group of Hindu soldiers, apparently motivated by radical Hindu ideology, carried out a terrorist strike against Muslims. As tragic as this isolated event was, papers with sympathies for the Congress party seemed to keep the story on the front page for a remarkable span of time.

3 Modi won re-election as Chief Minister of Gujarat on December 22, 2007. In the wake of the 11/26 attacks author Martha Craven-Nussbaum assessed the situation by writing in the *Los Angeles Times*, "...that's more bad news for India's minority Muslim population" and worrying about the response of Indian Hindus, likening their treatment of Muslims to racial profiling in the United States ("Terrorism in India has many faces," 11/30/08). This prompted *New York Times* columnist William Kristol to ask "Is it just that liberal academics are required to include some alleged ugly American phenomenon in everything they write?" ("Jihad's True Face" 12/1/08).

a fair consideration of the Hindu right's platforms and motivations. The mainstream Hindu right is not a second incarnation of National Socialism or a Hindu Taliban, and shows no signs of being a threat to representative democracy as a form of government. If we accept the reality and inevitability of caste-based and communal-based politics on the state level, then perhaps the Hindu right is an inevitable national expression of the clannish nature of local governance. When you think about it, a democratic system based on caste and community is no more or less genuinely democratic than American democracy, where the election of candidates depends as much on sound bites, media manipulation and shifting primary schedules as on issues.

Inspired, if not always faithful, to traditional Hinduism, the Hindu right has several millennia of pluralist heritage to draw from. As Nobel-prize winning economist and Nussbaum's own patron, Amartya Sen remarked in the *Economist* in late 2005 "India has been fortunate in having a long and powerful argumentative tradition", which he sees as one of the cornerstones of successful representative government. The Hindu-right thus does not fear democracy, dissent or pluralism; rather it is ideologically predisposed to accept them within certain parameters.

Moreover, the Hindu right wing, including both political parties like the BJP and cultural organizations like the VHP represent a dynamic stream of cultural and intellectual development that attempts to adapt and re-interpret social realities to modern times. They are in no sense simple reactionaries and, in some instances, their ambivalence towards certain aspects of Western culture is understandable when considered in context.

My first trip to Indian occurred not only at a political watershed, but at a time of penetrating cultural changes as well. In the early 1990s, there were only a few channels on television. The faces on the screen were Indian and the shows mostly consisted of cricket matches, newscasts and religious dramas. The next time I visited India in 1994, everything had changed. Starting with Rupert Murdoch's Star TV and followed by other channels like HBO and MTV, India was bombarded with Western programming, with all their attendant sexual imagery. By the time I next arrived in 2005, the trash-ification of India's airwaves had climaxed with the addition of Fashion TV, a 24-hour television fashion catalogue, whose program "Midnight Hot" showcased swimwear and lingerie, sometimes with topless models. The show became a cult hit with many young Indian men I knew.

The advent of Western television had an immediate impact on the way people dressed and acted. In Benares in the early 90s, most young men wore the traditional *kurta pajama* but by the mid-90s many had switched to Western shirts and slacks. TV has exposed average Indians to a wide range of foreign and sometimes perplexing images. No wonder some segments of Indian society feel that their traditional culture is under attack from the West.

In all the books written about the BJP and the Hindu right, few authors stop to appreciate the importance of the rise of the BJP in the development of true multi-party democracy in South Asia. The Congress Party and the Gandhi-Nehru dynasty at its head, has controlled the central government in New Delhi for most of the sixty years of Indian independence. Democracy as we usually envision it, entails offering the electorate a choice. Until the rise in the Hindu right in the 70s and 80s, Indian voters had little choice in national elections; different versions of the Communist Party held sway in certain states (e.g., West Bengal and Kerala) but they did not often threaten the Congress Party hegemony on the national level. The Hindu right, regardless of its many shortcomings, has created a true multi-party democracy on the national level. Once Western scholars and writers have attained enough distance to see the issue from a sober perspective — one in which they hold their personal political biases in check — they must, I believe, ultimately accept this development as beneficial to India and the world.

Tempest in a Teapot: The Darjeeling Tea Trade

In the distant past, invaders descended upon the Indian subcontinent from the mountains. Aryans, Mughals and Macedonians have all poured through the high passes of the Himalayas and the Hindu Kush in search of conquest on the fertile plains of India. Today, however, the invasion moves in the other direction. As the average daily temperature on the Indian plain climbs towards 100 degrees, middle-class Indian tourists from Calcutta, Delhi, and Hyderabad ascend the Himalayan foothills in droves. Hill stations like Manali, Simla and Monsoorie receive a flood of visitors in May, as Indian universities and schools release their students for summer vacation.

In May 2005, Deborah and I joined this yearly exodus and traveled by train and jeep to Darjeeling, a hill station in the foothills of West Bengal. Located at about 7,000 feet above sea level on a north-facing ridge, Darjeeling is so different from the Ganges River plain that we feel like we have arrived in another country. Natives of Darjeeling looked, sounded and acted differently from people in Lucknow. Their facial features tended to be more Asiatic and they spoke mostly Nepali, Tibetan and Tamang rather than Hindi. Himalayan people smiled more often than people from Uttar Pradesh did and they struck me as more laid-back. Shopkeepers did not shout at us as we walked through the bazaar, nor did they barter as contentiously as merchants in Lucknow did — a pleasant surprise.

Darjeeling's reputation rests on tea. Unfortunately, due to a hereditary arrhythmia of the heart, I was under doctor's orders not to drink any. Thus, when the idea of writing about Darjeeling tea arose, I was not sure I could write about a beverage that I did not personally enjoy. In the end, I decided to ignore my doctor's advice for a while, at least until I had finished my research. As soon as I arrived in Darjeeling, I went looking for a cup of the best Darjeeling tea. I found it in a shack on a hillside outside of town. I do not have a discerning palate for tea, but even I could tell that a cup of unadulterated Super Fine Tipped Golden Flower Orange Pekoe fresh from the first flush (the pre-monsoon harvest) was qualitatively different from any other tea I have sipped. It had a heady, floral aroma and no bitter aftertaste.

Darjeeling's tea is the result of the area's unique climate, which is perfect for tea bushes. For optimum yield and flavor, tea bushes should grow in an environment that does not exceed 30 degrees or dip below 13 degrees Celsius. Tea plants appreciate sunlight, but prolonged exposure to strong sun dries out the tips of the plant, which are the most flavorful part of the bush.[1] Darjeeling's high altitude and frequent cloud cover create optimal conditions that are neither too sunny nor too gloomy.

Light and temperature are only part of the reason that Darjeeling tea tastes so good, however. An expert on the chemistry of tea notes that, "The flavor (taste and aroma) of tea is constituted of more than 500 chemicals, the relative proportion of which depends on the vagaries of the weather."[2] The complexity of the taste of tea means that only a few locations on earth have an optimal combination of soil, sun and rain for black tea. Darjeeling is one of them.

The British discovered the benefits of Darjeeling's climate and began growing crops here in the early 19th century. As more and more British investors arrived from Calcutta to make their fortune in the tea trade, they created a genteel culture of planters and plantations that met in exclusive clubs and built extravagant villas on hillsides around Darjeeling. Today, some hotels still serve a Raj-style high tea complete with tasteless cucumber sandwiches. The Darjeeling Zoo also celebrates tea's role in the city's history. For a few rupees, tourists can dress up in fake Nepali tribal garb and pose near a scraggly tea bush as a photographer snaps their picture.

Happy Valley

The actual life of a tea laborer, or *mazdoor*, is much less glamorous. My first meeting with plantation workers took place on a hillside just outside Darjeeling, in the fields of the Happy Valley Tea Estate. From a distance, I saw a group of women carrying large wicker baskets along a narrow path. As I watched, they stopped by the side of the road, placed their baskets down, crawled inside them and fell asleep. I hated to wake them, but I wanted to ask them some questions about their work at Happy Valley. I called out to them, and slowly, three sleepy women emerged from their baskets, rubbed their eyes and asked me what I wanted.

---

1   Barua, D.N. "Crop Management and Nutrition," *Tea Culture, Processing and Marketing* M.J. Mulky and V. S. Sharma ed. (Bombay: Hindustan Lever Research Foundation 1993), p. 51.

2   *Ibid.*, Menon, K.K.G. "The Tea Industry in India — How to Redesign a Native," p. 6.

They told me that a *mazdoor* at Happy Valley earns about 47 rupees a day (about one US dollar). Tea plantations are also responsible for providing some medical care, housing, maternity leave and educational assistance for the children of workers. How often plantations live up to these regulations is a matter of debate. Most *mazdoor* told me that they live in houses provided by the tea estate, and receive up to three months off for maternity leave. These same women, however, complain that they receive little or no regular medical care and that they must pay for their children's education out of their own pockets.

Despite long hours under the hot sun and heavy baskets of tea that laborers must carry to the processing factory, tea picking is often women's work. Planters often feel that women are more dependable and have a lower rate of absenteeism. Men, when they work at all, usually work in the tea factory, operating drying and processing machines. Increased automation has meant fewer and fewer factory jobs, and many men now wile away (and sometimes drink away) their days at home waiting for their wives to come home from work.

On the other side of Darjeeling lies Fullbari Tea Estate, which claims to be one of the oldest tea plantations in the Darjeeling area. When I visited, I discovered that being "the oldest" could have more than one meaning. The first *mazdoor* I met at Fullbari was 74-year-old Unita Thapa. She has been working at Fullbari for 41 years. When I asked when she would retire, she did not understand the question. I asked again, but the idea made no sense to her. Finally, a passerby explained that there is no such thing as retirement for a *mazdoor*.

I asked Unita if I could take a photo of her. She reached in to her basket and removed a pair of sunglasses. Unita looked so comical when she put them on that I laughed involuntarily. She explained to me that she had only one eye — the other was lost years ago in a factory accident — and she did not want to appear in a photo with one eye missing. I apologized for laughing. "You look great," I said. "In English, we would say that you look very 'hip'."

Walking farther down the slope, I met another group of *mazdoor* coming in from the fields. I began to ask them questions about their work. An old woman climbed up the hill with a package of timber on her back. I asked her age and the other women told me that she was 70. I wanted to ask the women more questions, but the supervisor arrived. Suddenly, the women stopped talking. One woman, who had been telling me about the difficulty of affording education for her children, stopped speaking in mid-sentence and refused even to tell me her name.

The supervisor, a heavy man with a bad habit of gesticulating wildly with his sickle, asked me what I wanted. When I told him that I wanted to talk to the workers, he responded that if I had any questions I could ask him.

"But I don't want to ask you," I said. "I want to talk to them."

"They not speak English," he said.

"That's okay," I countered, "I know some Hindi and a little Nepali."

"No questions," he said flatly.

My objections were of no use; I could not ask the workers questions. The more I argued, the more the overseer waved his sharpened blade in my face. He spoke quickly in Nepali and I could not follow him. I was unsure if he was simply carelessly gesturing with his sickle or if I was being deliberately threatened. In any event, the *mazdoors* would no longer talk openly with me, and I left.

The Gathering Storm

If life is tough for the *mazdoors* of Darjeeling, it looks like things will only get worse. As good as Darjeeling tea tastes, the tea industry in West Bengal is in steep decline. At least three Darjeeling tea plantations, including Happy Valley, planned to close in 2005 alone. Worried planters are often negligent about paying wages to their workers and increasingly reluctant to provide the benefits dictated by law. As a result, labor unions in Darjeeling regularly threaten strikes and agitation over working conditions and contracts.

Underlying this industry-wide malaise are changes in the global tea trade. Darjeeling produces high-quality tea primarily for export to Europe and America. Although there is no shortage of demand for tea in the First World, stiff competition from African growers has resulted in a worldwide shift away from Indian teas. Between 1950 and 1990, tea exports from India grew scarcely 18 million kilograms. Compare this to a roughly 200-million-kilogram increase in exports from Kenya and Malawi, and the magnitude of the problem becomes obvious. In the largest tea market, Great Britain, Indian imports have fallen from 115 million kg. to 30 million kg., while Kenyan imports have grown by a similar amount.[1]

Some economists theorize that the problem lies in an archaic labor code, which grants plantation workers in the Darjeeling area higher wages and more extensive benefits than their African counterparts. Most tea workers in India receive extensive labor protections from the Plantation Labor Act of 1951. In West Bengal, the state government — Communist Party of India (Marxist) or CPI(M) — has enforced the requirements of this legislation strictly. *Mazdoors* in Darjeeling must receive a set of benefits that include healthcare, housing and education assistance.

Tea companies and planters see these labor laws as harmful because they increase overhead costs of tea harvesting and make Darjeeling tea uncompetitive in the global market. Moreover, they note, North Indian *mazdoor* suffer from high absenteeism and low productivity.[2] Statistics show that productivity in North Indian tea plantations (1,600 kilograms per hectare) is significantly lower than that in South-Indian plantations (2,000 kg/ha) and African plantations (e.g., Ma-

---

1 *Ibid.*, Venkatachalam, K. "Tea — World Market," p. 188.
2 See Kar, R. K. "Absenteeism among Tea Labour: A Case Study in Cultural Ecology," *Plantation Labours of North-east India*, Badra, R. K. ed. (Dibrugarh: N. L. Publishers 1997).

lawi with 2,146 kg/ ha).[1] This year, growers have attempted to introduce wages linked to productivity but have met stiff resistance from labor unions.

Continued erosion of worker benefits in an attempt to make Indian labor competitive could backfire, however. Strikes are common in Darjeeling and friction between management and labor is sometimes so acerbic that factories remain closed for months, which only makes productivity levels worse. The hills of West Bengal have a long history of labor strife and agrarian rebellion against the central government. In the 1960s, a violent rebellion of local agricultural workers against plantation owners rocked the Naxalbari subdistrict of Darjeeling saw.[2] The uprising spawned the Naxalite movement, a radical communist insurgency that continues to simmer in West Bengal, Bihar and Andhra Pradesh.

In the 1980s widespread unrest spread across Darjeeling as Nepali tribes agitated for the creation of "Gorkhaland," an autonomous homeland for Nepali speakers. This movement spawned the Gurkha National Liberation Front (GNLF). Today just one more political party in the vast ocean of Indian politics, the GNLF was once a full-blown separatist rebellion that the government suppressed with a brutal anti-insurgency campaign. As the tea industry continues to founder, it is probable that the future will see continued agitation for increased regional autonomy.

Disenchanted with a communist party (Communist Party of India Marxist or CPIM) that seems to have gone soft on its proletarian ideology, many field workers today look to a more potent brand of communism. Indian security forces already speculate that Naxalite rebels and Nepali Maoists have conspired to share resources, coordinate offensives and create a "red corridor" in India that stretches from the West Bengal Hills to the Eastern Ghats.[3]

Rebutting Marxist economists who saw agrarian India as rife with revolutionary sentiment, author Paul Brass wrote:

> It is clear that agrarian unrest in India is very much the exception rather than the norm and that it is the extraordinary stability of agrarian society in the face of caste divisions, considerable inequalities, and pervasive poverty that requires explanation.[4]

Rural India is a vast and diverse place and generalizations about it are difficult to make. Still, I question whether Brass' conclusions hold for the hills of West Bengal. The current economic and social conditions conspire to make contemporary Darjeeling fertile ground, not for tea bushes, but for civil unrest.

---

1 Menon, K.K.G. "The Tea Industry in India — How to Redesign a Native," *Tea Culture, Processing and Marketing*, Mulky, M.J. and Sharma, V. S. ed. (Bombay: Hindustan Lever Research Foundation 1993), p. 4.

2 Brass, Paul. *The Politics of India Since Independence* (Cambridge: Cambridge University Press 1990), p. 323.

3 *"Naksaliyon ke Khilaaf Teen Rajyon men Saajhaa Abhiyaan," Dainik Jaagaran*, 5/15/05, p. 2.

4 Brass, p. 330-331.

TAZO: THE REINCARNATION OF TEA

Into this dreary scene strides the Starbucks Corporation, like an over-caffeinated messiah miraculously walking upon a sea of espresso. Darjeeling has attracted the attention of a Starbucks subsidiary calling itself "Tazo: The Reincarnation of Tea." Tazo had made agreements with local growers to provide tea for their high-end Tazo products, which sport names like "Awake," "Calm" and "Lotus." The company has also funded high-profile humanitarian-aid projects in the Darjeeling area such as Collaboration for the Hope and Advancement in India (CHAI), a West Bengal-based social initiative. The Tazo website (www. tazo.com) claims that CHAI operates in 24 villages.[1]

I met with a representative of Tazo in Darjeeling, intending to ask her why Tazo resists adopting the Fair-Trade label, a certification granted by an independent monitoring organization (TransFair USA) indicating that production took place under humane working conditions.[2] My Tazo contact did not appreciate my questions and refused to answer them, however. I have since tried to contact Tazo by phone and mail, but have never received an answer about their fair trade policy. Although Tazo may have reincarnated high-end tea importing as a viable business venture in America, any hope for fair treatment for Darjeeling's *mazdoors* — at least according to the widely accepted standards of TransFair — remains sadly moribund.

NILHAT HOUSE

It is unfair to blame all the problems of the Darjeeling tea business on field workers, or on labor unions, or on the self-serving practices of Western business conglomerates. The Indian exporters themselves are also partly responsible for the current crisis. Many exporters cut Darjeeling tea with cheaper teas from Nepal, Sri Lanka and Africa. The result is a glut of adulterated "Darjeeling" tea that uses the Darjeeling name for marketing purposes but lacks Darjeeling's unique taste. Diluted "Darjeeling" tea gives the real McCoy a bad reputation and weakens the marketing power of the Darjeeling label.

---

1 See www.tazo.com. Oddly, "...more than half [of these villages] have no connection to tea gardens."

2 For more on Starbuck's relationship to its third world labor force, see Clark, Taylor. *Starbucked: A Double Tall Tale of Caffeine, Commerce, and Culture* (New York, Little, Brown and Company 2007) pgs. 170-198. Considering a similar free fall in global coffee prices, Clark notes that while the Fair Trade movement is admirable in its goals, it will probably have little lasting effect on the conditions of coffee growers. Recent volatility in the global price of coffee, in Clark's view, arises from numerous causes, such as America's withdrawal from the International Coffee Agreement in 1989, the sudden glut of Vietnamese *robusta* coffee and global weather patterns. Clark defends the charge that some of Starbuck's coffee growers use child labor, making the remarkable claim, "for rural children in Latin America, working with your family to harvest coffee is as much a part of growing up as naptime or Little League is in America," *ibid.* p. 179.

Many Americans and Europeans have probably never tried authentic Darjeeling tea. If they had, they might be willing to pay a few extra dollars for its distinctive flavor. The Indian government has passed The Geographical Indicator of Goods Registration and Protection Act, which would brand Darjeeling tea and require all tea sold as Darjeeling tea to contain a high percentage of tea from Darjeeling itself. To be effective, however, this Act awaits recognition of international-trade organizations and governing bodies. Like French Champagne, Darjeeling tea may someday be an authentic and valued commodity that does not lie about its origins.

To find out more about the tea-export business, I took a trip to downtown Calcutta. For over a hundred years, most Darjeeling tea has ended up at the tea auction that takes place every Monday and Tuesday at Nilhat House on R.N. Mukherjee Road. There we met Mr. R.K. Kasera, a 4th-generation tea exporter, who showed us the various chambers and functions of Nilhat House. Administered by the Calcutta Tea Traders Association (CTTA), the weekly tea auction takes place in small auditoriums, where buyers bid on pre-published lots of tea from tea estates throughout Bengal. Different types of tea come up for auction at different times of the day. Darjeeling tea goes on the block on early Monday morning, cheaper CTC tea in the early afternoon.[1] Upstairs in the sampling room, workers packed small bags of tea that represented the next week's offerings. The CTTA sends the samples to registered buyers who then test them and plan their bids.

"Registered buyers?" I asked Mr. Kasera, "Registered by whom?"

The CTTA, of course, Mr. Kasera told me. It requires a half-million rupees to become a registered buyer and another three lakh rupees (a lakh, is equal to 100,000) as a security payment. This steep fee is required of everybody, even a 4th-generation tea exporter like Mr. Kasera. Moreover, registration by the CTTA is selective and they reserve the right to reject applicants for any reason at all.[2] The Calcutta tea auction is not an open market at all but a clique of well-connected Bengali traders.

Mr. Kasera supported the Geographical Indicator Act, believing that it would eventually raise the value of Darjeeling tea. He was less enthusiastic about the Labor Act of 1951. He said that this legislation artificially raises the cost of tea. In fact, he estimated that he pays 15 cents of "social cost" for every kilogram of tea that he buys. When I described for him the conditions for field workers that I saw in Darjeeling, he responded by saying, "The government should take on these costs. Why are we responsible for this problem? That is why we have a government."

---

1 CTC stands for Crush, Tear, Curl and refers to the method by which the tea-leaf is processed. CTC teas tend to be cheaper than teas processed by other methods.
2 See http://www.cttacal.org/rules.asp, the CTTA's website.

Before I left Mr. Kasera's office, he offered me a cup of tea. He told me it was from Darjeeling, but it was bitter and did not taste like the Darjeeling tea I had tasted. Perhaps somebody had mixed it with African tea. As I sipped, I thought about 74-year-old Unita Thapa with her one eye and missing teeth, working herself to death in the fields of the Fullbari Estate. Then I thought about Mr. Kasera and his anger over 15 cents of "social cost." I put my cup down and decided at that moment to stop drinking tea. The doctor was right; it does not agree with my heart.

The Song Remains the Same: Bombay, Business and the Protestant Work Ethic

For some people, India holds an ongoing fascination that does not lessen with time. In March 2006, retired former US Ambassador and Assistant Secretary of State for South Asia Phillips Talbot returned to India at the age of 91 to attend a meeting of the Asia Society's 16th Asian Corporate Conference in Bombay.[1] I had met Phil on several occasions in America and he arranged for my wife Deborah and me to attend the conference as well. Prime Minister Manmohan Singh and other dignitaries were scheduled to speak at the opening dinner, and the occasion gave us a perfect excuse to travel to one of India's most storied cities.

You cannot fly from Lucknow to Bombay directly, so we boarded the Pushpak Express for the 24-hour train trip and spent the night rolling through the dusty hills of Madhya Pradesh.[2] During the long ride, I caught up with my reading. Although I had visited Bombay once long ago, I knew the city mostly through books. Bombay is a massive city and most recent books about it are appropriately weighty. In the last half-century a number of thick volumes have appeared, attempting to approximate the extensive sprawl of the city with large numbers of pages. Well-known author Salman Rushdie, a Bombay resident by birth, has set many of his novels (e.g., *Midnight's Children*) in Bombay. All of his books — including his latest, *Shalimar the Clown* — are amusing page-turners and are immensely

---

1 I should also mention that Phil is a former fellow and an honorary trustee of the Institute of Current World Affairs, to which I also belong and which provided funding for the initial research for this book. Phil is the author of many books on India including, most recently, *An American Witness to India's Partition* (Delhi: Sage 2007).

2 With the proliferation of domestic airlines in India, I am certain that this will change soon, or has already changed.

popular with both Indians and Westerners. His work is too vaudevillian for my taste, however. When I reach the conclusion of one of his books, I often feel like I have finally heard the (mildly amusing) punch line of a 900-page knock-knock joke.

Suketu Mehta's *Maximum City* offers a more sober look at contemporary Bombay. Mehta, a non-resident Indian (NRI) living in New York City, returned to the city of his birth to write the book. Although *Maximum City* had its moments, it disappointed me. Mehta is of Indian origin, but he is perhaps only as authentically Indian as I am authentically Irish — meaning only in the genetic sense and without any accompanying cultural insight (set me down in Dublin without a map and I might as well be in downtown Saigon). Mehta's take on Bombay is thus sadly pedestrian; it is easy to imagine any visitor having similar experiences. He deliberately and somewhat disingenuously seeks out prostitutes and gangsters to lend his middle-class, wine-sipping existence some grit.

Ironically, the novel *Shantaram* by the Australian author Gregory David Roberts has a more authentic voice. An escaped convict, Roberts fled to Bombay in the 1980s to evade the Australian police. With limited resources, and suffering bouts of heroin addiction, he ended up in one of Bombay's slums, living in a small hut without running water or electricity. While thus down and out, he learned fluent Hindi and Marathi and opened an amateur medical clinic (he had almost no formal training) for the residents of the slum. Local gangsters had other plans for him, however. They soon learned about Robert's troubled past and enlisted him as an enforcer for a shadowy underworld kingpin named Kheder Bhai. His adventures in the Bombay mafia make for interesting reading, especially when he takes a job as a gunrunner for the Mujahideen in Afghanistan. Beyond the true-crime stories, Roberts displays a universal curiosity about everything around him, from beggars, to lepers, to film stars. The result is a broad, sometimes disturbed, portrait of the city painted by a man in the midst of an epic battle with his own demons.

Perhaps the best literary depiction of Bombay is not a large book, but the short stories of a rarely translated writer from Kashmir named Saddat Hasan Manto. Writing in Urdu around the time of partition in 1947, Manto was an obscure and little-liked literary figure (many of his contemporaries considered him a pornographer) that died penniless, of alcoholism, in 1955. For those who take the trouble to dig up the few English translations of his work, however, Manto is a profound discovery — tawdry, heart wrenching, Brechtean, and unsparing in his grimness. He wrote about the Bombay he knew, a city of prostitutes, pimps, gangsters and hedonists, a city where "no one takes any interest in anyone else. If you are dying in your room, no one will ask about you. Even if one of your neighbors is murdered, you can rest assured you won't hear about it."[1]

I was thinking about this passage as Deborah and I checked into The Strand Hotel on the Bombay waterfront. The Asia Society's conference occurred in the middle of a five-day test match between the Indian and English cricket teams and the hotels were booked with cricket fans. I remembered spending a lost weekend as a student at The Strand and, as no guidebook listed it, rooms were still available. Unfortunately, it seemed as if the staff had not changed the bedding or painted the walls in the decade since I last stayed there. Our room was tiny, the TV did not work and the closet was only three feet tall. Strangest was the shower, which stood in such close proximity to the toilet that washing put you in danger of falling in. I wondered whether anybody would notice if we *did* die in this room.

If The Strand was somewhat uncomfortable, however, it at least lay at the center of Bombay's nightlife district. We stopped in at Indigo, a trendy watering hole, for a cocktail. The first thing that struck Deborah about the crowd was its wardrobe. Both the *deshi* (local) and *videshi* (foreign) women at Indigo showed just as much élan and style as women in New York City. At the bar, we met a British NRI (non-resident Indian), in town for the cricket match. When Deborah told him that she had been living in Lucknow, he was incredulous. "Lucknow!" he said. "Wow! What do women do on Saturday night in Lucknow?"

"They iron their burqas," Deborah quipped.

Back in our tiny hotel room, I thought about my upcoming meeting with Phillips Talbot. Phil is an impressive individual and he has offered me invaluable advice on numerous occasions. I remember meeting Phil one night for dinner at the Century Club in Manhattan.[2] After dinner, I walked with Phil to Grand Central Station, where I intended to hop the 5-train back to the Bronx. When I offered to hail a cab for Phil for the ride back to his Upper East Side apartment, he would not hear of it but insisted on taking the bus.

I gazed for a moment at Phil, who, in his tenth decade of human life, was a bit unsteady on his feet. When I asked him why he was taking the bus, he replied, "Because it is only a dollar."

Displaying my unfortunate habit of blurting out impolitic questions I asked, "What are you saving it for, Phil?"

He looked perplexed for a moment, as if he did not understand the question. "For my children," he answered finally.

---

1 Manto, Saadat Hasan. *Bombay Stories*, translated by Matthew Reeck and Aftab Ahmed (publication pending), p. 52.

2 The Century Club appears briefly in Vonnegut's novel *Slapstick or Lonesome No More!* where the grand "haven for men of power and wealth" becomes a social club for people with the middle name Daffodil. See Vonnegut, Kurt. *Slapstick: Or Lonesome No More!* (New York: Delacorte Press 1976), p. 182.

I wanted to reply that his children, all successful individuals in their own right, would survive without his taxi fare, but I bit my tongue. I realized that I was witnessing a deeply entrenched part of Phil's personality, a sense of duty that did not recognize even the existential limitations of human endeavor.

A short time later, I was flipping through a copy of Max Weber's *The Protestant Ethic and the Spirit of Capitalism*, a landmark work on the relationship between religious doctrine and fiscal behavior, when I came across the following passage:

> If you ask them what is the meaning of their restless activity, why they are never satisfied with what they have, thus appearing so senseless to any purely worldly view of life, they would perhaps give the answer, if they know any at all: "to provide for my children and grand-children." But more often and, since that motive is not peculiar to them...more correctly, simply that business with its continuous work has become a necessary part of their lives.[1]

Fairly or unfairly, Phil, a practicing Presbyterian, has since become a symbol of the Protestant work ethic for me, an embodiment of this restless acquisitiveness I find so strange. By way of contrast to Phil, I am immune to the Protestant work ethic. Had I been in his position on that night I would have taken the taxi, perhaps even taking a ride around Central Park just for the fun of it. Thrift does not come easily to me, and thrift without a terrestrial motive, as displayed by Phil, seems akin to madness. Of course, this difference also partially explains why Phil lives on the Upper East Side and I spend my time in the Bronx.

THE CONFERENCE

The next morning, Deborah and I took a taxi to the Grand Hyatt, a five-star hotel near the airport where the Asia Society had scheduled its conference. The Hyatt is miles from The Strand and for over an hour we crawled through in nightmarish traffic through miles of slums. In much of the city, squatters had taken over the sidewalks and built rows of two-story, tin shacks that stretched along the streets, long slivers of misery and dysentery.

Writer Fareed Zakaria had recently remarked regarding economic development in India, "You can feel the change even in the middle of the slums."[2] Looking at the endless progression of ramshackle huts with ragged inhabitants staring hopelessly back at me over open sewers, I was skeptical. When a beggar girl approached our taxi at an intersection, I thought I would test Zakaria's claim by asking her if she "felt the change." Before I could speak, however, she pressed her face against the window and broke into song.

Jingle Bells Jingle Bells,

Rupee deejee-ay! (Please give money)

---

1 Weber, Max. *The Protestant Ethic and the Spirit of Capitalism* (New York: Scribner 1958), p. 70.

2 Zakaria, Fareed. "India Rising," *Newsweek*, 3/6/2006, p. 35.

Santa Cruz Santa Cruz,

Mujhe dejee-ay! (Please give it to me).[1]

Her musical composition amused me but I did not want to encourage her begging. I applauded her effort and waved to her as the taxi drove off.

Once we reached the Hyatt, repeated security checks delayed us further. By the time we did get inside, the Prime Minister's guards had locked the door to the auditorium and we were directed to an adjacent room with a live video feed. In his usual somnolent speaking style, Prime Minister Singh made special mention of Phillips Talbot's return to India and a few other innocuous remarks. A long list of additional dignitaries (including the Governor of Iowa) blew extensive remarks about "strategic partnerships" into the already sufficiently hot air of Bombay.

In the speeches and in private conversation with delegates during the reception that followed I heard the same statistic over and over again — the emerging Indian middle class was made up of over 300 million people. I did not know where this statistic came from, but the delegates to the conference seemed fond of it.[2] Three-hundred million is approximately the population of America, and perhaps the delegates liked to think that the direct foreign investment they were promoting had created a little America in Asia, a group of 300 million people with enough income to buy toothpaste, cell telephones and skin whitening cream (a popular cosmetic in South Asia) and to charge it all on their credit cards — now offered in large numbers by Indian banks.

Most delegates believed that direct foreign development would soon have a broad effect upon the poor in India and the atmosphere of the conference was permeated with a sense of mission that could only be called "Mahatma Gandhi Syndrome." The Western executives I met felt not only that they were making money from their Indian investments, but that they were also lifting up the suffering Indian underclass. I had found this attitude in Uttar Pradesh as well. I once spoke to an American woman who bought, packaged and exported herbal tea in Lucknow. She was so proud of the imagined effect that her activities were having on the rural poor that it was only with great reluctance she admitted that her selfless toil on behalf of the downtrodden was also highly profitable.[3]

---

1 Santa Cruz is a neighborhood in Bombay.

2 As it turns out, the delegates were exaggerating. The size of the Indian middle class is anywhere between 55 million and 250 million, depending upon the definition of "middle class." The higher estimate represents households with an income of 70,000 rupees a year, the lower represents household with an income of over 140,000 rupees. See Sridharan, E. "The Growth and Sectoral Composition of India's Middle Class: Its Impact on the Politics of Economic Liberalization," *India Review*, Vol. 3, No. 4, 2004. Cited by Guha, p. 689.

3 Similarly with Anand Giridharadas' article on Reliance owner Mukesh Ambani, "Indian to the Core, and an Oligarch," *The New York Times, Sunday Business*, 6/15/2008, p. 1. Giridharadas' article begins with Ambani watching his cricket team play from a private box and wondering, "Can we really banish abject poverty in this country?"

The next day, on my way to the second day of the conference, my taxi stopped at the same intersection where the same beggar girl was holding out her palm. Seeing me through the car window, she smiled in recognition. She approached the car and began another, more complex rendition of "Jingle Bells," now with the accompaniment of another young girl.

Jingle Bells, Jingle Bells,

Roti Chahi-ay! (We want bread)

This time I could not resist them and rolled down the window to hand them a few coins. They grabbed the money and inserted their hands into the cab; asking for more and resisting any attempt to roll the window back up. Several more beggar children joined them, all holding down the window so that I could not escape them. The driver turned around in his seat, "The air conditioning is running! You are wasting the air conditioning!" he yelled frantically. I tried to pry their fingers off the glass, but the beggar girls saw this as an opportunity to hold my hand. They laughed and started singing louder, now confident that I liked their rendition of Jingle Bells. "Jingle Bells Jingle Bells *Rupee Deejee-ay!!!*" By the time the light turned green and the car sped off, they had lightened both my heart and my pockets.

BHOLU: EX-PICKPOCKET

Back at the Strand Hotel, I managed to get two stations on the television by fiddling with the knobs. Unfortunately, there was not much to see except cricket. Between overs, I noticed that one station was playing a new commercial for a credit card issued by the State Bank of India. The ad showed a young man staggering through the streets of a large Indian city with a heavy load on his back. The next scene showed the same man struggling to push a cart up a steep hill while children harassed him. Finally, the ad depicted the man with a load of bricks on his head, working at a construction site. At the end, the young man's name and occupation appeared on the screen as "Bholu: Ex-pickpocket." The screen then flashed an image of the new State Bank of India's credit card with the caption, "Welcome to a cashless world." The next morning I found a printed version of the ad in the newspaper in which a rickshaw puller named Babu (also labeled an "ex-pickpocket") struggled to drag a fat, smug-looking man and his daft-looking son up a hill.[1]

---

1 The ad begs the question how, in a cashless world, these passengers intend on paying Babu, who is surely unable to process a credit-card payment. The ad also makes me wonder about Babu's future. If he is no longer able to engage in petty theft and day labor is shameful, the only viable option for him is to update his skills and learn to perpetrate credit-card fraud. This, in fact, is what many people in Babu's position have done. International credit-card companies have issued over 40 million cards to Indian consumers over the last 15 years and credit card fraud of all types is rampant. See *Times of India, Lucknow Edition*, 5/29/05, p. 1.

If the brave new world of the State Bank of India is cashless, it may also be heartless. While the ads intended to show the poetic justice of former criminals reduced to thankless employment, they contained a disturbing subtext. The day laborers portrayed in these ads are condemned to their tasks by their own ethical failings. Blue-collar work appears as a shameful activity, the result of prior indiscretions. This idea is not an invention of the State Bank of India, of course; it is the philosophical lynchpin of the worst aspects of the caste system, the only difference being that Bholu's fault is in this life rather than in the previous one. As one editorial about these ads in the *Hindustan Times* remarked, "It is as though India has taken its worst, most deeply entrenched, most retrograde aspect and held it up as a virtue."[1]

Watching these messages on television about Bholu, ex-pickpocket, I had a type of epiphany about economics, Weber, religion, India and capitalism. Max Weber argued that religious doctrine has an indirect influence on people's attitudes towards money and commerce. He suggests that Calvinists in Reformation Europe developed a new and unique attitude towards the accumulation of personal wealth that resulted in capitalism, meant here not as a system of commerce, but as a psychological state, the *spirit of capitalism*. Capitalism for Weber meant more than just a system of free trade and investment. It meant that the acquisition of personal wealth was not only acceptable — in a way that it had not been in Catholic Europe, which often glorified poverty — but an unqualified spiritual asset.

I wondered how India fit in with this scheme. In the introduction to *Protestantism and the Spirit of Capitalism* Weber mentions India and Indian civilization surprisingly often, but only by way of excluding it from the Western practice of capitalism proper. India has developed numerals, he suggests, but not accounting, and it has discovered statecraft but not nationhood; India has knowledge of commerce but not industry in the proper sense. The spirit of capitalism never possessed India as it had Europe, Weber argues, and Indians were not predisposed to modern capitalism by virtue of their culture.[2]

Weber admits, however, that he has little understanding of Indian thought and that he must rely on faulty and partial translations of Indian religious texts. Moreover, his understanding of Indian culture had no personal element to it; he had never traveled to India. I wondered whether he would have re-written sections of his book if he could see India today, with its soaring Sensex stock exchange and burgeoning IT industry. From what I saw at the Asia Society's business conference, Indians take to capitalism as readily as fish to water.

While Calvinism and Hinduism are different in many respects, they share similar solutions to a theological conundrum called The Problem of Evil or theo-

---

1 Roy, Anita. "Pickpockets All," *Hindustan Times: New Delhi Edition*, 4/22/06, p. 10.
2 Weber, Max. *The Protestant Ethic and the Spirit of Capitalism* (New York: Scribner 1958).

dicy. In summary, the Problem of Evil admits a seeming rational inconsistency between an all-powerful benevolent God and a suffering humanity. How could a kind-hearted deity, for example, allow a young, seemingly innocent child to develop a debilitating health problem? You are left with a God who is either limited in power or who is jarringly unsympathetic to our, sometimes pathetic, human condition. Or, as the playwright Archibald MacLeish quips in his drama *J.B.*:

If God is God, He is not good,

If God is good, He not God,

Take the even, take the odd.[1]

The Problem of Evil runs like a recurring theme through much of Christian theology. Calvin sidesteps the issue by postulating an unforgiving predestination. Every individual is fated for paradise or damnation and nothing — not sacraments, nor priests nor Christ himself — can prevent it. All of creation conspires to promote the glory of a mysterious and aloof God, whose ultimate designs are hidden from both the saved (or "the Elect" in Calvinist lingo) and the damned.

In human society we can only know the saved from the damned by their fortunes. Like the Old Testament Jehovah, the Calvinist God rewards his chosen with prosperity in this life. This means that a believing Calvinist needed to show his elevated spiritual status with constant industry and the obsessive accumulation of wealth — wealth not generated for enjoyment but for spiritual reasons. To participate in the glory of God a person had to follow a "calling" and work steadily within a certain profession.[2]

There was no reason to lose too much sleep over the plight of the economically destitute in Calvinist thought.

> ...it [the spirit of capitalism] gave him [the believing Calvinist] the comforting assurance that the unequal distribution of the goods of this world was a special dispensation of Divine Providence, which in these differences, as in particular grace, pursued secret ends unknown to men. Calvin himself had made the much-quoted statement that only when the people, i.e. the mass of laborers and craftsmen, were poor did they remain obedient to God.[3]

Hinduism has a similar approach to the Problem of Evil. The Laws of Manu explains that the caste system arises from the sacrificial vivisection of a primeval man, *Parusha* (see "Caste and Communal Poltics of Lonesome No More!" above).[4] An individual's caste and fortunes in life arise from the workings of *karma*, literally action, but meaning in the context of Hinduism, accumulated spiritual merit or de-merit. A person's misfortunes in this life are ultimately temporary and one

---

1 See MacLeish, Archibald. *J.B.* (New York: Houghton MIfflin 1989).

2 Calvin and other Protestants constructed the idea of "calling" from obscure biblical and Apocryphal references, particularly in the Book of Ecclesiasticus, the Wisdom of Jesus ben Sirach.

3 Weber, p. 177.

4 See Lanman, p. 57.

need not fret unnecessarily on their behalf. "Those who are wise lament neither the living nor the dead," says the *Bhagavad Gita.*[1]

Hinduism, like Calvinism, tends towards determinism; transcendent forces beyond human comprehension map the course of our lives. Other elements of Weber's characterization of Calvinism are also present in mainstream Hinduism. The idea of work for work's sake, for example, is not foreign to the Hindu religion. In fact, the idea that one must work without attachment to the "fruits of work" as expressed in the *Bhagavad Gita* sounds almost identical to the Calvinist's quest for wealth for the sake of wealth.[2] Effort in worldly affairs is a part of an individual's natural course through life. *Artha*, or wealth, is one of the four legitimate goals of life, pursued by a fully mature householder.

When the religiously conservative Bharatiya Janata Party arose in the early 1990s, it struggled to develop an economic platform in accord with Hindu religious ideals. The result, "integral humanism" includes elements of economic isolationism (*svadeshii*), but, in general, accepts free-market economics without serious issue.[3] For most Hindus, their traditional culture and religion is no barrier to modern economic life, and, in certain aspects, Hinduism seems equivalent to Calvinist Protestantism as a socio-religious inducement to entrepreneurship.

Which brings us back to Bholu: Ex-Pickpocket. In these advertisements I saw the unlikely marriage of the Protestant work ethic and the Hindu concept of metempsychosis. The rich deserve their wealth while the poor are poor because they are predestined for damnation (or reincarnated sinners). In the face of the man in the rickshaw, I could see the offspring of this union, the 300-million-strong Indian middle class that the delegates at the conference were so fond of mentioning, a middle class that is too often overconfident, smug and without a sense of responsibility to the poor.

HELLO AND GOOD-BYE

Before we left Bombay, we had dinner with Phil Talbot at an Italian restaurant in the lobby of the Grand Hyatt Hotel. The meeting was both a reunion and a farewell. While Phil was returning to India, my wife, Deborah, was making plans for her escape. After months of power failures, mysterious insects in the bathroom, lizards on the walls, ants in the cupboard, exploding generators, daily political agitations, bad internet connections, dust storms, 120-degree heat, undrinkable water, dysfunctional plumbing, bacterial dysentery, and a wide array of additional inconveniences that make up daily life in Uttar Pradesh, she

---

1 Prabhupada, Swami Bhaktivedanta, trans. *Bhagavad Gita as it Is* (New York: Bhaktivedanta Book Trust 1972), p. 21.

2 *Ibid.,* p. 103.

3 See Hansen, Thomas. "The Ethics of Hindutva and the Spirit of Capitalism," *The BJP and the Compulsions of Politics,* Hansen, Thomas and Jaffrelot, Christophe ed. (Delhi: Oxford University Press 1998).

had reached the end of her patience. *The Strand Hotel* was the final straw; she had bought a return ticket to America and would depart several days after the conclusion of the conference.

Over dinner I asked Phil about his meetings in the 1940s with Mahatma Gandhi. As a researcher and later, as a journalist, Phil met all the well-known personages of the Independence movement, including Mahatma Gandhi, Jawaharlal Nehru, Mohammad Jinnah and Sarat Bose. Knowing that he had met each of these famous people personally, I asked Phil if there were any anecdotes that he could tell about them. I wanted to hear his impressions about Gandhi's bald head, Nehru's aloofness, Jinnah's tippling and Bose's reputed ill-temper. Phil was every inch the diplomat, however. His recollections were almost purely factual, polite, and lacked any subjective element.

Phil's careful way of speaking was the result of years as an ambassador and a member of the Kennedy and Johnson administrations. All diplomats, after all, speak in a manner designed not to offend. The political argot placates rather than provokes, suggests rather than insinuates, evades as often as it engages. I knew that discretion was a professional requirement for people like Phil, but I could not help but feel disappointed.

Throughout my visit to Bombay, the song of the street children echoed in my head. As I discovered with literature about Bombay, the greatest truths are often contained in the shortest expressions. I found the most profound insight on India's economic future encapsulated, not in any of the speeches of Manmohan Singh, but in the verses of the children on the street corner. "Jingle bells, jingle bells, *Rupee deejee-ay.*" In this ditty I heard all the elements of the Indian entrepreneurial spirit, the willingness to innovate, the ability to adapt, the strength to persevere, the boldness to demand, and the stoicism to do it all with a smile. More importantly, these girls were too young for the State Bank of India to accuse them of being ex-thieves.

Their version of *Jingle Bells* was also a sad song. The rising tide may be lifting some boats in India. It may be lifting 300 million of them, if you can believe it. The tide is not, however, going to lift these girls any time soon — let's be honest — ever. Even if these girls live as long as Phillips Talbot, not one of them will ever rent out a room at the Grand Hyatt, go for a vacation in Goa, or have a drink at *Indigo.* Nor will any of the large corporations at the Asia Society's conference ever offer them work, maintain (or even build) their slum's sewage system, provide them comprehensive health care or award them a pension.

The *depth* of India's poverty often escapes the experts' attention. If these girls and millions others like them can expect only unending deprivation in their life-times, then all of the recent economic development probably holds little interest for them. They are not "feeling the change." Worse, on TV and in the movies they can see the *nouveau riche* of Bombay and Bangalore enjoying the fruits of an economy that excludes them. Impoverished Indians, especially in a wide band of eastern India called the Red Corridor, have thus increasingly looked to left-wing political movements and a resurgent Naxalite (Maoist) insurgency for their future. The Naxalites and associated groups are responsible for a dramatic upswing in violence over the last several years. The trouble in states like Andhra Pradesh and Chhatisgarh had become so pronounced by 2006 that Prime Minister Singh called it "...an even greater threat to India than militancy in Jammu and Kashmir..."[1]

If an Indian countryside overrun by a popular Maoist insurgency sounds fantastic, it also sounded like a far-out scenario in Nepal ten years ago. The possibility of widespread rural chaos gives the issue of wealth distribution added urgency. How and when the recent economic windfall will spread to the less fortunate is still an open question, and one for which nobody seems to have a viable answer. Meanwhile, the Naxalites widen their popular support, improve their tactics and acquire sophisticated weaponry. In their determination to reap the benefits of Ricardian economic theory, the corporations at the Asia Society's conference run a distinct chance of inadvertently proving Marx right instead.

In the week after the Asia Society wound up its annual conference, the Sensex (Bombay stock exchange) passed 11,000 for the first time, India lost the five-day test match to England, leftist rebels attacked a police station and jail in the impoverished state of Chhattisgarh, 300 million Indians decided how to spend their disposable income, two beggar girls on a street corner and millions just like them wondered where their next meal would come from, Sonia Gandhi resigned her post in parliament, the Prime Minister traveled to Amritsar to visit the Golden Temple, Phillips Talbot left for Goa to visit friends and Deborah boarded a jet and returned to New York City. As for myself, I bought a train ticket for the long ride back to Lucknow, Uttar Pradesh — the other India — where development is scattershot and five-star hotels are few, but where your neighbors will surely notice your passing.

---

1 "Code Red: Naxals, the biggest threat," *Hindustan Times*, 3/26/06, p. 17.

Sona's Blue Refrigerator

One morning at breakfast, I looked over the top of my copy of the *Times of India* to see my servant Sona crouched on the floor eating her morning *paraathaa* (flatbread). Servants in Lucknow habitually sit on the floor and I had willfully repressed my feelings of repugnance for this practice, telling myself that "When in Rome...." On this morning, however, seeing Sona crouched on the ground while I sat at the table was unbearable.[1]

It might have been all the empty chairs; my wife had left for America and did not plan to return. We had separated and my life seemed empty. To make matters worse, many of my friends had left for the Himalayas to escape the summer heat and I felt isolated, depressed about my marital problems, and in need of some companionship.

So on that morning, I asked Sona if she would like to join me at the table.

"*Nahin Bhai, nahin*" she said, shaking her head vigorously. No, brother, no.

I tried again. "Sona," I said, "I know that this is normal in your culture, but I find it strange to have you sitting over there like that. Please come sit here with me."

She smiled shyly, stood up and mounted the chair next to me, the legs of her four-foot ten-inch body dangling above the kitchen tiles. She seemed nonplussed.

"Have you never sat in a chair before?" I teased her. Then, in a fit of inspiration, I added, "See, now we are *baraabar* (equal)!"

"Yes *bhai, baraabar*," she said with an expression I could not read.

---

[1] I realize the term servant sounds archaic and insensitive to the Western ear. The Hindi word (*naukar*) remains in common usage, however, and does not carry the same negative connotations as it does in the West.

The next morning, with no encouragement from me, Sona made her breakfast and joined me at the table.

"*Bhai*," she said, looking with a grimace at her *chai* (tea), "There is not much sugar in my tea."

"The sugar is in the cabinet." I answered.

"Yes, I know," she said. "Go get some, *bhai*. I am tired."

This was only the first of a list of extraordinary demands that Sona made on me over the next few days. In fact, once Sona got used to sitting on chairs, she did little else, and the furniture she was now so fond of reclining upon remained un-dusted. She asked for a sari as a gift for the Divali holiday. When I bought her one, she told me that color was wrong and that I should get her another one. Unnerved by her sudden change in attitude, I decided that I had to put my foot down. At breakfast a few days later, I looked across the table at her, and said hesitantly "Sona...maybe you should sit on the floor today."

She pretended not to hear me. That evening I came home to find her sleeping on the sofa with the air conditioner running full blast. As I watched her lying there, I realized that something irreversible had occurred in our relationship. I was out of my depth. I did not know what to do with her. I could not bring myself to fire her and I was not sure I could survive in Lucknow making my own meals but, on the other hand, I did not want to pay her for nothing.

Asking somebody to eat a meal with you does not sound like a very daring act, but for a white foreigner to become involved in the life of a low-caste woman in this area of north India cut across a number of barriers and violated a number of taboos. I worried that my experiment in social egalitarianism would end in disaster. I told a friend, a Western researcher, that I had invited Sona to sit at my table and had tried to break down the barriers of caste and class. My friend thought I had made a serious mistake and that I was breaking the *dharma*, the rules of society.

Sona had always been difficult to deal with in her own charming way. She may have been low-caste and illiterate, but she always stood her ground when an argument occurred. On one occasion, I had sent her to the market during the monsoons to buy me mangoes. Mangoes are a delicacy in Lucknow and I craved a particular local variety. She returned with mangoes that were soft and almost in-edible. I let her know that I was displeased and I insinuated that she had bought rotten mangoes and pocketed the difference.

She would have none of it. She told me that mango season was nearing its end, mango prices had skyrocketed and she was lucky to find any at all. I did not believe her. After a series of sharp exchanges, I told her that, if she were not going to be honest going to the market, I would do it myself.

She shrugged. "Go ahead," she said. "You go to the market and buy your own mangoes."

At that point, I was ready to fire her. Before I did, however, I had to put my mind at ease about the correctness of my position. I went to the market and, much to my horror, discovered that Sona was correct. The mango season had ended and mangoes, when they could be found at all, had extraordinary prices.

I returned, crestfallen, to my apartment. I had a hard time admitting my mistake. Sona, knowing what had surely happened at the market, found the few, squishy mangoes that I had managed to buy in the back of the refrigerator.

"Ah yes," she said flashing her betel nut-stained smile, "very nice mangoes you have bought, *bhai*. They are wonderful! Where did you find them?"

She kept her job. Moreover, she never let me forget my mistake. "Are you going to buy mangoes?" She would ask me each time I was going out the door.

I had to wait a few months to get my revenge. One morning I walked out of my study to find Sona lying on the floor, theatrically clutching her stomach. "Oh, *bhai*," she said. "I need to go to the doctor."

I suspected that her rolling around on the ground was a performance. She probably needed some sort of medication and was too proud to ask me for the extra money, so she was pretending to be at death's doorstep. Still, having often been in the position of being a struggling writer without health insurance in America, I understood her problem and was more than willing to help, with or without the theatrics.

I loaded her into a rickshaw and took her to the nearest clinic. The doctor performed a perfunctory examination and recommended a series of diagnostic tests. A few days later Sona showed up with the test results in her hand. Illiterate, she could not read the results and asked me to tell her what the form said. Holding the paper before me, I saw that Sona suffered from *e. coli*, an everyday bacterial infection often contracted from unsafe drinking water and easily treated with antibiotics. That was not what I said to Sona, however.

"Oh, Sona," I said, "You do not have long."

"What do you mean?" she asked.

"This is very serious," I said with a wink. "Perhaps you should spend some time with your family..."

Winking did not mean anything to her, however, and she began to cry. Suddenly I felt mean spirited and tried to explain that it was just a stupid joke. My explanation did not make any sense to Sona, however, and, in the heat of the conversation, I could not remember the necessary phrases in Hindi. Sona thought I was just trying to make her feel better about her failing health and only cried harder. It took a long time to sort it all out. By the time it had blown over, I had learned my lesson — there was nothing funny about a sudden illness ending your life for people like Sona; she had probably seen this type of death often enough.

Not long after I invited Sona to sit in a chair, she insisted I buy *kabaabs* at least once a week. Lucknowi *kabaabs* are renowned throughout India. The chef pulverizes and spices the meat, then cooks it on a skillet with oil. *Paraathaa*, or flat bread, cooked on the under-side of a wok-like pan, usually accompanies the *kabaab*. Although I began my sojourn in India as a vegetarian, I found it impossible to maintain my dietary restrictions when faced with Lucknowi *kabaabs*. Sona showed me the best *kabab* shops in Lucknow and told me exactly how I must order them. I would take a rickshaw to the nearest *kabab* shops and return with a large box of them. By eating *kabaabs*, Sona was being a bad Hindu and I was being a bad vegetarian. Together, we shared a vivifying sense of transgression.

Sona had three sons and a day-laborer husband. She had married when she was 15 and a tattoo on her left wrist displayed the name of her husband, which tradition forbade her to speak aloud. Her entire family was physically diminutive. Sona herself stood under five feet tall and her sons peaked at an inch or two over five feet. One day I found her placing a bamboo-like plant in my freezer. She told me that she fed her children stalk-like plants, believing that they would make her sons grow taller.

Sona taught me so much about Indian life that a complete list of lessons learned would be impossible to write. One of the greatest benefits she bestowed upon me (without realizing it) was teaching me how to speak a more idiomatic Hindi. I learned Hindi and Urdu in university classrooms and formal language programs. Over the last decade or so, I have had various teachers from different backgrounds. All of my teachers were educated and upper class, however. Even as I gained enough proficiency to read a newspaper and follow an Indian movie, I remained sadly unable to communicate effectively with the common man (*aam admii*) on the street. Idiomatic language or slang confused me and any variation in dialect would leave me unable to follow a conversation.

Sona spoke only a local variety of Hindi, full of strange idioms and words borrowed from the local Awadhi dialect. Her vocabulary was earthy and practical. She did not know the word for "international," for example, but she knew countless terms for spices, fabrics, fruits and vegetables. She used one of these terms, *Kadduu* (pumpkin) as a nickname for me. I assumed pumpkin was a mild term of endearment in Hindi as it is in English and did not object when she referred to me as *Kadduu-ji*, Mr. Pumpkin, even in front of company. Only later, when one of her fellow maidservants began giggling uncontrollably at her use of this term did I finally understand that being a pumpkin was not a compliment at all. In the local slang, *Kadduu-ji* meant roughly, Mr. Blockhead.

I am sure that the reader wonders, given all of Sona's unpleasant behavior towards me, why I continued to employ her. Perhaps it was a sense of guilt over having a servant in the first place. Admittedly, I could not live with the thought of having caused her and her children misery by replacing her. It was much more than this, however. As time went on, I found that Sona was indispensable in countless ways. For example, attaining cooking gas was difficult in Lucknow.

Gas shortages were common and if I did not arrive at the gas office at just the right time and offer the men who worked there some fawning compliments and some *bakhshish* (money that is half tip, half bribe), it could take me weeks to fill up an empty gas canister. Sona made the entire process much easier. She had a connection on the local black market and could procure a full gas canister within a day for a reasonable price.

Beyond cooking gas, Sona became my closest confidant. She taught me about Lucknow, its food and its customs, and especially the life of the poor. Although she was manipulative and took every opportunity to separate me from my money, she also took responsibility for me, smoothing over misunderstandings between the neighbors and myself. She lectured me about eating the right thing at the right time. You should not eat any fish between May and August, she said, because they were likely to be contaminated. Buying mangoes out of season was a waste of money, as was smoking. Sona defended her habit of obsessively chewing betel nut, however — even though most of her teeth had turned an unhealthy shade of red as a result — claiming that betel nut made her vigorous.

In Manil Suri's novel *The Death of Vishnu*, an alcoholic fix-it man named Vishnu falls fatally ill and lies unconscious on a stairwell in the Bombay apartment building where he works. As the novel progresses, the neighbors argue about who is going to pay his medical bills and the price of his impending funeral. Vishnu's inconvenient death brings out the worst in the residents of the building and they show themselves as ridiculous, petty, and vicious.[1]

One night, one of the residents, Mr. Jalal, has a dream in which Vishnu reveals himself as an incarnation or avatar of God.

> Mr. Jalal saw a sun emerge from behind Vishnu, and was surprised he could look straight into its molten white center. As he watched, he saw two suns, then four, then eight, and sixteen. The suns kept multiplying, and rising into the air, until the sky was covered with suns, and there was no more blue to be seen, just the brightness of incandescent discs stretching from horizon to horizon and pouring their brilliance down on him.[2]

The dream convinces Mr. Jalal that God has incarnated himself as Vishnu and he attempts to convince his wife and others that they should worship the dying man as God himself.

Suri's novel illustrates something essential about the emerging middle class in urban India. Higher salaries and social status also have the unfortunate effect of keeping people apart. In our apartment building, I barely knew my neighbors. A few would attempt conversation in the elevator, but this was the exception rather than the rule. After attaining the wealth needed to live in a comfortable life, my neighbors erected walls around themselves, engaging in inane small talk

---

1 Suri, Manil. *The Death of Vishnu* (New York: Perennial 2001).
2 *Ibid.*, p. 147.

in the lobby on occasion, sometimes extending wedding invitations to each other, but mostly keeping the world at bay through their impeccable *tameez* (manners).

For the isolated residents of my apartment building, servants functioned as important conduits of information, carrying gossip from one flat to the other, sharing or withholding information according to their whim or trading it for their benefit. From Sona I learned that the large Shiite man on the ground floor was insane, probably schizophrenic, and that I should avoid riding the elevator with him (she was right, he would later threaten to beat me with a bamboo stick). I learned that the woman across the hall drank to excess when her husband was not home, and that the milkman often cheated his customers by cutting the milk with water. Sona may have fudged the grocery bill on occasion — probably on regular occasion — but she was worth twice what I paid her.

Moreover, like Mr. Jalal in *Death of Vishnu*, I also saw something mysterious, almost transcendent, in my servant. In Sona, I found the remarkable conjunction of unrepentant immorality with genuine generosity. Side by side with her daily, petty thefts and deceptions lay a sense of fairness and decency; nastiness and warmth existed in her seemingly without any contradiction. She was the best and the worst, profundity and pettiness, kindness and cruelty all rolled inside a single sari. The juxtaposition of deception and excellence, love and larceny, created a crack in my moral universe through which I sometimes imagined I could glimpse divinity. "I am also the gambling of cheats and of the splendid, I am the splendor," says Krishna in the *Bhagavad Gita*.[1]

One evening Sona insisted I give her 20 rupees (about 50 cents) for a rickshaw ride home. I objected that she lived down by the river, a short distance away, and that the most any rickshaw driver would ask was 5 rupees.

She paused for a moment. "How do you know I live by the river?" she asked sharply.

"You told me yesterday," I answered.

She smiled. "I did not know that you understood so much. Your Hindi is better than I thought. I will have to be more careful." She thought for a moment. "I still need 20 rupees, brother," she said at last, "I brought you cigarettes yesterday and you never paid for them."

"You said that one of the neighbors gave them to you for free, because he was trying to quit," I said.

Sona's lips curled around her rotting teeth in a snarl, and she spoke clearly and deliberately, so that there could be no mistake.

"I LIED," she said.

Eventually, I visited her in her house by the river and came to know her children. Once, she even accompanied me to the bazaar, a brazen act in a gossip-

---

1 Prabhupada, A.C. Bhaktivedanta trans. *Bhagavad Gita: As it Is* (New York: Bhaktivedanta Book Trust 1972), p. 174.

addicted city where married women did not venture out into public with strange men. While we shopped for vegetables, I heard somebody ask, "Who is this woman with her *farang premi* (foreign lover)?" Sona did not seem to care; poor, low-caste women in India are not exactly members of polite society to begin with.

When I told Sona I was leaving Lucknow, she cried. I almost cried too. In a strange way, she had become my best friend. I gave up my apartment in Lucknow because I wanted to spend the Christmas holiday in Christian Goa. Sona did not understand why I could not stay in Lucknow and I could not explain that I wanted to be somewhere where December 25 meant something. Sona was a survivor, however, and while she might have been upset about my departure, she was not going to let me go without working it to her advantage. As I started selling off the furniture, I often found her in the kitchen looking mournfully at my pale blue refrigerator. Like most people in her settlement, she did not own one.

"What will you do with the fridge?" she asked.

"Sell it, I guess," I said.

Then her face would wrinkle and her eyes would get hard. "It's a nice fridge...," she would say and then sigh heavily.

Eventually I made a deal with her. She could have the refrigerator. In exchange, she must manage the selling of my furniture and belongings. It was an even trade in the end. I would never have sold half the furniture if she had not helped me. Sona knew everyone in the building; she seemed to know half of Lucknow. Before long, there was a regular parade of potential buyers marching through my living room. Furniture that I thought was worthless ended up being the object of bidding wars.

Once in Goa, Christmas was a disappointment. The Goan Christians certainly celebrate the holiday, but not in any way that I recognized. There was no eggnog, Christmas caroling, or stockings hung by the chimney, and there certainly were no snowmen or ice-skating. On Christmas Eve, I ended up at a party at Vagator Beach with a group of extremely stoned Europeans, dancing to the head-numbing sound of Goan Trance music played at an incredible volume.

The next day my cell phone rang. It was Sona calling to wish me *Christmas mubaarak ho* (blessed Christmas).

"I am glad you remembered me, Sona," I said.

"Yes," she answered, "whenever I look at the refrigerator, I think of you...but it needs some repairs, brother, and you should really send me some money to fix it."

Dramas of Progress: Lucknow in Indian Cinema

I tried to leave India in February 2007. I had been in Asia for over 25 straight months, my funding had dried up and I was almost out of money. Moreover, I was fatigued. In the last months of my residency in India I had traveled from one end of the subcontinent to the other, had met everybody from fanatic Muslims in Kashmir to the hippies of Goa, and I had found trouble — financial, professional, and personal — in every location. It was time to go home.

If I was done with Hindustan, however, Hindustan was not quite done with me. In Bombay, the immigration officer refused to let me board my flight home; I had failed to register with the correct office in Lucknow, thus breaking several strictures on foreign residents. Out of money and luck, I ended up living in a rundown section of Bombay, in a dismal dungeon named Hotel Fortune, while I tried to cut the necessary red tape and procure an exit permit that would allow me to leave the country.

During this period, my days started with a trip to the Foreign Residents Registration Office, where I stood in line for hours only to be ignored by a series of humorless bureaucrats. I never had the right form, or the correct number of Xerox copies of my passport, or the right size passport photos. The next day would start in the same way, stand in line, confront rude clerk, fill out incorrect form, repeat.

The evenings were not much better. I did not know many people in Bombay and had no money to enjoy myself anyway. I ate mostly *chaat*, a spicy street food with countless regional varieties. Excellent Bombay *chaat* could be had for a pittance around the corner from Hotel Fortune and, after years in Lucknow, my gastro-intestinal track was finally up to the task of digesting it. After dinner, I headed for Metro Theater, where tickets to a film sold for anywhere between $1 and $4. I thus spent a great deal of time watching Indian films during my last week in India. During that time and since I have returned to America, I have found a virtual India, a stage upon which Indian film makers act out India's fears and hopes. On a corner of this imaginary stage I even found Lucknow, the city of Nawabs, which has a special role in the cinematic dramas of contemporary India.

INDIAN CINEMA PAST AND PRESENT, MAINSTREAM AND ALTERNATIVE

When most people speak of the Indian film industry, they mean the Bombay movie business. Bombay, or Bollywood as it is often called, is the largest film industry in the world, producing many more titles per year than Hollywood. Although many Indian states, including, Telagu and Bengal also have film industries, the Bombay Hindi film industry dominates the Indian market. Bombay studios distribute their productions throughout the country and Bombay film stars are national — and increasingly international — celebrities.

Film music means so much to people that often, like teenagers who define themselves by the bands they listen to, Indians show passionate and unassailable tastes in film soundtracks. At Ram Asari's Sweet shop near Hazratganj, the storekeeper handed me a CD of his favorite film music and insisted I listened to it as soon as possible. When I listened to it, it included old film songs rarely heard anymore. At various points the music on the CD stopped and short advertisements for Ram Asari's Sweetshop (founded in 1805) played. Until recently, most popular music in India came from the Bombay film industry and Indians remember many films (e.g., *Ashiqi* or "Courtship," a terrible film with a great soundtrack) for their music, not their plot.

The average Bombay film differs from American and European films in many respects. They are longer, usually running about three hours with an inevitable intermission in the middle, and they usually contain several extravagant song and dance numbers. The typical Indian film follows a formulaic plot, involving a boy-meets-girl story that, after a bewildering number of twists and turns, ends in a happy union. Films often include at least one dance number in which a famous "item girl" dances a single dance and then disappears. Although depictions of sex are usually taboo in Indian films, and even kissing was rare until very recently, many films contain a "wet sari" number in which an actress gets caught in a monsoon downpour and gyrates suggestively in a soaked silk sari while belting out a love song in a head-splittingly high octave.

Indian film had not always been so formulaic. In the 1950s through the early 1980s innovators like Satyajit Ray complemented the Bombay film industry with alternative films with all the artistic *gravitas* of Western art house movies. This parallel movie world eventually petered out, when the Bombay *masala* film — with its mixture of predictable and sometimes stolen plots, endless song and dance numbers and the same, big name stars endlessly re-imagined — attained a position of almost unopposed dominance.

In the last decade or so, I have watched filmmakers both within and without the Bombay film industry try to break this familiar mold and strike out in new directions. Some directors have challenged the squeaky clean subject matter of the average Indian film, even taking on subjects such as divorce in films like *Kabhi Al Vida Na Kahanaa* (Never Say Goodbye, 2006) and AIDS in *Phir Milenge* (We'll Meet Again, 2004) and *My Brother Nikhil* (2005). Others have altered traditional narrative, adopting non-sequential storytelling as in the film *Salaam-e-Ishq* (Love's Goodbye, 2007), which tells six loosely related stories at once in a manner reminiscent of the recent Stephen Gaghan film, *Syriana*.

Other recent films have brought new genres of films from the West into Indian cinema. The 2005 psychological thriller *Being Cyrus*, starred Saif Ali Khan as an apparently innocent young man who takes a job as an assistant to a famous painter. The surprise ending, in which all is not as it seems, is reminiscent of the 1995 film "The Usual Suspects". Even science fiction has arrived in Indian cinema in the form of *Koi Mil Gaya* (Who Did You Meet? 2003), an Indian version of Steven Spielberg's ET and *Krish* (2006), an Indian retelling of the Superman myth.

The gamble does not always pay off. Bombay's standard fare has a devoted following and when producers alter the usual cinematographic formula and fail provide stirring drama the result is sometimes commercial and artistic disaster. Vishu Chopra's *Eklavya* (2007), a story about a dysfunctional royal family in Rajasthan, reduced the film time to two hours and nixed the musical numbers. Unfortunately, the result is a film so heavy that it sinks like a stone. Without music or comic relief it becomes a gruesome MacBeth-like palace bloodbath minus the weird sisters, or the fun.

Some of the greatest Indian filmmaking in the last twenty years, in my opinion, has occurred when Indian filmmakers avoided the Bombay filmmaking establishment in its entirety.[1] Such was the case with the 1994 Film *Bandit Queen*, a film produced by NRI Indian talent with British backing. A powerful and thinly fictionalized account of the early life of Phoolan Devi, a UP dacoit (gangster) who goes on a killing spree against upper caste Indians in the wastelands in the extreme south of the state, *Bandit Queen* broke new ground in the realistic portrayal of India's underclass.[2] Gritty and heartbreaking, with excellent performances by Seema Biswas and Nirmal Pandey, the film reconstructs from Devi's own words the life of a low-caste woman who will not follow the rules.

Bandit Queen and the recent *Slumdog Millionaire* (2008) show what heights Indian actors and filmmakers can attain when left to pursue artistic quality rather

---

1 Such is the case with Deepa Mehta's *Water* (2005), an Oscar nominee in the foreign film category. *Water* was produced in Canada and was never released in India.
2 After her capture, Phoolan Devi spent time in prison for her part in the murder of 22 people in the village of Behmai in 1981. Eventually released, she successfully ran for Parliament in 1996 but died by assassination in New Delhi in 2001. Reportedly, Devi did not like *Bandit Queen*.

than domestic commercial success. In *Slumdog Millionaire*, Scotch director Danny Boyle who directed Vikas Swarup's novel *Question and Answer*, a fictional account of the popular game show *Kaun Banayega Crorepati* (roughly, Who Wants to be a Millionaire) into an Oscar-winning phenomenon.[1] *Slumdog Millionaire* depicts the hardscrabble lives of *basti* (illegal settlement) denizens and strikes a delicate balance between serious social realism and Horatio Alger fable. The success of the film seemed to anger Bollywood superstar Amitabh Bachchan, who remarked on his blog that it presented India as a "third-world, dirty, underbelly developing nation" and suggesting that its critical acclaim was due in part to Boyle's Hollywood connections.[2]

Of course, Bachchan has a great deal to lose if the Bollywood film industry fractures into a series of smaller audiences that seek more sophisticated films from sources other than Bollywood. Indian cinema has a small cast. Most big productions showcase a small number of actors and actresses over and over again. Indicative of the incestuous casting practices of Bombay films are the Three Khans, Shah Rukh Khan, Saif Ali Khan and Salman Khan. Any initiate to Indian films first must differentiate between the three, as at least one of them is likely to appear in any mainstream Bombay release.

Due to overexposure, I developed a negative impression of Amitabh Bachchan. Bachchan, or as he is affectionately sometimes called, the Big B, is a large man attached an even larger PR machine. The Big B has become a ubiquitous presence in India, appearing on so many advertisements and billboards that it is almost impossible to go through the day in India without coming face to face with his goatee or hearing his paternal growl on television.[3] Perhaps part of my aversion is jealousy; Bachchan is so popular in India that when he was hospitalized for a temporary stomach malady in 2006, his medical condition dominated the news headlines for days.

As for Indian cinema's leading ladies, the current crop of Bollywood belles — Rani Mukerjee, Karishma Kapoor, Ashwariya Rai, et al. — are easy on the eyes, but I find the sirens of former ages even more interesting. My idolization of Indian actresses culminates in a fascination with Madhubala, India's answer to Marilyn

---

1 A *crorepati* is one who owns a *crore*, or 10 million rupees. Depending on the exchange rate, this works out to about $220,000 American dollars. A crore currently has much greater purchasing power than a million dollars in the urban United States.

2 Bachchan later denied criticizing the film, claiming that he did not actually write the "underbelly" comment, he just posted it on his blog. See "Bachchan denies Slumdog Criticism" http://news.bbc.co.uk/2//hi/south_asia/7832705.stm, 1/16/09.

3 I am a big fan of Hritik Roshan, however. The star of both the groundbreaking *Koi Mil Gaya*, and the 2006 sequel, *Krish*, Roshan may be the rare Bollywood star who would go over as big in Hollywood as in India. What strikes me most about Roshan is his comic potential. His draw laughs with his facial expressions rivals that of Jim Carey. Add to this his considerable physical attributes and his athletic dancing ability and India may have a star with true potential on the international stage. Like Owen Wilson, Roshan has a face that almost automatically elicits a smile.

Monroe and the star of *Mughal e Azam* (The Great Mughal), and dovetails with my interest in historical dramas. While films with present day settings document the dreams of contemporary Indian society, historical settings serve as a stage for the imagined origins of Indian culture and can function as a telltale window into the Indian soul.

LUCKNOW: DRAMAS OF PROGRESS

Lucknow has a special place in the history of Indian cinema. Although rarely chosen as the location of a film, the city's occasional appearances are often memorable; the history of the city serves as a backdrop for filmmakers' historical reflections and fantasies. Lucknow becomes the repeated setting for the final gasp of Mughal-era culture before the Great Mutiny of 1857 and the rise of the British Raj. This occurs in both large commercial endeavors such as *Umrao Jaan* and in smaller "art house" films such as *Shatranj ke Khelari*.[1] As seen in these films, Lucknow inhabits a corner of the Indian psyche as a setting for dramas of progress in which the past gives way to the future.

Lucknow found itself on the outside of Indian film culture in the early days of the industry. A 1937 survey of production companies found Lucknow was home to a single company while Bombay boasted 34 and Madras 36.[2] In 1960, however, Guru Dutt produced a delightful romantic comedy, *Chaudhvin Ka Chand* (The Full Moon) set in contemporary Lucknow. Typically long at almost three hours, the film boasts impressive song-making, opening with a musical tribute to Lucknow's charms, "In search of a goal, There wanders every traveler," and continuing with several memorable dance numbers. *Chaudhvin Ka Chand* tells the oft-told tale of mistaken identity leading to matrimonial mix-ups, but defies easy characterization by delivering a surprisingly tragic ending.

Lucknow reappears in Satyajit Ray's 1977 Film *Shatranj ke Khelari* (The Chess Players), which features the city's unique historical role in the history of India. Set in the final days of the Kingdom of Oudh as the British scheme to dethrone the fun-loving King Wazed Ali Shah, *Shatranj ke Khelari* tells the tale of two refined Lucknowi gentlemen playing endless games of chess. The upheaval around them only serves to annoy the two men, who would prefer to play on obliviously.[3] Based on a work by the renowned Hindi novelist Premchandra, *Shatranj Ke*

---

1 Film historians Rachael Dwyer and Divia Patel would place both films in the 'courtesean' genre, a group of Indian films they characterize as "...one of the most popular genres, in terms of their box office success rather than the number of films produced." Dwyer, Rachel and Patel, Divia *Cinema India: The Visual Culture of Hindi Film* (New Jersey, Rutgers University Press 2002) p. 69.
2 Barnouw, Erik and Krishnaswamy, S. *Indian Film* (New York, Oxford University Press 1980) p. 104.
3 The film notes the difference between the standard and the older Indian rules of chess. The archaic rules of the game — still used in parts of India — did not allow pawns to advance two ranks on their initial move. Echoes of these rules are found in the practice of capture-in-passing (*en passant*) and in the Indian Defenses, by which Black opens with

Khelari includes arresting animated segments and narration by a young Amitabh Bachchan.

Film critic Sumita Chakravarty describes *Shatranj ke Khelari* as a dramatic struggle between history and culture, the former represented by the British and the latter by Ali Shah.

> Ultimately, "history" and "culture" remain separate rather than inform one another. "History," appropriated by Outram [the British official], becomes the province of the strong, "culture" the domain of the weak.[1]

In the film's pivitol scene, a distraught minister arrives at the palace to inform Ali Shah of the impending British takeover, arriving in the middle of a *kathak* dance performance. As the dancer whirls to the sound of the tabla drum, the king watches enraptured; perhaps he sees something in the performance of greater importance than the British East India Company, something more enduring than the British Empire itself. In the end, suggests the film, culture will trump history.

> The haunting beauty of the song, the camerawork that renders the pyrotechnics of the dance, and the graceful movements of this art form are certainly assertions of cultural/national pride in the face of the humiliation of colonization. It is the supreme moment of the aestheticization of history.[2]

In Ray's hands, Wazed Ali Shah becomes a poet-king who cultivates the arts as his kingdom falls around him, convinced that redemption for Oudh lays in the durability of its music and poetry, not the vigor of its monarchy. In one memorable scene, he tells the British resident that citizens of his kingdom sing songs that he himself has authored. He then wonders aloud if Queen Victoria has written any songs that her subjects know by heart.[3]

Ali's personal ideal of leadership, while pathetic in the context of the story, is not at all absurd. For the king, the important part of leadership is not signing treaties, waging war, public work projects or any of the other activities usually associated with political power. For him, *tameez aur tahazeeb*, Oudh's culture, is the sum of his legacy. Art's ability to touch the hearts of his subjects is more significant than any reform he could orchestrate via his treasury or his army. And the king might be right; laws and treaties do not rule the daily lives of people;

Knf6 usually followed by g6, deliberately abandoning the mid-board to White. Also called the Coward's Defense for its supposed pusillanimity, the Indian Defense has enjoyed a renaissance in contemporary tournament play.

1 Chakravarty, Sumita, *National Identity in Indian Popular Cinema 1947-1987* (Austin, University of Texas Press 1993) p. 188.

2 *Ibid* p. 190.

3 The Nawab's claim is no empty boast. Some scholars place the origins of *thumri*, or Hindustani light-classical music, in the courts Lucknow's nawabs. See Garg, Lakshminarayan. *Sangiita Vishaarad* (Hathras: Sangeet Karyalaya 2004), pgs. 232-240. Pandit Ravi Shankar specifically credits the court of Wazid Ali Shah with the distinctive innovations that characterize the style. See Shankar, Ravi. *My Music My Life* (New York, Simon and Schuster 1968) p. 33.

rather the mysterious forces of culture order daily existence. The truly effective ruler in the view of Ray, Premchandra and perhaps the historical Ali Shah, is the person who cultivates and adds to the cultural milieu.

Historians of Indian film note that films by artists such as Satyajit Ray are financially small-time. They neither cost a great deal to make nor earned much at the box office; *Shatranj ke Khelari* cost about half of what Bombay films of the same period cost and earned much less once released. Once critic summed up the failure of the film to connect with many Indians,

> Thus Ray's portrait of the fall of Oudh is a sardonic one. Dissecting colonialism in a way that is equally applicable to neo-colonialism, it seemed to some observers to be extraordinarily timely. But if it did not at once enthrall Hindi film audiences, reasons are not hard to find. Indians could not readily derive emotional satisfaction from its version of history — nor, for that matter, could the British. If it had no villains, it had no heroes either — and no action climax, such as many may have yearned for.[1]

If chess players failed to excite the average Indian film fan, however, an account of how Lucknow's women survived the Mutiny proved both popular and resilient. The story of Umrao Jaan had the added advantage of focusing on the subject of Lucknow's famed courtesans. Nineteenth-century Lucknow was the home of *tawaif*, professional, geisha-like courtesans who entertained well-bred men in extravagant brothels (*kotha*). Men of repute in Lucknowi society would gather for special parties (*mahfil*) where these highly trained women would sing, recite poetry, dance and play musical instruments. *Tawaif* were no simple streetwalkers; they were refined women who required months of courting and demanded expensive gifts before granting any man access to their physical intimacies.

Late 19th century Urdu writer Mohammad Ruswa made the *tawaif* of Lucknow the focus of his novel *Umrao Jan Ada*, the story of a village girl pressed into a scandalous life by trickery.[2] The 1981 film version of the novel entitled *Umrao Jan* and starring the sultry actress Rekha, perpetuated the myth of Lucknow as a place of illicit love, clandestine meetings and Urdu love poetry whispered *in sotto voce*.

> ...if culture must subsist in time and place, it is Lucknow of the nawabi era that represents the best of the Hindu-Muslim amalgam. Although courtesans were located in all parts of India, it is Lucknow that popular culture has identified as their representative site. For the minority Muslim population and for Indians generally, Lucknow connotes the "civilized" outpost or remnants of bygone Muslim imperial splendor, the elegance of the Urdu language, and lived social grace.[3]

1 Barnouw, Erik and Krishnaswamy, S., *Indian Film* (Oxford, Oxford University Press 1980) p. 242.
2 Ruswa, Mohammad Hadi. *Umrao Jan Ada* (Hyderabad: Disha Books, 1993).
3 Chakravarty, Sumita S. *Indian Popular Cinema 1947-1987* (Austin, University of Austin Press 1993) p. 288.

Umrao Jan was so popular that that a remake of the film, starring former Miss World Ashwariya Rai, was released in 2006.[1] Oddly, the producers of the 2006 version of *Umrao Jan* opted to shoot much of the film in Rajasthan rather than Lucknow. The filmmaker, J.P. Dutta responded to criticism that his film crews had overlooked Lucknow by insisting that his crews filmed in Lucknow for over 60 days. "Other films...were shot in the city because they couldn't afford to shoot on elaborate ostentatious sets. I chose to shoot in Lucknow," said Dutta.[2] Still, the 2006 version will not look familiar to anyone who has lived in the city. The set looks like a palace rather than a brothel, the air is too clear and the streets too uncluttered; anyone who had ever visited the city would know that the setting of *Umrao Jaan* 2006 *cannot* be Lucknow.

This prejudiced me against the film but I could not resist it in the end. Rai is stunning and does an adequate job approximating *kathak* dance moves. The male lead, Abhishek Bachchan, the son of The Big B, makes a fine nawab and the real-life romance between himself and Miss Rai — they married in 2007 — adds an additional layer of modern soap opera to the production. The dialogue was simpler in the new *Umrao Jaan* than in the earlier film and I reached for my dictionary less often. This made watching easier for somebody with limited linguistic skills, but the richness of the language was gone. The courtly Urdu of the Kingdom of Oudh seemed more artificial, more divorced from its roots.[3]

In the imaginary universe of the Indian cinema, Lucknow became the backdrop for historical fault-lines, the fading Mughal era and also the waning power of the British. The 1965 Ivory-Merchant production, *Shakespeare Wallah* — Satyajit Ray provides an excellent, haunting score — tells the story of a small troupe of Shakespearean actors touring post-Independence India and playing to dwindling audiences. Mr. Buckingham (Geoffrey Kendal), his wife (Laura Lidell) and daughter, Lizzie (played by the charming Felicity Kendal), cling to an ideal of Anglican gentility in a new nation that has rejected it in favor of native cultural ideals. The Raj era is over, and with it, much of people's interest in British theater. The film opens at the La Martiniere School in Lucknow as the Buckinghams entertain a bored and defiant-looking group of students. The troupe later moves on to other parts of India, giving performances to dwindling and increasingly disre-

---

1 I wondered whether the world depicted in *Umrao Jaan* still existed in Lucknow. Reportedly, the *tawaif* survived the Mutiny of 1857 and Independence but went extinct during the austerity of the Nehru era. I also heard rumors that *tawaif* still operated in Lucknow in private, secret clubs on the outskirts of the city. I could not determine whether these rumors had substance or were simply the wishful thinking of lonely men. Notably, the film *Chaudhvin Ke Chand* (1960) presents the *tawaif* as a contemporary reality.

2 "Umrao Jaan gets flack in Lucknow" www.realbollywood.com 11/4/06.

3 The new version omits one of my favorite folk sayings in Hindustani, *agar ghora ghas se dosti karega to kayega kya?* "If the horse makes friends with the grass, then what will it eat?" I learned it from the 1981 *Umrao* and have since found it a useful expression when circumstances require that you take temporary advantage of an acquaintance.

spectful audiences. His daughter finds love in the arms of Sanju (a young Shashi Kapoor), an Indian playboy whose jealous kissing cousin (Madhur Jeffrey) is a vindictive Bollywood actress.[1]

In the film's pivotal scene, Sanju's jealous lover (Jeffrey) enters the theater during a performance of *Othello* and deliberately creates a commotion by posing for a horde of photographers. When Sanju apologizes to Mr. Buckingham after the show, the latter describes the event as a "victory of film over theater," a sign of the changing times. In the end, Lizzie leaves India for England, a symbol of the final vestiges of the Raj-era returning home. As she waves good-bye from the deck of the departing ship, she has a vision of Sanju sitting by her side as they play the piano together and sing, "Do Re Me..." In her reverie, Sanju stops her and changes the scale to *Sa Re Ga*, the *swara* (notes) of the Hindustani octave. In the future, suggests the film, art in India will mean Indian art.[2] Perhaps, the notes Sanju sings were always in the background waiting to be heard. The last King of Oudh, Wazad Ali Shah, knew that when the sound of the British bard had fallen silent, the song on the lips of the peoples of India would be his.

---

1 Shashi Kapoor returns the Lucknow for the forgettable *Junoon* (1978), a labored costume drama about English women captured by rebels during the Mutiny of 1857.
2 See Barnouw, Erik and Krishnaswamy, S. *Indian Film* (New York, Oxford University Press 1980) p. 248. *Shakespeare Wallah* documents the real-life careers of the Kendalls and their former employee, the film star Sashi Kapoor.

THE UPSIDE-DOWN TREE TURNS UPSIDE DOWN: ON GOING HOME

When I finally did board an airplane in Bombay and returned to America, I had a hard landing. Unable to find work, I freelanced briefly for a local paper and tried to piece my life in America back together. Soon after my return, Deborah announced she was divorcing me. Soon afterwards, the police in Ogunquit, Maine, where my family has a summer house, arrested me and charged me with driving under the influence of alcohol. I was later exonerated of the DUI charge (the hearing officer decided I was not a drunkard, just a very bad driver), but my marriage was irreparable and I spent much of my time during those first months in a state of cultural and personal disorientation. If it had been at all possible to return to Lucknow — that city I had so many complaints about — I would have done so without a second thought.

Much had changed in the two and a half years I had been gone. I was used to how things worked (or did not work) in India and some days the United States seemed almost like a foreign country to me. I had become addicted to the chaos of Asia; I missed the lack of regulation and standardization, the spicy food, the Bollywood films, and even the steamy monsoon weather. When the temperature dipped below 75, I reached for a sweater; food without curry was almost inedible to me, films without choreographed song-and-dance routines seemed to lack something and our American habit of meticulously obeying traffic rules struck me as limiting. I started out my stay in India with the idea that it took courage to leave home for such an extended time. I ended up discovering that leaving was the easy part — coming home took courage.

Missing India, I went to the local bookstore and browsed the shelves for books on Asia. Mira Kamdar's *Planet India* epitomized the tone of many of the new books about India on the shelf:

As India, a rising civilizational giant, gains economic and political power, its cultural clout will increase as well. One day soon, when a critical mass of the talent, the money, and the market is in Asia, a tipping point will be reached, and India will move from joining the game, or even winning the game, to inventing new rules for new games. Then things will get interesting.[1]

Almost everyone she interviews in her book shares her unflagging optimism about India (the one exception, oddly enough, is New Age guru Deepak Chopra). She admits, "Amid the celebratory din surrounding the emergence of India, it is rare to find a dissenting voice..."[2] After 300-odd pages of this unrelenting panegyric to India's glorious future, I could only picture the author by imagining a woman dressed in a cheerleading costume with the world "Planet India" emblazoned across her bosom in sparkling, red letters.

Like Kamdar's book, most recent coverage of India contained good news. The economy was growing at a healthy rate, the government in New Delhi was economically progressive, and the usual problems with Pakistan, Kashmir, inflation and labor unrest, if they were not getting better, at least did not seem to be getting appreciably worse. Nobody could deny India's potential.

The news was so good, however, that some people had adopted what writer Edmund Luce calls "a pre-mature spirit of triumphalism." Dark clouds still sat on India's horizon. Higher education, for example, remained a crucial problem. In America, most Indian people were highly educated and extremely motivated — so that Americans sometimes assumed all Indians held an advanced degree in technology or science. They often did not realize that higher education in many parts of India itself, including Uttar Pradesh, was in a state of complete disarray. A few prestigious technical institutes dotted the landscape. Otherwise, most universities I saw in north India often closed due to student agitations, student government elections, confrontations over exams or a host of other reasons.

Lucknow University suffered from a horrific violence problem. Students physically assaulted professors and were then in turn victimized by groups of young criminals who were students in name only. The type of dysfunction Americans expect only in inner-city high schools was endemic in the universities of some parts of India. This had resulted in a whole generation of Indians who had lost out on a quality education. And when you consider that the growth India has enjoyed in the Internet and computer industries depends on education, the threat posed by a troubled education system to India's economic options cannot be underestimated.

India as long had a legacy of weak schooling for its young, even as it has promoted high-quality government-financed universities. But if in the past a largely poor and agrarian nation could afford to leave millions of its

1 Kamdar, Mira. *Planet India* (McMillan Library 2007), p. 96.
2 *ibid*, p. 86.

people illiterate, that is no longer the case. Not only has the roaring economy run into a shortage of skilled labor, but also the nation's many new roads, phones and television sets have fueled new ambitions for economic advancement among its people — and new expectations for schools to help them achieve it.[1]

An even more serious problem was the environment. A leading environmentalist, Jared Diamond, made some provocative comments about development in the third world in his recent book *Collapse, How Societies Choose to Fail or Survive*:

> People in the Third World aspire to First World living standards....
> Third World citizens are encouraged in that aspiration by First World
> and United Nations development agencies, which hold out to them the
> prospect of achieving their dream if they will only adopt the right policies,
> like balancing their national budgets, investing in education and infra-
> structure, and so on. But no one in the First World governments is willing
> to acknowledge the dream's impossibility: the unsustainability of a world
> in which the Third World's large population were to reach and maintain
> current First World living standards....What will happen when it finally
> dawns on all those people in the Third World that First World standards
> are unreachable for them, and that the First World refuses to abandon
> those standards for itself?[2]

In other words, this dream many of us had for Asia, of a place where a bulging middle class of 400 million Indians and 400 million Chinese all drive SUVs and use washing machines was a pipe dream, for the planet has neither enough fuel for 800 million more SUVs nor water for 800 million more washing machines.

If Diamond is correct in suggesting that third-world development has a looming, impassable environmental horizon — one which, Diamond takes pains to point out, we cannot reasonably expect some well-timed technological innovation (e.g., hydrogen fuel cells) to save us from — then we were all guilty of selling snake oil. It meant that all the economic forecasts about the rise of Asian mega-economies, in which India and China grow to become two-billion-consumer-strong twin Titans of world industry, were only a numerical fantasy, the result of thinking that had taken place in a bubble.

In the September 21, 2007, edition of *The Wall Street Journal*, commentator Mary Kissel advanced the novel theory that the Chandni Chowk market near the Jama Masjid in New Delhi was not chaotic; it just appeared to be. Behind the apparent disorder, in Kissel's opinion, was a mysterious organizing principle at work — Adam Smith's invisible hand. Where most people saw a simple jumble of shops, Kissel saw the magic of the market.

> There's no government imposing order. And why should it? As Smith
> said, there's a "certain propensity" in human nature to "truck, barter and

---

1 Sengupta, Somini. "Push for Education Yields Little for India's Poor," *New York Times*, 1/17/08, p. 1. Sengupta notes that the annual Pratham survey of 2007 finds little improvement in public schools in India from previous years. *ibid*, p. 1, 16.

2 Diamond, p. 496.

exchange one thing for another," so it's natural that a certain kind of system guided by an "invisible hand," results.[1]

The idea of India directed by a mysterious invisible hand or force, some disembodied force of capitalism, struck me as fantastic. Yet, thousands of educated people read it and believed it. Next to this idea, the belief that human life followed the dictates of an invisible, transcendent *Brahman*, did not seem so strange.

It occurred to me at that moment that the upright tree was as mythical as the upside-down one. Progress, the ideal that informs economic policy and international aid in India, was only another philosophical belief among many. Progress holds that improvements in global living standards are open-ended; things will always get better. This rests not on any inviolate rule of economics or physics, but on simple optimism. As Oliver Wendell Holmes once observed:

> The attempt to lift up men's hearts by a belief in progress seems to me, like the wish for spiritualism or miracles, to rest on not taking a large enough view or going far enough back.[2]

I began writing this book by imagining India as a tree, growing from the ground to the sky, from poverty to progress. I realize now that I was in error. The analogy is faulty in many ways and the goal itself, universal material development, may be, as Diamond argues, an environmental impossibility. Conversely, the traditional, upside-down tree is more believable than it once seemed. If the global economy cannot make India into a first world economy, then the traditions India alone will survive to make sense of people's lives, order society and create social cohesion. The fabric of Indian society is remarkably resilient, adapting what it likes from foreign influences and shaking off the rest. India adopted music and architecture from the Mughals, but passed on large-scale conversion to Islam. Similarly, India is happy for the train, roads and courts that the British left behind — perhaps too happy, as all three of them could use an update — but Christianity made few inroads into the Indian heartland.

This century, a new foreign influence arrived on the subcontinent, American-dominated globo-culture. As with the Muslims and British before us, we imagine that India will adopt our culture, not only our music and our clothes, but our social ideals and cultural values. As with former invasions, this one will probably end in failure. Indians will continue to follow their customs and their religion.

---

1 Kissel, Mary. "Passage to India: Adam Smith in a Delhi Market," *Wall Street Journal* 9/21/07. Kissel ignores the extensive and interesting literature on organized complexity and its relation to unplanned cities. See Johnson, Stephen. "The Myth of the Ant Queen," Miller, Richard and Spellmeyer, Kurt, eds. *The New Humanities Reader* (New York: Houghton Mifflin Company 2006), p. 274.
2 Seldes, George. *The Great Quotations* (New York: Simon & Schuster 1969), p. 783.

The central trunk of our imaginary tree will wither in time, but branches growing from the sky and rooted in the earth will support it in its periodic decrepitude.[1]

At the conclusion of Vonnegut's *Slapstick or Lonesome No More!*, America has ceased to exist in any recognizable form. States have become feudal fiefdoms engaged in a constant state of internecine warfare; modern industry and commerce have ground to a halt. Due to a lack of fuel, Americans ride donkeys rather than automobiles. Slavery is again common. Yet the novel ends on an oddly upbeat note, as one of the characters (with the middle name Oriole-2) travels across the former nation of America, supported by members of her state-mandated caste.

> She would encounter relatives everywhere — if not Orioles, then at least birds or living things of some kind. They would feed her and point the way. One would give her a raincoat. Another would give her a sweater and a magnetic compass. Another would give her a baby carriage. Another would give her an alarm clock.[2]

Economic fortunes will rise and fall, *Slapstick* suggests. Given the planet's environmental problems, they may fall more often than they rise in the near future. In the end, all that will remain is our culture. In a time of political and economic decay, only our network of relationships between individuals and groups sustains us. India — with its almost infinite variety of castes and sub-castes, clans and communities — is perhaps better prepared than our own country for this scenario.

Bettering their lot is a goal of most Indians. Given their belief in the recurrence of human life, however, Indians are famously (or perhaps infamously) in no hurry. The law of *karma* is inviolate; justice, in the Hindu view of life, can take thousands of years, but it is inevitable. This tendency to take the long view makes some Indians skeptical about the latest development schemes. When talking to members of the Scavenger caste in India, I asked them about a plan to build a new sewage system in Lucknow, a project that would make their government-contracted work cleaning sewage pipes obsolete. They were not worried. They had seen development workers come and go with a wide variety of plans, and they had all failed to replace them. They saw it all as just another temporary headache, one that they would outlast.[3]

This propensity to wait, this lack of urgency, may be wise. India is an ancient country; it has seen invaders come and go. It has survived the Greeks, the Mughals and the British. And for many Indians in Uttar Pradesh, the latest developments in Delhi, the call centers of Bangalore and the glitz of Mumbai, and the

---

1 "Progress has not followed a straight ascending line, but a spiral with rhythms of progress and retrogression, of evolution and dissolution." Seldes, George. *The Great Quotations* (New York: Simon & Schuster 1969), p. 783.

2 See Vonnegut, Kurt. *Slapstick: Or Lonesome No More!* (New York City: Delacorte Press 1976), p. 243.

3 See the chapter entitled "The International Museum of the Latrine" above.

Western programming that they see on their TVs, are just one more invasion, one more foreign influence with limited scope and self-serving intentions that their family and their caste will see rise and fall.

Perhaps the rising economic tide we so often hear about will not rise as high or reach as far into the interior of India as we have been lead to believe. When and if that happens, the winners will be the political parties that always took the promises of the global economy and the culture of the West with a grain of salt. In the end, if the dreams of progress offered by globalization turn out to be less ideal than promised, most Indians will be left with their family, their caste and their religion. In this case, India will one day have to get back to its roots; it will, like myself, have to come home.

Selected Bibliography

Akbar, Khatija. *Madhubala* (UBS Publishers and Distributors 1997).

Awadhesh, Mishra, ed. *An Advanced Hindi Magazine Reader* ed. (Varanasi: Abhaas Prakashan 1994).

Besant, Anne, trans. *The Bhagavad Gita: Text and Translation* (Theosophical Publishing House 1998).

Brass, Paul. *The Politics of India Since Independence* (Cambridge: Cambridge University Press, 2004).

Chin, James. The AIDS Pandemic: The Collision of Epidemiology with Political Correctness (Abingdon: Radcliffe Publishing Ltd. 20007).

Disputes Over the Ganga: A Look at Potential Water-related Conflicts in South Asia (Kathmandu: Panos Institute 2004).

Eliade, Mircea. *Yoga: Immortality and Freedom* (New Jersey: Princeton University Press 1969).

Fayez, Ahmed. *Dast e Sabaa* (Aligarh. Educational Book House 1997).

Fonesca, Isabel. *Bury me Standing: The Gypsies and their History* (New York: Knopf 1995).

Forbes-Mitchell, William. *Reminiscences of the Great Mutiny 1857-59* (New Delhi: Asian Educational Service 2002).

Fyzee, Asaf A. A. *Outlines of Muhammadan Law* (Delhi: Oxford University Press, 2003).

Gibbon, Edward. *The History of the Decline and Fall of the Roman Empire* Volume II (New York: Penguin 1995).

Gopal, Sarvepalli, ed. *Anatomy of a Confrontation: Ayodhya and the Rise of Communal Politics in India* (London: Zed Books 1990).

Guilaume, A. *The Life of Muhammad: A Translation of Ibn Ishaq's Sirat Rasul Allah* (London: Oxford University Press 2002).

Gupta, Dipauter, ed. *Caste in Question* (New Delhi: Sage Publications 2005).

Hansen, Thomas Blom and Jaffrelot, Christophe, eds. *BJP and the Compulsions of Politics in India* (Delhi: Oxford Unviversity Press 1998).

Hussein, Abid Saliha ed. *Anees ke Marsiay* (New Delhi: Tariqi Urdu Bureau 1990).

Imtiaz, Ahmad, ed. *Divorce and Remarriage among Muslims in India* (Delhi: Manohar 2003).

Jaffrelot, Christophe. *The Hindu Nationalist Movement in India* (New York: Columbia University Press 1993).

Jeffery, Patricia and Jeffery, Roger. *Confronting Saffron Demography: Religion, Fertility and Women's Status in India* (Gurgaon: Three Essay Collective 2006).

Kamdar, Mira. *Planet India* (McMillan Library, 2007).

Khan, Muhammad Muhshin. *Sahih al Bukhari* (Kazi Publications 1979).

Luce Edward. *In Spite of the Gods: The Strange Rise of Modern India* (New York: Doubleday 2007).

Manchester, Frederick, trans. *The Upanishads: Breath of the Eternal* (New York: Mentor 1975).

Mandelbaum, David. *Society in India* (Berkeley: University of Chicago Press 1970).

Manto, Saadat Hasan. *Bombay Stories*, translated by Matthew Reeck and Aftab Ahmed (publication pending).

Metcalf, Barbara Daly. *Islamic Revival in British India: Deoband 1860-1900* (New Delhi: Oxford University Press 1982).

Matthews, David. *The Battle of Karbala: A Marsiya of Anis* (New Delhi: Rupa & Co. 1994).

Mulky, M.J. and Sharma, V. S., eds. *Tea Culture, Processing and Marketing* (Bombay: Hindustan Lever Research Foundation 1993).

Nagarkar, Kiran. *Cuckold* (New Delhi: Harper Collins 1997).

Naipaul, V. S. *India: A Wounded Civilization* (London: Penguin 1979).

Nandy, Ashis with Shikha Trivedy, Shail Mayaram, and Achyut Yagnik, eds. *Creating a Nationality: The Ramjanambhumi Movement and Fear of the Self* (Delhi: Oxford Press 1995).

Narain, Harsh. *The Ayodhya Temple–Mosque Dispute: Focus on Muslim Sources* (Delhi: Penman Publishers 1993).

Nash, Ogden. *Candy is Dandy: The Best of Ogden Nash* (London: Andre Deutsch 1983).

Nussbaum, Martha Craven. *The Clash Within: Democracy, Religious Violence, and India's Future* (London: Belknap / Harvard University Press 2007).

Parry, Jonathan. *Death in Benares* (New Delhi: Cambridge University Press 1994).

Pathak, Bindeshwar. *Road to Freedom: A Sociological Study on the Abolition of Scavenging in India* (Delhi: Motilal Banarsidas 1991).

Pickthall, Marmaduke, trans. *The Glorious Koran* (New York: New American Library) p. 254.

Prabhupada, Swami Bhaktivedanta, trans. *Bhagavad-Gita As It Is* (New York: Bhaktivedanta Book Trust) 1972.

Ruswa, Mohammad Hadi. *Umrao Jan Ada* (Hyderabad: Disha Books 1993).

Suri, Manil. *The Death of Vishnu* (New York: Perennial 2001).

Swami Pavitrananda, trans. *Siva-Mahimnah Stotra* (Pithoragarh: Advaita Ashrama 1976).

Thapar, Romila. Somanatha: *The Many Voices of a History* (London: Verso 2005).

Trautmann, Thomas R. *The Aryan Debate: Debates in Indian History and Society* (New Delhi: Oxford University Press 2005).

Vonnegut, Kurt. *Slapstick or Lonesome no More!* (New York City: Delacorte Press 1976).

Woodroffe, John. *Principles of Tantra* (Kessinger Publishing, 2003). Published under the name Arthur Avalon.

INDEX